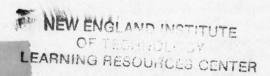

BLOOD MAGIC

BLOOD MAGIC

THE ANTHROPOLOGY OF MENSTRUATION

EDITED, WITH
AN INTRODUCTION BY
THOMAS BUCKLEY AND
ALMA GOTTLIEB

University of California Press
Berkeley · *Los Angeles* · *London*

University of California Press
Berkeley and Los Angeles, California

University of California Press, Ltd.
London, England

Copyright © 1988 by
The Regents of the University of California

Library of Congress Cataloging-in-Publication Data
Blood magic : The anthropology of menstruation
  edited, with an introduction by Thomas Buckley and Alma Gottlieb.
     p.   cm.
    Bibliography: p.
    Includes index.
    ISBN 0–520–06085–7 (alk. paper)
    ISBN 0–520–06350–3 pbk.
      1. Menstruation—Cross-cultural studies.   2. Menstruation—
  -Folklore.   3. Menstruation—Social aspects.   I. Buckley, Thomas.
  II. Gottlieb, Alma.
  GN484.38.B56 1988
  305.4—dc19   87-12529
                                                           CIP

Printed in the United States of America
  2 3 4 5 6 7 8 9

In memory of
VICTOR W. TURNER
teacher and friend

Contents

Acknowledgments

This book results from the cooperation and efforts of many individuals and organizations, and we are grateful to all of them.

We thank, first, the contributors to this volume. Laura W. R. Appell, Carol Delaney, Chris Knight, Frederick Lamp, Emily Martin, and Vieda Skultans have all written new essays especially for this book; Denise L. Lawrence has significantly revised an earlier publication (as have the editors). We have been enriched through our association with all of these colleagues.

Our title, *Blood Magic*, is Aletta Biersack's translation of a Paiela (Papua New Guinea) term for menstrual practices. We thank Professor Biersack (Department of Anthropology, University of Oregon) for bringing it to our attention.

We are also grateful to the journals *Africa*, *American Ethnologist*, *Anthropological Quarterly*, *Grassroots*, and *Man* for their permission to reprint, in part or in whole, work that originally appeared in them. We thank, as well, Melbourne University Press and Muller, Blond & White Ltd. for permission to reprint illustrations originally published by them.

Many others—colleagues, friends, and family—have rendered invaluable services to us, and we wish especially to acknowledge their work. Marjorie Mandelstam Balzer, Aletta Biersack, Rose E. Frisch, Gillian Gillison, Barbara B. Harrell, Terence E. Hays, Martha K. McClintock, and Deborah Winslow, all of whom have made important contributions to the anthropology and biology of menstruation, contributed much to the present volume as well, and we thank each of them.

Special thanks are due Florence Gottlieb for her generous contribution in typing the final manuscript, a job she did with great skill and aplomb, and to William Gottlieb for his proofreading services. Marjorie Hurder also cheerfully took on a considerable amount of typing when help was needed, and Brenda Lenoir assisted in this seemingly endless task as well; we are grateful to both for their work. We also wish to thank Barbara Cohen for preparing the index.

Through a Faculty Development grant and through granting a leave of absence to Thomas Buckley, the University of Massachusetts at Boston furthered work on this volume in most useful ways. We thank the university and its Department of Anthropology. Likewise, we thank JoAnn D'Alisera who served as a research assistant to Alma Gottlieb during a critical stage in the editorial process, and the Research Board of the University of Illinois, which awarded the funds for her assistantship.

Finally, Philip Graham, Jorunn Jacobsen Buckley, and Jesse Buckley have all been unstinting in their good-humored support, Philip and Jorunn reading our work when readers were most needed. As in everything, we thank all three.

Editors' Note

Our names appear on this book in alphabetical order, not as first and second authors. Although the original idea for the book was Alma Gottlieb's, we have collaborated equally in every aspect of its production. Selection of and correspondence with contributors, editing of the various chapters, the labors of manuscript preparation and publication have been shared equitably. The introductory chapter, "A Critical Appraisal of Theories of Menstrual Symbolism," is likewise the result of full collaboration. That one name must come first in print is a fact of language—not, in the present case, a reflection of our relative contributions.

T. B./A. G.

What are we to make of the red symbolism which, in its archetypal form in the initiation rites, is represented by the intersection of two "rivers of blood"? This duality, this ambivalence, this simultaneous possession of two contrary values or qualities, is quite characteristic of redness in the Ndembu view. As they say, "redness acts both for good and ill."

—V. Turner (1967a:77)

PART I

INTRODUCTION

1

A Critical Appraisal of Theories of Menstrual Symbolism

Thomas Buckley
Alma Gottlieb

The topic of menstruation has long been a staple of anthropology, for this apparently ordinary biological event has been subject to extraordinary symbolic elaboration in a wide variety of cultures. The symbolic potency so often attributed to menstrual blood and the exotic-seeming stringency of rules for the conduct of menstruating women have placed menstruation in the foreground of anthropological studies of "taboo" and, more recently, of symbolic "pollution." Menstrual taboos have been seen by turn as evidence of primitive irrationality and of the supposed universal dominance of men over women in society. The widespread occurrence of menstrual taboos and their cross-cultural similarities has spurred a search for their universal origins, once identified with the very wellsprings of social organization (Durkheim 1897:50) and, more recently, of religious thought (Douglas 1966:6).

Yet for all of the significance attributed to menstrual symbolism by anthropologists and others, and for all of the fascination with which its origins and functions have been pursued, little has been firmly established. While menstruation itself has at least a degree of biological regularity, its symbolic voicings and valences are strikingly variable, both cross-culturally and within single cultures. It is perplexing, then, that the study of menstrual symbolism has been limited by a paucity of detail regarding such variations, by imbalances in ethnographic reporting, and by overly reductionistic theoretical frameworks.

Heretofore the majority of ethnographic reports of menstrual customs and beliefs have been restricted to terse statements on "the" meaning of menstrual blood—seen always as symbolically dangerous or otherwise defiling—and to normative accounts of the practices instituted to contain the perceived negative potency of the substance. These analyses have great predictability, for again and again they center on the concepts of *taboo* (supernaturally sanctioned law) and *pollution* (symbolic contamination). Repeated ethnographic reports of the taboos that are seen to constrain menstruous women because of the imputed malevolence of menstrual discharge have contributed in important ways to the development of powerful general theories of pollution. The availability of such theory, as well as ethnographic tradition, has assured the collection of more data on menstrual taboos and further elaboration of pollution theory through these data. The anthropological study of menstruation has thus tended toward redundancy.

During the past decade, however, in response to a fresh current of interest in the lives of women, new anthropological approaches to the topic of menstruation have begun to emerge. These have not yet resulted in new general theories of menstrual symbolism, its origins, or its functions. Rather, recent work demonstrates in broadly diverse ways the types of considerations that will now have to be accommodated by any general theory of menstruation as a cultural construct—if indeed such an all-encompassing theory remains desirable or possible. These considerations include the varying contexts of menstrual symbolism, the ambiguity of much of this symbolism, the possibility of intracultural diversity in its meanings, and the interface between biological and cultural systems in the making of human society. In taking up these general considerations, new specific lines of inquiry must also be opened to investigate specific systems of meaning in culture: intragender variations in these systems, the service of menstrual symbolism in the interest of women as well as men, and so on.

The essays that make up the present volume are, we hope,

representative of the scope and spirit of such new cultural-anthropological approaches to menstruation. In general, the authors of the following chapters neither deny the usefulness of all received theory nor suggest singular alternatives to it. Rather, they tend to acknowledge the relevance of earlier contributions while hazarding a long look beyond them. From the results they achieve it seems clear that to transcend the limitations in received theory demands a more balanced and comprehensive ethnographic base than that which has been available. For this reason, while being both theoretically informed and informative, most of the following essays are very much grounded in ethnographic specificity and, not coincidentally, most are based in recent field research. Much of this fieldwork has focused on women and much of it was undertaken by women. Together these two shifts away from what until recently has been the dominant fieldwork situation redress some of the limitations in previous ethnographic reports and theoretical formulations alike (see also Gregory 1984).

A second movement away from earlier styles in the study of menstruation is signaled by the openness of investigators to biocultural considerations in symbolic analyses. Though positing no form of biological determinism, many of the cultural anthropologists represented by the following studies acknowledge and analytically integrate the roles of human reproductive biology in the cultural construction of menstruation. In this regard the potential fruitfulness of interdisciplinary inquiry is considerable.

The acknowledgment of both the traditional male-focused structure of ethnological inquiry and the potential usefulness of biocultural perspectives raises unsettling issues regarding the past study of menstruation and, more generally, the present status of anthropological (and biological) knowledge. It is here that the study of menstruation, a seemingly limited topic, can reveal a profound and broad intellectual import. For the studies presented in this volume cumulatively suggest that the critical cross-cultural study of menstruation must now be taken to include the study of anthropology, and even of biology, as themselves cultural—that is, symbolic—sub-systems.

Although such implications have consequences for anthro-pological work far beyond the apparent confines of the topic at hand, these general implications are perhaps best demon-strated through concrete substantive studies. Thus the foci of the chapters that follow remain firmly fixed on menstruation and closely related phenomena, and within clearly defined cultural contexts. In order to locate these chapters within the spectrum of earlier studies to which they are responding, we turn first to a selective review of the received literature on menstruation.

EXPLAINING MENSTRUAL TABOOS

> A menstruating [Gisu] woman must keep herself from contact with many activities lest she spoil them: she may not brew beer nor pass by the homestead of a potter lest his pots crack during firing; she may not cook for her husband nor sleep with him lest she endanger both his virility and his general health. A menstruating woman endangers the success of rituals by her presence. . . . At first menstruation . . . she must be se-cluded at once from normal contacts, particularly from contact with men of the village, her agnates. During the time that she is menstruating she must not touch food with her hands: she eats with two sticks. (La Fontaine 1972:164–165)

For anthropologists and nonanthropologists alike, the most compelling aspect of the comparative study of menstruation has surely been the widespread existence of "menstrual taboos." Again and again, ethnographers have reported that menstrual blood and menstruating women are viewed as dangerous and/or offensive among the peoples they have observed. Accordingly these perceived contaminants are re-ported to be kept at bay by broadly similar sets of injunctions and prohibitions, almost all of which have been interpreted to be oppressive to women. So striking has been the near universality and exoticism alike of these menstrual taboos and, perhaps, so resonant with the feelings of men and women in literate cultures that the ethnographic findings themselves have entered into popular culture as truisms. Such truisms are promulgated today, in the wake of feminism, by a spate of popular books. Statements found in Paula Weideger's *Menstruation and Menopause* (1977) are typical of this group of writings:

> The menstrual taboo is universal. (P. 85)

> Generally, the object of a taboo may be a source of good or evil, but in the case of menstrual blood the ascriptions are almost universally evil. (P. 89)

> The menstrual taboo exists as a method of protecting men from danger they are sure is real (the source of which is in women), and it is a means of keeping the fear of menstruating women under control. (P. 92)

These sorts of statements are interesting for a variety of reasons. They evidence the influence of cultural anthropology on popular culture in the West; they are concise summaries of suppositions that underlie much psychoanalytic and anthropological work, as well as being prominent in popular imagination; and, like so much popular wisdom, they are at once partially true and highly simplistic.

"The menstrual taboo" as such does not exist. Rather, what is found in close cross-cultural study is a wide range of distinct rules for conduct regarding menstruation that bespeak quite different, even opposite, purposes and meanings. Many menstrual taboos, rather than protecting society from a universally ascribed feminine evil, explicitly protect the perceived creative spirituality of menstruous women from the influence of others in a more neutral state, as well as protecting the latter in turn from the potent, positive spiritual force ascribed to such women. In other cultures menstrual customs, rather than subordinating women to men fearful of them, provide women with means of ensuring their own autonomy, influence, and social control. "The menstrual taboo," in short, is at once nearly universal and has meanings that are ambiguous and often multivalent.

This multivalence appears to be inherent in the very term *taboo* as analyzed by Steiner (1956). Probing the semantic sphere of the Polynesian word *tabu* and its variants (compare Durkheim 1897:57), Steiner observed that the Polynesian root *ta* means "to mark" and that *pu* is an adverb of intensity, and he translated *tabu* (*tapu*) as "marked thoroughly" (1956:32). This etymology shows a lack of unilateral stress on either negative or positive dimensions, and Steiner accordingly suggested that concepts of "holy" and "forbidden" are inseparable in the many Polynesian languages. There is no polarity of meaning inherent in the term *tabu*, which, on the contrary, implies a fusion of two concepts that Western views tend to distinguish. Furthermore, the logical opposite of "tabu" is neither "sacred" nor "defiled" (both of which are encompassed within "tabu") but "profane," in the sense of "common" (Steiner 1956:36, 82). (For a critical discussion of anthropological usage of "tabu," including Steiner, see Keesing 1985.)

Steiner's discussion of taboo and its potential multivalence has rarely been considered by writers on menstrual taboos outside Polynesia. We suggest that the poverty in understanding the variable meanings of the menstrual taboo, both within and between cultures, has been in part the result of an emphasis on monocausal explanation. The very wide—if not universal (see Appell, chapter 4)—distribution of menstrual taboos has given rise to a linked set of cross-cultural questions, all entailing causal explanation: How can we account for the presence of menstrual taboos, both as universals and in a comparative sense? What are their origins? Can we predict what types of societies will be most likely to elaborate upon them in striking ways?

Despite the considerable cross-cultural variety in the "shape" and meaning of menstrual taboos, answers to such questions and related predictive hypotheses reflect a limited number of causal theories and explanatory approaches. The range of these may be suggested through considering a few of the many received studies that seem to us particularly exemplary: theories that view "the menstrual taboo" as both reflection and source of female oppression; as evidence of neurotic complexes; and as means for addressing any of several practical problems in social life.

TABOO AS OPPRESSION OF WOMEN

Perhaps the most pervasive interpretation of menstrual taboos in both the popular and professional literature has been the one that equates the notion of "taboo" with "oppression" and hence menstrual taboos with the suppression of women in society. This perspective, however, seldom recognizes the fact that taboos surrounding the menstrual cycle may restrict the behavior of others more than that of the menstruating woman herself. Again, it is one that usually regards the isolation of menstruating women as, by definition, a sign of lower status. Finally, it is a perspective that often treats taboos as no more than rules prescribing certain behaviors rather than as parts of religious systems that may have wide cosmological ramifications. Such collapsing of distinct taboos and rules into a single category for analysis has often reflected, ironically, an underlying androcentrism in explanations of menstrual taboos as means for the suppression of women in society.

We may take as representative of the female oppression theory the work of F. W. Young (1965) and Young and Bacdayan (1965). In explaining how he classifies societies in terms of the status of women, Young (1965:155) writes that the "menstrual taboos that often apply to native women throughout their middle years may function as a mechanism for reducing the status of women in contrast to that of men." "May" as used here is deceptive. It obscures the fact that Young—like many others—*presupposes* a correlation between menstrual taboos and low female status, for if such a correlation did not exist, how could the taboos function as mechanisms to reduce status? Yet Young neither specifies how "low female status" might be defined nor tests the correlation he presupposes. Rather, in a work with Bacdayan (Young and Bacdayan 1965), he asserts that the menstrual taboos, taken as a single category of symbolic features, reflect both men's fear of women and weak solidarity among men themselves and are therefore imposed by men upon women in order to assure male dominance of society. This explanation—one that has entered into popular Western commentaries on

menstrual taboos (e.g., Delaney, Lupton, and Toth 1976)—
depends for its strength on a disregard of certain crucial
analytic distinctions.

It is necessary, for example, to distinguish between two
varieties of menstrual taboos that are often lumped together,
as they are in the work of Young and Bacdayan. Some taboos
restrict the behavior of menstruating women themselves,
whereas others restrict the behavior of other people in relation
to such women. The threats that are culturally attributed to
menstruation must likewise be analytically separated. We
need to ask, for instance, if a taboo is violated, will the
menstruating woman harm someone else or herself? If the
former, a danger to others is indicated; if the latter, the *vulnerability* of the woman. Frazer pointed out long ago
([1950]1963:260) that these two kinds of dangers associated
with taboos are quite separate, and we urge that they be
treated as such.

Deborah Winslow (1980), for example, demonstrates the
importance of this distinction in her analysis of menstrual
taboos and menarche rituals among several groups in Sri
Lanka. Among Buddhists in Sri Lanka, the experiences of
menarche and menstruation are held to evidence women's
threat to cosmic purity and, hence, to society. In contrast,
among Sri Lankan Catholics they are signs of women's *vulnerability* to threats posed by cosmos and society. Although
on the surface the rituals attending menarche among both
Buddhists and Catholics are similar, the rituals mean quite
different things to the people who participate in them, and
these meanings rest on distinct cultural constructions of
womanhood: dangerous among Buddhists; endangered
among Catholics. Such distinct constructions in turn suggest
an equally distinct social status for Buddhist and Catholic
women.

In contrast to Winslow's attention to the specific (sub-)cul-
tural contextualization of menstrual taboos and of their social
functions, many writers taking cross-cultural approaches
have ignored such contextualization and have thereby col-
lapsed diverse categories of rules and taboos into a single
concept of "menstrual taboo."

As an example, we take the work of William Stephens (1961). Stephens (pp. 393–394) identifies five classes of taboos: those against menstrual blood as itself dangerous; those that require the isolation of menstruous women; those that prohibit menstrual sex; those that prohibit menstruous women's cooking, especially for their husbands; and a general category of "other" taboos. However, having distinguished these categories, Stephens then conflates them in order to come up with a composite "score" for the relative presence or absence of menstrual taboos (the "menstrual taboo," again) in a given culture. This score comprises the statistical base for testing various hypotheses, including one to the effect that menstrual taboos are not strong in societies in which women make significant economic contributions (Stephens 1962:121).

In fact, Stephens finds no correlation between the economic contributions of women and the presence of menstrual taboos. Yet this is not surprising in view of his conflation of taboo types. It would seem most likely that taboos against menstruating women working in farming, food processing, crafts, and so on (all lumped together in Stephens's "other" category) would be far more pertinent to the hypothesis than would, say, taboos against sexual intercourse during menstruation. The statistical conflation of distinct taboo types—insistence on "the menstrual taboo," however sophisticated—undermines the logical base of Stephens's and comparable cross-cultural studies.

As we will see later in this chapter, the assumption underlying Stephens's collapsing of rules and taboos is that these taboos serve to oppress women. Yet this assumption is problematic.

In cataloging the potential victims of menstrual pollution, accounts hinging on suppression of women unilaterally stress the effects of menstruation on men. Yet women themselves are often culturally defined as vulnerable to menstrual pollution, not only that of other women but of their own menstrual blood as well.[1]

One menstrual custom that has repeatedly caught the anthropological imagination and has often been singled out as indicative of low female status is that of "menstrual seclusion": the isolation of menstruous women, often in special shelters, that seems once to have been widespread (Stephens 1967). Yet, as Rosaldo (1974:38) observed, "pollution beliefs can provide grounds for solidarity among women," and depending on the cultural context, menstrual seclusion "huts" can themselves be sanctuaries. We must consider the degree to which accounts of such seclusion have been inflected by the pride of missionaries and other colonialists in putting an end to what *they* perceived as an evil, rather than by the lived experiences of women in "menstrual huts."

We find, on close examination, that little is actually known of such episodes of seclusion. "Menstrual huts" have widely been among the first of indigenous features to be relinquished by native peoples upon contact with outsiders from the West (e.g., Balzer 1985; Buckley, chapter 8).[2] Reports that are available suggest wide cross-cultural variations in both seclusion practices and women's experiences of them. Price (1984) found that Saramaka women of Surinam mildly resent their mandatory seclusion yet maintain the practice, although others nearby have abandoned it, because they also find this ritual contribution to communal welfare somehow fulfilling. In contrast, most women of Mogmog Island in the Pacific atoll of Ulithi "enjoy this break from their normal labors and spend the time happily talking or weaving" (Patterson 1986:490). Their large *ipul*, or "women's house," is equipped with looms and serves as a community center for women, as viewed in a photograph by David Hiser (in Patterson, 490–491) showing three women and a child occupying an *ipul*.

While scattered reports such as these are suggestive, to our knowledge there have been no detailed studies of women secluded in menstrual huts, and a great many questions go largely unexamined in received ethnographies and cross-cultural studies. Are most secluded women in "solitary confinement," or is seclusion more often communal, as on Mogmog? Do women usually "resent" their seclusion, as in Price's (third person) accounts? Or do they, as in Patterson's, usually "enjoy this break from their normal labors"? Do they widely perceive it as a "break" from men as well? What do women do during this time? Some, at least, talk and weave, meditate (Buckley, this volume), cook (Gottlieb, this volume)—do others just mope?

Although such questions are rarely answered in the ethnographic literature, we do find many suggestions that seclusion is not always onerous. Among the Djuka of Dutch Guiana (Kahn 1931:130), the Warao of Venezuela (Suárez 1968:2–6), the Kaska of western Canada (Honigmann 1954:124), and others, menstrual seclusion has been seen as bringing women sexual autonomy and opportunities for illicit love affairs. (The frequency of this claim suggests that not all men, either, view all menstrual taboos as binding.) Other accounts, such as those received by A. L. Kroeber from a Yurok Indian woman (see Buckley, this volume), suggest that menstrual seclusion is viewed by some women as a means toward spiritual and even economic ascendancy: that is, toward enhanced rather than lowered status.

We may not be certain, then, that menstrual seclusion in separate shelters arises from the desire of men to suppress women in society. The possibility should not be ruled out that women themselves may have been responsible for originating the custom in many societies, as Martin suggests in chapter 7 (compare Leacock 1978:270). There is also a possibility that such seclusion, when practiced, may sometimes in effect be voluntary, a cultural option to be exercised by women in their own interests rather than those of men. We know this to be the case for other menstrual taboos in certain instances. For example, according to Barrett (1976:172), Pomo Indian women observed only quasi-voluntarily menstrual taboos relating to the making of baskets. There were culturally defined means for opting out of these taboos if the woman desired to continue working on her baskets during her period. Such voluntarism in following prescribed menstrual customs suggests that Pomo women, at least, found the taboos against work somehow desirable.

To assume that prohibiting women from working—or, in the case of menstrual seclusion, from having contact with men—is always a form of suppressive discrimination against women is rather limited. As Gottlieb and Martin argue (this volume, chapters 2 and 7), taboos against women working, cooking, having sex, and so on can as easily be interpreted as boons to women as means of suppressing them.

In much of the literature, when women have been described as being prohibited from contact with something in the male domain—a man's hunting gear, say—it has been interpreted as an indication of male dominance manifested by women's exclusion from prestigious activities. Conversely, however, when it is forbidden for men to have contact with something in the female domain—such as menstrual blood— it has been interpreted in an opposite manner, as a sign of female inferiority. The two kinds of actions, or taboos, would seem parallel, yet the anthropological interpretation of them has been binary. Thus the desirability and benefits of some menstrual taboos for women, the possibility that these taboos enhance rather than suppress women's influence and power, have generally been ignored by investigators (but see Lawrence, this volume).

We are not arguing here the reverse of current explanations: that rather than originating in an urge to suppress women and increase male solidarity, menstrual taboos uniformly arose to empower women and enhance female solidarity. Instead we are arguing that the social functions of menstrual taboos are culturally variable and specific. If one society views these taboos as a means of subordinating women (e.g., Delaney, this volume), a second as giving women access to gender-exclusive ritual powers (e.g., Lamp, this volume), and a third ambivalently, as both containing and enhancing the power of women (e.g., Buckley, this volume), can we legitimately lump all three together as societies practicing menstrual taboos toward the suppression of women?

We are suggesting, then, that "female oppression" models of menstrual taboos, in their simpler forms at least, are inadequate. As Schlegel has written, "It may be that some cultures have used menstruation to explain and justify the inferior status of women; but that is a culture-specific trait and cannot be generalized to all cultures having menstrual taboos" (1972:93). To assume that the presence of menstrual taboos is a universal indicator of relative female "status"—however that may be defined—is tautological and, moreover, simply does not fit specific ethnographic cases.

TABOO AS NEUROSIS

The theory that menstrual taboos by definition oppress women has been adopted by at least some of another group of writers, those utilizing a psychoanalytic approach. In contrast to the more purely anthropological version of the taboo-as-oppression theory, however, psychoanalytic explanations do have the capacity to deal with menstrual taboos as symbolic representations (rather than as purely functional sociological mechanisms); hence these taboos are seen as subject to unlimited transformations and aptly expressed within a religious context. Based on a theory of (putatively) universal unconscious content and process, psychoanalytic theory aims at once to account for the near-universality of menstrual taboos and their inter- and intracultural diversity. Cultures, here, may be understood as analogous to dreams. In both forms single motivating themes (e.g., "castration anxiety") are voiced, according to psychoanalysts, through virtually unlimited numbers of symbolic associations, by projection, condensation, identification, and other processes first postulated by Freud (1955).

Freud himself wrote little on either menstruation or menstrual taboos (see Skultans 1970:646). Neglecting these topics entirely in his essay, "Female Sexuality" (1931), he dealt with them in a single footnote in *Civilization and Its Discontents* (1930:36). Here Freud located the origins of menstrual taboos in the "organic repression" of a sexual attraction felt by men toward women during their periods. While this theory has had little influence upon the anthropology of menstruation, the more general connection drawn in psychoanalytic theory between contemporary Western neuroses and "primitive" belief systems has had considerable

impact. (For other psychoanalytic treatments of menstruation, see Horney 1931; Deutsch 1950.) Perhaps the most am-
bitious anthropological attempt at a cross-cultural explanation
of menstrual taboos from a psychoanalytic perspective has
been that of William Stephens (1962). We address his work
critically here because it exemplifies many of the pitfalls awaiting those who attempt to apply classic Freudian theory on so
wide a scale.

Stephens hypothesizes that men's "castration anxiety" is
responsible for menstrual taboos because he presumes that
"the sight or thought of a person who bleeds from the genitals
(a menstruating woman) is frightening to a person who has
intense castration anxiety" (1962:93). He hypothesizes that
the greater the number and variety of menstrual taboos in a
society, the stronger the castration anxiety among men in that
society.

Stephens (1962:119) concedes that there is no way to test
directly for the presence or absence of castration anxiety, as
it exists at the level of the unconscious. He is thus compelled
to test his theory indirectly, through indices claimed by
psychoanalysts to be correlated closely with castration anxiety
and, by Stephens, to be more measurable. He chooses several
such indices: maternal seduction of sons, strong punishment
of masturbation/strict training regarding sex, and strict paternal authority. These, he predicts, will be present in propor-
tion to the stringency and elaboration of menstrual taboos.
Through statistical tests he claims a correlation between these
three indices and the proliferation of menstrual taboos in
specific societies.

But Stephens's correlations are statistically weak and more
suggestive than conclusive, and their relevance is highly controversial (e.g., Paige and Paige 1981:240–245). A long and
still unresolved debate in anthropology has been waged over
whether or not the "Oedipus complex" (of which castration
anxiety is an important part) can even be said to exist in
non-Western societies (e.g., Parsons 1969). It is not untoward,
then, to question the centrality of the concept to Stephens's
and others' comparative statistics.

There is a second, unexamined yet critical assumption in

Stephens's work that, like the Oedipus complex, demands close scrutiny. Approaches like his imply that menstrual taboos were created by men for their own benefit. This implication rests on the unspoken assumption that men write the cultural script and that women simply and obediently recite their lines. As more data on women's roles in cultures are gathered, this assumption appears groundless as regards, at least, certain spheres of social life (e.g., Collier 1974; Etienne 1977; Lederman forthcoming). It is highly problematic where menstruation is concerned as well. In the present volume, for example, Denise Lawrence (chapter 5) demonstrates that in the Portuguese village she studied even stringent menstrual taboos may be in the interests of women and may be manipulated by women toward their own ends.

There is a second body of psychoanalytic theory regarding menstruation and its symbolism. Bettelheim (1954), considering data on men's rituals that simulate women's reproductive processes by inducing heavy flows of blood, suggests that it is reproductive (or "vaginal") envy, rather than castration anxiety, that characterizes both the male response to menstruation and the taboo systems culturally enacted to contain perceived menstrual threat (compare Montgomery 1974). Although this theory grants far more creative psychological power to women than do those based in castration anxiety, it still portrays women, who apparently must suffer the taboos most directly, as a priori the passive victims of male-created symbolic systems.

To some extent the male bias underlying these psychoanalytic approaches to comparative menstrual beliefs is inherent in classic Freudian theory itself (e.g., Van Herik 1982). Later psychoanalytic writers have followed suit in focusing on the "hormonal onslaught" that is said to occur before and during menstruation and to cause profound neurotic disturbances. For instance, Isidor Silberman (1950:258) has written: *"The woman, during each menstrual period, regresses to pregenital levels in response to psychological experiences arising out of hormonal onslaught"* (emphasis in original; compare Chadwick 1932; Montague 1957:196).

Such formulations, however, fail to consider the ways in

which Western women's menstrual and premenstrual anxieties may be products not of biochemistry but of the highly specified cultural setting of contemporary industrial society, as examined by Martin in chapter 7. A view parallel to Silberman's has been adopted by contemporary medical investigators of the "premenstrual syndrome" (PMS); however, in fact the "hormonal onslaught" central to such theories has been found to be far more extreme during ovulation than during menstruation or the paramenstruum (Burley 1979: 837), although no ovulatory taboos have yet been noted in the ethnographic literature. Second, such explanation of menstrual taboos as means of containing the biologically in-duced negative psychic energies of women is weakened by the extraordinary bias of this formulation. Simply put, such theories are no more than rationalized means of blaming the (apparent) victim.

Although psychoanalytic explanations such as Stephens's for the origins of menstrual taboos have been weakened by varieties of biases and overly reductive analyses, they do have one undeniable strength: their ability to address the taboos themselves as symbolic, and especially religious, representations. This strength is wholly absent in the last group of explanatory theories of menstrual taboos that we consider: those proposing one or another form of pragmatic explanation.

TABOO AS PRAXIS

Perhaps the most seductive of all explanations of menstrual taboos is the related set of theories that locate the origins of menstrual taboos in rational responses to practical problems, as defined by Western observers: utilitarian strategies that have been *extended*—in the view of the writers, irrationally—to a vast assortment of apparently unrelated domains in culture. Such theories imply that practical responses to the demands of bioecological actuality—say, successful hunting—have been culturally extended to cover religious endeavors.

The notion that such hypothesized extensions of causally

singular taboos have been both extraordinarily broad within given cultures, on the one hand, and have been accomplished in an extraordinarily similar manner cross-culturally, on the other, suggests weakness in this implicit theory of extension. There must be, it would seem, a more parsimonious and less speculative means to account for both the range of menstrual taboos and their cross-cultural similarities than through the unprovable hypothesis of fortuitous convergent extension (compare Montgomery 1974:145). Further, it might be hoped that such means would not depend upon the supposed "irrationality" (Leacock 1978:270) of cultural construction, its astonishing *rationality* having been so convincingly argued (e.g., Lévi-Strauss 1966, etc.). Here we examine two varieties of practical explanations for the origins of menstrual taboos, both of which depend upon an implicit or explicit theory of extension in making their causal cases.

Menotoxins

One line of cultural argument from "practical reason" (Sahlins 1976) that has been recently resuscitated in the medical literature is based on the alleged bacterial toxicity of menstrual blood itself. This theory was first proposed in 1920 by a physician, Bela Schick, who posited the existence of what he termed bacterial "menotoxins" in menstrual blood. Anthropologist Ashley Montagu (1940, 1957) brought Schick's hypothesis to the attention of anthropologists, suggesting that menstruating women indeed wither plants, turn wine, spoil pickles, cause bread to fall, and so forth because of chemical components in their menstrual blood. Thus, Montagu argues, taboos against women engaging in a variety of actions during their menstrual periods may have originated as reasonable responses to closely observed physical facts. Clellan Ford (1945:12–13) likewise explains the common taboo against menstrual sex as arising from medical risks to men from hypothesized menotoxins.[3]

Ford's and related theories have two profound weaknesses. First, although they might conceivably account for the origins of taboos in some cultures against menstrual sex, or wine making, pickling, and the like, accounting for the origins of *all* menstrual taboos through these theories demands that people in widely dispersed areas and epochs have all made the same empirically based observations concerning the effects of menstruation, and that is not only improbable, but as we will see, untrue. In addition to near-universal homogeneity in empirical observation, completely nonuniform, irrational extensions must also be invoked if menotoxins are to be held responsible for widespread taboos against other activities that are clearly *not* endangered by any postulated "menotoxicity": for example, the taboo against participation in public rituals by menstruous women in some cultures and, at the same time, rules that *enjoin* women to participate in such rituals specifically *during* their menstrual periods in other cultures (e.g., Mead 1970:417). Such diversity in the symbolic coding of menstruation suggests its arbitrariness and cultural relativity, rather than motivation by any single physical phenomenon.

Meanwhile, the hypothesis of menotoxicity itself remains controversial at best. After having first been postulated by Schick and then popularized by Montagu, the theory slumbered until 1974, when a British physician (Reid 1974) reawakened it and issued a challenge to medical researchers to test it. A few researchers responded, some supporting the theory and others raising skeptical queries (Davis 1974; Pickles 1974; Bryant, Heathcote, and Pickles 1977), but to date no more definitive studies have been conducted that would either prove or disprove the theory. Indeed reproductive biologists and biological anthropologists seem little interested in, or are unaware of, the hypothesis (Martha McClintock, personal communication, 1984; Linda Klepinger, personal communication, 1984).

This brings us to our second objection to the theory of taboo as based in toxicity, as postulated by Ford and Montagu. In light of the failure of biologists to agree on the very existence of menotoxins, there seems a strong possibility that theories based in these hypothesized bacteria tell us more

about the ways in which our own culture symbolizes perceived threat than about any cross-cultural actuality. Menotoxins, that is, may be no more than the symbolic terms of a
folk-biology of pollution, a "scientific" symbol for forces
coded elsewhere and at other times in other terms—as spiritual contamination, psychic poison, or divine punishment.

In any case, menstrual discharge has by no means been
universally coded as toxic, and other peoples hold quite opposite theories. Far from viewing menstrual blood solely as a
dire physical poison, the Imperial Romans, according to
Pliny, held that it encouraged the fecundity of wheat fields
(pace Montagu), and they used it in a variety of therapeutic
topical applications. Pliny notes its use in treatment of a wide
spectrum of medical conditions, including gout, goiter,
hemorrhages, inflammations of the salivary glands, erysipe-
las, furuncles, puerperal fever, hydrophobia, worms, and
headache (in Novak 1916:273). Vosselmann (1935:86–92) offers a long list of menstrual remedies from a variety of other
cultures for ailments ranging from epilepsy to infants' eye
diseases, including use of menstrual blood in dressings for
open sores and wounds in Morocco. Such usage, according
to Vosselmann, is not all prescientific. French physician R.
Jahiel, contemporary with Vosselmann, used subcutaneous
injections of menstrual blood in treating "menstrual liver-bile
syndrome" apparently with some success (Vosselmann 1935:
118). Whether or not Dr. Jahiel used only the menstrual discharge of virgins in his injections is not stated, but this seems
to have been the preferred substance in most agricultural and
medical applications remarked upon by Pliny and in the many
cultures surveyed by Vosselmann (compare Durkheim 1897:
56). This preference for the blood of virgins suggests, again,
that what is involved in all of this is symbolic, rather than
practical, reasoning (see also Knight 1985).

Menstrual odor

Menstrual blood may or may not be toxic, but it does have a
distinct odor, and several authors have argued recently that

menstrual taboos may be explained by this fact. One school of thought (March 1980; Nunley 1981) holds that menstrual taboos originated in observations that animals either attack (bears) or are repelled by (white-tailed deer) humans exuding a menstrual scent. Kitahara (1982) has extended this in his theory that menstrual taboos are most stringent and numerous among hunting peoples (compare Child and Child 1985).

As these scholars recognize, however, empirical research on menstrual odor has been informal and inconclusive (March 1980; Nunley 1981). Moreover, even *should* white-tailed deer and perhaps other ungulates be shown definitively to be repelled by menstrual blood, the fact that people hunt many other kinds of game in various regions must be taken into account. The odor avoidance hypothesis would have to be proved for these other animals—and more surely than it has been for white-tailed deer—in order to afford solid grounds for a general cross-cultural theory of the origins of menstrual taboos. (In fact, some peoples have deemed menstrual blood *attractive* to nondangerous animals such as rabbits [Novak 1916:273].) Even if this were accomplished, other logical difficulties remain.

First, odor theory might account for the origins of hunting-related menstrual taboos against activities such as menstrual sex, which would spread the odor to hunters, or against menstruous women touching men's hunting gear or cooking for hunters; but the theory is incapable of shedding light on the origins or functions of other taboos that clearly have nothing to do with the "natural" effects of menstrual odor—such as the Greek Orthodox taboo against menstruating women receiving Communion.[4] By the same token, it is not only menstrual sex that is denied hunters but, very widely, intercourse with any woman before the hunt; nor, again, are women in many societies prohibited from touching men's gear only while menstruating, and so on. While it is possible to propose hunting as some kind of primal activity that informs all others in all cultures (but see Tanner 1981), it is inelegant to do so: Occam's razor cuts sharply here. We are stuck with the fact that although few of the world's peoples are hunters, most have at least some menstrual taboos.

It has been argued, however, that while this is the case, hunting peoples tend to have far more, and more stringent, menstrual taboos than nonhunters (Kitahara 1982). Although the cross-cultural data base indeed seems to suggest that this is the case,[5] it does not necessarily follow that this is a result of attractive and/or repellent qualities of menstrual odor (contra Child and Child 1985); there are other, symbolic rather than utilitarian, possibilities (Balzer 1985). Until these can be more thoroughly explored, neither menstrual odor nor the occupation of hunting can be unequivocally identified as universal roots of menstrual taboos. In the meantime we are faced with the many native exegeses that explain the antipathy between menstruous women and male hunters, not in terms of odors but in terms of spiritual force (e.g., Shostak 1981:239); menstruous women seem to be held to weaken hunters physically and spiritually far more often than they are held to make hunters smell badly and thereby drive off game (see Snowden and Christian 1983:50 for data from Pakistan, India, and Egypt, where women claim that menstrual blood emits no distinctive odor). That is, menstrual taboos are overwhelmingly justified by the peoples who observe them in (broadly) religious terms rather than in the practical terms of odor management or, for that matter, of bacterial theory.

Taboo as practical masquerade

From the point of view of the two groups of practical theories just reviewed, the embedding of menstrual taboos in religious systems merely masks their utilitarian origins. Religion from this point of view is a kind of smokescreen created to ensure the adherence of simple peoples to procedures that guarantee their physical survival: procedures that, presumably, these peoples—seen by turn as acutely observant and blatantly irrational—would otherwise ignore.

Such practical explanations as those reviewed earlier implicitly deny the ability of peoples to discriminate between "rules" and "taboos" (see Gottlieb, chapter 2) and obscure the necessity of dealing with menstrual taboos *as* taboos, religious or parareligious constructions, and not merely as social or ecological rules. The Beng of Ivory Coast are probably not unusual in distinguishing between things "taboo" (*sõ pɔ*) and rules that by local standards are commonsensical. If menstrual taboos are extensions of practical rules, as utility theorists argue, why should people not observe them without the threat of *spiritual* sanctions? What we are insisting here is that menstrual taboos—where they indeed comprise taboos and not merely rules—must be analyzed *as* taboos. Embedded as they are in systems of thought, it is in the realm of the symbolic, we suggest, that their origins lie. To assume that people cannot distinguish between practical rules (like the Beng rule that menstrual sex is to be avoided because it is messy) and taboos (like the Levitican taboo that sanctions menstrual sex with spiritual retribution) is to deny the very nature of religion itself.

In short, menstrual taboos are quite different from menstrual rules. When stated as taboos they must have some kind of spiritual or mystical foundation that is apart from any practical effects that might be their by-product. In order to understand such taboos it would seem that systems for symbolically constructing reality, and their religious expressions, must be analyzed first and that the practical implications of these systems cannot be seen a priori as generative of them.

It may well be that many forces have been at work in generating and shaping menstrual customs and ideas—that menstrual taboos themselves are overdetermined by a plethora of psychological, ecological, and social factors. As a result these taboos may function in the management of anxiety, in safeguarding subsistence, and in the management of health and social organization alike; that is, they may be reflective of a variety of human concerns whose origins and functions probably cannot be exhausted by any single causal or functional explanation. But above all, menstrual taboos are cultural constructions and must first be approached as such—symbolic, arbitrary, contextualized, and potentially multivalent whose meanings emerge only within the contexts of the fields of representations in which they exist. We turn now to an examination of the literature that has attempted this.

UNDERSTANDING MENSTRUAL
SYMBOLISM

We have seen that many comparative studies of menstrual taboos base their analyses in a collapsing of distinctions between a variety of rules and religious structures, without inquiring into the specific meanings given these by the cultures in which they are practiced. The entire basis of such analyses can be called into question on logical grounds. If various menstrual taboos seem alike (or at least comparable) to an outside observer (or reader of ethnographic accounts) but are perceived differently within their own cultural contexts, can they then be compared as equivalents (compare Evans-Pritchard 1965a; Eggan 1954)?

Symbolic analyses attending to menstrual taboos as comprising culturally specific subsystems of signification seem to offer firmer grounds for understanding the semantic diversity of menstrual taboos. In terms of general theory, the notion of "pollution" has historically been the most central in such cultural analyses.

MENSTRUATION AND POLLUTION

An abundance of symbolic analyses of menstrual taboos has been built on the concept of "pollution"—symbolic contamination. These studies posit (correctly or incorrectly) that menstrual blood and menstruous women are culturally defined as dangerous to established order (in various senses)—if not universally then at least widely enough to constitute a justifiable generalization. Because menstrual blood and menstruous women are perceived as dangerous, taboos have been devised to contain their energies and keep these from spreading beyond a limited place in the order of things. Among anthropologists utilizing a pollution model in the study of menstrual customs and beliefs two lines of analysis have been followed, independently or in conjunction with each other. The first of these stresses the symbolic structures of pollution concepts in diverse cultures; the second emphasizes the sociological correlates of such symbolic structures.

Both lines of analysis have been pursued by Mary Douglas, an anthropologist perhaps best known for her work in general pollution theory. Although Douglas has written no extended work solely on the topic of menstrual pollution, her broader investigations of pollution (1966, 1972) and of body symbolism (1968, 1970) place her foremost among theoretical contributors to the comparative cultural-anthropological study of menstruation.

THE SYMBOLISM OF MENSTRUAL POLLUTION

In *Purity and Danger* (1966) Douglas proposes that the cultural coding of a substance as a pollutant is based in a shared perception of that substance as anomalous to a general symbolic, or cultural, order. Pollutants are coded as "dirt," symbolic "matter out of place." As such, pollutants are at once a product of a specific symbolic order and a danger to it. As dangers to symbolic order, pollutants are also perceived as dangers to social order given that for Douglas—following Durkheim—the symbolic system has functional goals in the maintenance of society. Hence the acknowledgment of pollutants in cultural systems is accompanied by prohibitions the intent of which is the protection of *social* order from disruptive forces symbolized by culturally defined anomalous substances.

Menstrual blood is a particularly apt candidate for analysis in terms of this theory. As blood itself, menstrual discharge is "out of place," breaching the natural bounds of the body that normally contain it. All forms of human bloodshed may be coded as polluting (and are in many cultures; see Durkheim 1897:48 ff.), but menstruation is generally found especially so. Menstrual blood does not issue randomly or accidentally, as does the blood of wounds, but from a single source and to some extent regularly and predictably (but see later discussion)—if, unlike other products of elimination, uncontrollably. Again, in flowing from the reproductive organs of women such blood, rather than signaling a threat to life, is recognized by most peoples as signaling its very possibility.

Finally, in the vast majority of the world's societies men have a virtual monopoly on routine or ritual forms of bloodletting: hunting, butchering, warfare, rituals involving sacrifice, mutilation, and scarification alike (Rosaldo and Atkinson 1975). Thus the fact that menstruation may be the only act in which women normatively and routinely let blood may, depending on the culture, constitute a symbolic anomaly. In all of these senses, then, there is a compelling tendency to perceive menstrual blood as "out of place," and more so than other sorts of blood. Hence in terms of Douglas's theory, menstrual blood is perceived as a dire pollutant whose effects must be contained through stringent taboos.

In a follow-up article to *Purity and Danger*, Douglas (1972) revised her initial theory of pollution somewhat. Responding to the work of Tambiah (1969) and Bulmer (1967), Douglas argued that although all pollutants are anomalous in terms of a given symbolic order, not all symbolic anomalies must be coded as polluting. Rather, anomalies are simply "powerful," according to Douglas, their power being granted a negative or positive valence to be determined through specific cultural analysis rather than being attributed cross-culturally. An entity deemed polluting in one culture might, for example, be deemed holy in another (see our earlier discussion of Steiner).

In either case, however, the issue remains "power" and is therefore, as in Douglas's original scheme, an essentially religious matter (1966:49). Two issues are thereby addressed. First, the constitution of laws regarding pollution as supernaturally sanctioned taboos, rather than as mundane rules, becomes comprehensible through recognition of "power" as a concept grounded in spiritual notions (as, for instance, is the case in Polynesian *mana*). Second, in keeping with Durkheim's theory of the relationship between religion and society (1915), the matter of containment of extrahuman power links neatly with the social functions of taboos such as menstrual ones. For Douglas consideration of a symbolic anomaly and religious attention to it lead directly to a consideration of sociological functionality.

The sociology of menstrual pollution

The social functions of religious symbolism were broadly explored early on by Durkheim (1915), and his student Marcel Mauss went on to outline a specific model for a sociological analysis of human body symbolism (1979). Mauss's premise was that symbolically elaborated body concepts mirror the society in which they occur. This insight has been further developed by investigators working on a variety of specific problems in body symbolism, including menstruation.

Other than Durkheim himself (1897), one of the first proponents of a Durkheimian perspective in menstruation studies was Meggitt (1964). Meggitt pointed out that the Mae Enga of New Guinea place unusually strong emphasis on the polluting nature of menstruation, in comparison to other nearby peoples. Meggitt proposed that menstrual pollution serves the Mae Enga as a metaphor for their distrust of outsiders, of which a man's wife is, in this virilocal society, the prototype, as the Enga "marry their enemies."

This kind of analysis, which posits a close relationship between ideas about the body social and the body physical, was greatly extended in the work of Mary Douglas (especially 1970). Pollutants such as menstrual blood that are given meanings within religious systems bespeak, for Douglas, the sociosymbolic logic primary to religion itself (1966:6 ff.). By this route Douglas moves firmly back from arbitrary symbolic processes to the determination of those processes by social facts.

In particular Douglas hypothesizes that beliefs about menstrual pollution are found in a restricted number of societies and take on analogous meanings throughout these societies. Menstrual blood is seen as polluting when it symbolically encodes an underlying social-structural ambiguity regarding women and things female. On the one hand a society may have a consciously developed *ideology* of male superiority but, on the other, it may also permit women access to at least some kinds of power, thereby in a sense undermining its own ideology of male dominance. The common fact of menstruation among all women challenges the social order of a male-dominated society and defines and bounds a female subgroup within the society, thereby creating a new separate and dangerous order. Here is a social situation, then, that contains a powerful contradiction, and Douglas suggests that it is in such societies that strong concept of menstrual pollution will arise, signaling the contradiction.

Most recently Balzer (1981) has taken up Douglas's theory, documenting subtly and precisely just how this theory can be used to explain Siberian Khanty menstrual taboos in the wider context of Khanty society. Others have drawn on Douglas's central insight as well, offering variations on its theme. Raymond Kelly (cited in Ortner and Whitehead 1981:20–21) suggests that women are viewed as polluting in societies in which men are dependent on them as sources of prestige—economic, political, or social. Sanday (1981) has also been influenced by Douglas and by Meggitt as well. She proposes that a society will view menstruation as dangerous and polluting if it holds a negative view of its environment as dangerous—threatening starvation—and a concomitant negative relationship with neighboring groups in that environment. Like Meggitt, Sanday predicts that the view of menstrual blood as dangerous mirrors ideas about the outside world, with those ideas being projected onto women's bodies.

Finally, a recent book on reproductive ritual by Karen and Jeffrey Paige (1981) makes further use of Douglas's interpretation. Like Douglas, these authors seek to predict what types of social structures will generate menstrual taboos with (supposedly) concurrent notions of pollution. Paige and Paige postulate that in tribal and band societies one finds the seclusion of menstruous women when there is an unstable economy and, hence, an unstable political base. In this situation, the Paiges hypothesize, men attempt both to maintain control over and to dissociate themselves from women's reproductive cycles. These men seek to demonstrate that they have more of an interest in the society as a whole and in keeping it together in the face of economic hazard than they do in their own narrow conjugal concerns (Paige and Paige 1981:209–254).

The paired theories of menstrual pollution—symbolic and sociological—that have been summarized here have been crucial in shaping current anthropological understanding of menstrual customs and beliefs. How justified is this influence, and in what ways might anthropology now be ready to move on to new theoretical approaches to the topic?

THE LIMITS OF POLLUTION THEORY

Pollution theory, and especially Mary Douglas's initial foray into it (1966), has made notable contributions to knowledge both in anthropology and in other fields, such as the history of religions. Its usefulness, however, is not unbounded. To begin with, there is a clear limit to the fruitfulness of analyses of menstrual blood as "matter out of place," and not recognizing this leaves the replicative analyst open to the dreadful inquiry, "So what?" What, for example, lies beyond the structural grasp of symbolic grammars in the lived experiences of people, once these grammars and their anomalies have been fully explored (see Bruner and Turner 1986)?

The anomalies themselves pose further problems. Although Douglas, in her 1972 article "Self-Evidence," agreed with her critics that symbolic anomalies themselves were of neutral valence, to be "swung" either positively or negatively by the cultural system that determined their anomaly, the possibility that symbols anomalous to one subsystem within a culture could find a securely structured place within an alternate subsystem was not taken up (compare Buckley, this volume). Analyses following Douglas in finding menstrual blood, for instance, polluting because it is anomalous to *the* symbolic system can thus be both overly idealistic and simplistic.

As regards the sociological components of Douglas's overall theory of pollution, the one most frequently utilized by other investigators, there are equivalent problems. The focus on solidarity in male-dominated analytic domains of social action reflects a methodological prejudice, in classic social anthropology, for formal social structures as against informal modes of social organization. "Real" society has been located in large-scale analytic domains—politics, economics, kinship, religion—that are seen as dominated by men occupying named statuses imbued with authority. The often informal structures through which the influence of women may be exercised have customarily been disregarded as inconsequential to this "real" society, as have been formal structures dominated by women (but see, e.g., Weiner 1976). When they have been acknowledged at all, such female-dominated formal structures, and the seemingly more frequent informal ones, have usually been viewed as comprising futile "shadow" societies, generated by male domination and alienated from "real" society (e.g., Wolf 1972). In short, until recently society has been analytically treated as a result of and vehicle for male action.

This effect constitutes the sociological dimension of the cultural theory critiqued earlier: that women are the passive recipients of male-created cultures. It is this male-focal vision of culture and society that underlies analyses of pollution as an index of social-structural tension. The social vision itself, as well as the way in which pollution ideas have been related to it, may reflect the relative domination of the ethnographic record by men, to some extent as anthropologists and, even more, as informants. It is men who have by and large defined menstruation as polluting, and the typical ethnography rarely tells us what the women of the culture at hand think of their own menstrual periods, and those of other women. Thus there hardly seems much solid cross-cultural evidence to support a generalization such as the following, found in a popular text: "There is everywhere a sense that menstruation is unclean. And everywhere women seem to have internalized this attitude to feel shame or unease concerning the natural workings of their own bodies" (Hammond and Jablow 1976:7).

In two of the rare studies that do report the attitudes of individual women toward their menstrual cycles, we find much more variation than this sort of generalization indicates. The Syrian Orthodox Jewish women studied by Kharrazi

(1980) express deep ambivalence, while a portion of Skultans's Welsh sample (chapter 6) apparently feel entirely positive about their periods: far from perceiving them as being
polluting, these women find in their periods confirmation of
their own positively valued womanhood. There is a clear
need, then, to consult female informants before reaching any
conclusions regarding the status of menstruation as an accepted pollutant in any given society.

However careful Mary Douglas herself may have been in
attributing the notion of menstrual pollution only to certain
types of societies (those in which there is evidence for strong
structural ambiguity regarding women), others have not been
so careful. Indeed, when one consults the index of an ethnography, if reference to menstruation is included at all, it is
almost invariably included under the rubric of "menstrual
pollution." One has the impression that most, if not all,
societies view menstruation as a source of pollution, in extension of Douglas's general theory, and that there is no more
to be said. Yet it is clear that the situation is hardly that
simple, and that the very power of pollution theory, coupled
with Western societies' own codings of menstrual blood as a
pollutant, has perhaps created "dirt" where none previously
existed, or existed only for some people and/or in some contexts in a given culture. The elegance of pollution theory itself
can thus manufacture the illusion of overwhelming negativity
in symbolic systems where menstruation may be coded ambiguously or even positively.

In the West we are accustomed to thinking of menstruation
as largely negative. It is "the curse" or, more fully, "the curse
of Eve": a part of God's punishment of women for Eve's role
in the Biblical Fall (Wood 1981).[6] We are not alone in holding
such a view, but it is hardly a universal one. Niangoran-
Bouah (1964:52) reports, for instance, that among the Ebrié
of Ivory Coast it is forbidden to collect fruits of trees protected
by their owners with certain mystically powerful objects. If a
man disobeys this taboo he is afflicted with impotence until
he confesses to the owner; if a woman picks the fruit she is
afflicted with amenorrhea—*losing* her period (rather than en-

during it for eternity like the daughters of Eve) until she confesses. In this case menstruation would appear to be the female counterpart of the masculine erection: associated with fertility, not pollution; desirable, and traumatic to lose. As the Ebrié case shows, menstruation is by no means coded as a universal negative.

Moreover, the widespread exclusive use of males as ethnographic informants tends to place analytic stress on the vulnerability of men to female pollution and the consequent efforts of men to distance themselves from the sources of such pollution. Yet the consistency of reported male testimony regarding menstrual pollution disguises complexities of various kinds.

First, where there is a documented ideology of menstrual pollution, close reading often reveals that not all men are deemed vulnerable to a woman's polluting influence, but only certain classes of men—for example, husbands (e.g., Thompson 1985:706) or old men (Gottlieb, this volume). Second, women are not alone in being suspected of contaminating influence during their periods; often their husbands must share the ritual restrictions incumbent upon their menstruating wives, as among the Hadza of Tanzania (in Douglas 1968:23). The !Gwi of southern Africa, by the same token, initiate the husbands of menarcheal women together with their young wives, the two being scarified and decorated in identical manner (Silberbauer 1963:21–22). Such cases as those of the Hadza and !Gwi suggest that although pollution may be an issue in a given culture, other matters may be equally of concern. Most pertinent here is a notion of *shared substance* between husband and wife, which is quite similar to that shared substance stressed by anthropologists in analyses of the *couvade* (symbolic joint pregnancy and birth labor) which the menstrual practices of the Hadza and !Gwi resemble (see Rivière 1974–75).[7]

Both Hadza and !Gwi men (at least) do view menstruation as polluting. The meanings of menstruation cannot be exhausted in either case through a simple theory of pollution, however, for in both there is at least one other constitutent—

the idea of shared substance. As we suggested for "taboo," culturally constituted symbolic anomalies such as menstrual blood may gather meaning from two directions at once to be both negative, or polluting, and positively powerful. The shortcoming of pollution theory in the analysis of menstrual meanings is that it can too easily obscure, through its own elegance, such potential multivalence. In explanations of menstrual symbolism through it, understanding too easily escapes us. We illustrate this crucial point through further ethnographic examples.

Ritual uses of menstrual blood

The heuristic value of interpreting menstrual blood as an anomalous substance whose power is gained through its relationship to other items in a symbolic structure is clear (Gottlieb forthcoming); again and again menstrual discharge has indeed been granted the extraordinary powers of the anomalous, or "liminal" (Turner 1969). The symbolically constituted power of menstrual blood makes it, "naturally," in Douglas's terms (1970), a prime substance for manipulation in rituals. At the same time, its frequently multiple meanings as well as its symbolic arbitrariness suit it for use in a variety of rituals with diverse and even contradictory intent, both intra- and cross-culturally.

As a culturally specified pollutant, menstrual blood is an obvious candidate for ritual use with the negative intent of bringing harm to others, especially through witchcraft. Thus among the Mae Enga, it is held that "menstrual blood introduced into a man's food . . . quickly kills him, and young women crossed in love sometimes seek their revenge in this way" (Meggitt 1964:207). Similar alleged uses of menstrual blood may be cited for any number of cultures, in most of which—as in New Guinea—avoidance of this substance is conjoined with a fear of those who are reputed to *seek* contact with it for unscrupulous purposes. Menstrual witchcraft, where it is reported, need not necessarily be voluntary. For example, in China, according to Ahern (1975:194–195), people say that menstrual blood adheres to the ground, making it dangerous to walk on the streets. The use of menstrual blood in witchcraft thus seems to exist within a continuum of negative effects and manipulations all reflecting a clear underlying notion of pollution. Quite opposite effects and ritual manipulations have also been reported, however, that cannot be resolved through pollution theory.

Probably the most commonly reported *positive* use of menstrual blood is in the manufacture of various kinds of love charms and potions. These occur in cultures as diverse as the medieval farmers and shepherds of southwestern France (Ladurie 1979:32), the Beng of Ivory Coast (Gottlieb, this volume), and rural whites in the United States. Kirksey (1984:32) gives the following fictional but ethnographically informed rendering of a conversation in Southern Illinois:

> "You remember your Uncle Skinny and your Aunt Jac, don't you?"
> "Yes, ma'am," Ward said. "I remember them pretty well."
> "Maybe you don't remember this, but your Uncle Skinny snuck around on your aunt a lot. That is, till she come to me, said that Skinny was stepping out on her, said she wanted to keep him at home. So I told her to put a spoonful of her 'time of the month' in his coffee regularly. If she did, he'd never leave her. Of course, you know what happened, I'm sure. Your uncle died in your aunt's arms, loving her to the very end."
> Ward was shocked to hear the tale, but he remembered his Uncle Skinny's often docile, loving manner toward Aunt Jac.

We also find accounts of *men* using menstrual blood to ensure the fidelity of their wives, as Pliny reported for Imperial Rome (in Novak 1916:273). These accounts seem better analyzed in terms of a theory of shared substance, as discussed earlier, than one of pollution. Their sense would not seem exhaustible by this or any other single cross-cultural theory, however, for the accounts themselves arise within a literature replete with positive uses of menstrual blood that cannot be explained through a notion of shared substance—such as the medicinal uses described earlier—but, rather, seem to have in common only the general theme of "power."

Such power has been specified through a variety of metaphors—"pollution," "shared substance," and others. Among such metaphors that of "life force" (Kuper 1947:107) is perhaps most striking. In this case menstrual blood is viewed as an emblem or manifestation of creative power, particularly in the sense of fertility. Thus the use of menstrual blood in fertility rituals is widespread (and, it would seem, conceptually linked to the use of this substance in love charms). The Nigerian Tiv use menstrual blood in the *imborivungu* ("owl pipe") ritual, which also involves human sacrifice (Lincoln 1975:51 ff.). Menstrual blood is mixed with that of a sacrificial child in a ritual pipe as a central act in an elaborate ritual through which the farms surrounding a ritual center are blessed, and their fertility—and that of the women who inhabit them—ensured. (For other examples see Poole 1982:105; Jetté 1911:257, 403; Yalman 1964:135.)

The use of menstrual symbols in the enhancement of life force (in the sense of fertility) seems to point in two directions at once: toward a better understanding of pollution, when it is manipulated toward the protection of life, and toward an appreciation of folk-biological components in culturally specific menstrual meanings. This complex, even dialectical, situation may again be illuminated through ethnographic examples.

Menstrual blood is often used in symbolically powerful objects the purpose of which is to keep life-threatening forces at bay. Among the Kwakiutl, for example, "the malignant power which menstrual blood was believed to have for human beings extended to monsters; therefore when women were traveling, they kept some menstrual blood in a bit of shredded bark to be used to poison a monster should one appear" (Ford 1941:35). In this instance the polluting powers of menstruation are linked with its status as a symbol of life force to be manipulated in such a way that its very negativity protects life itself.

We suspect that such a dialectical relationship between the negative and positive poles of symbolic menstrual power is found more commonly than has been remarked upon. An example is provided by the well-studied Asante of Ghana. According to Rattray (1927:74–75, 211, 234, 271), menstruating Asante women are subject to numerous taboos, some of which are kept under pain of immediate, automatic death. The strength of menstrual pollution may, however, be used by priests in assuring their own safety. Asante priests manufacture fetishes (*kunkuma*) of brooms defiled with menstrual blood, and "a priest is supposed to be safe without any other protective charm provided he has with him his *kunkuma*" (Rattray 1927:14). The logic appears simple enough: potent, negatively valued substances such as menstrual blood may be manipulated for positive ends by those who are themselves spiritually potent enough to reverse the valence and make it positive. Yet the Asante case exhibits further complications.

Although the Asante view menstrual blood as definitively polluting, subject to "one of the greatest and deadliest taboos in Ashanti" (Rattray 1927:13), they also celebrate menarche with an elaborate ritual for individual girls in which the menarcheal girl, among other things, sits in public view beneath an umbrella (a symbol generally reserved for kings and other dignitaries), receiving gifts and congratulations and observing singing and dancing performed in her honor (Rattray 1927:69–74). Within Asante society, then, menstrual symbolism is highly complex. Menstrual blood itself causes dire pollution (especially to ancestral altars), yet menarche is celebrated with profound honors and, moreover, priests use menstrual blood toward positive ends. Among the Asante as among comparable peoples, we are in a realm far beyond the grasp of any simple model of menstruation-as-pollution.

We suggest that such diversity in meaning is strongly tied to indigenous conceptions of the biological function of menstruation in the reproductive cycles of women. Though this has been symbolized in different ways among different peoples, particularly widespread conceptions focus on the symbolic role of menstruation in human fertility. When they are found these ideas further undermine the utility of a simple pollution model of menstruation.

Menstruation and gestation

In the medieval European interpretation of Aristotle's biology, menstrual blood was held to be the "matter" to which semen supplied "form," creating the fetus (Wood 1981:715–719). In this system excess menstrual blood was retained in the womb, providing the basis for lactation at parturition (Wood 1981). The basic elements of this folk-biological theory of conception and lactation are widespread, found in many cultures that, like medieval Europe, also view menstrual blood as a pollutant.

For example, the Paiela of New Guinea have a highly elaborate theory of conception in which menstrual blood is held to be "bound" slowly by semen introduced into the womb through repeated intercourse (Biersack 1983). (Also see Evans-Pritchard 1932:407 on the Azande of the Sudan; O'Flaherty 1980:42 on fourth-century India; and Laqueur 1986 on Europe through the Renaissance.) The Mohave Indians of southern California give an added twist to this general theory, viewing the blood of parturition as "a sort of supermenstruation, expelling all at once the accumulated menstrual blood of ten missed periods" (Devereux 1950:253), and deeming this blood polluting, as they do menstrual blood.

Such folk theories—and they are both numerous and widely distributed (see Ford 1945)[8]—both complicate efforts to analyze menstrual symbolism purely in terms of a theory of pollution and, at the same time, inform that theory. The negativity of menstruation is necessarily made ambiguous by the inclusion of the menstrual cycle among the reproductive processes, which is generally viewed quite positively. Ernestine Friedl (1975:29) remarks that the very occurrence of menstruation can be interpreted as a sign of death, insofar as it is a signal that a new life has not been conceived. Friedl finds an explanation of menstrual taboos and notions of menstrual pollution in this connection between menstruation and death (but see Gottlieb, chapter 2, for a different view).

We hypothesize that where the fetus is held to be menstrually constituted, one will find strong menstrual taboos and assertions of pollution. This is based on the supposition that such taboos and ideologies reflect a notion that the proper role of menstrual blood is in the formation of new life, and that its flow beyond the boundaries of women's bodies marks a missed opportunity for procreation. Our hypothesis would illuminate the observation of Vosselmann (1935:79) that "without a doubt this blood that is so useful . . . when it was retained in the womb lost these [useful] qualities as soon as it began to escape from it" (our translation). In this way the presence of menstrual taboos and notions of menstrual pollution, far from signaling the inherent pollution of the female principle as has so often been postulated, may instead point toward a more complex and far-reaching conceptual system that includes elements of folk-biology to constitute the basis for the meaning of the taboos themselves.

This would seem to be the case in Swazi culture, as reported by Kuper (1947; also see Wright 1982 on the Navajo): "menstrual blood is . . . considered part of the foetus that grows within the womb—its discharge is analogous to a miscarriage" (Kuper 1947:107). In keeping with our hypothesis, the Swazi say that menstrual blood can pollute crops, cattle, and men alike. However, Kuper continues (1947:107),

> In certain situations . . . menstrual blood is not destructive, but is considered a life symbol or rather a life force; thus the recurrence of menstruation after a woman gives birth "washes her" and enables her to cohabit again with her husband, and after a death in the family circle, a man should not cohabit with his wife until she has menstruated.

In this case menstruation both pollutes and purifies: "The verb (Z[ulu]) *geza*, to wash, purify after death, is a euphemism for menstruation. The flow of blood pollutes women yet also cleanses after death or bearing a child" (Kuper 1947:107). (A parallel understanding occurs in certain rabbinical commentaries among Orthodox Jews, as in this Talmudic scholar's verse: "As yeast is good for dough, / so is menstruation good for women"—cited in Vosselmann 1935:121.)

Our hypothesis may explain a certain percentage, but undoubtedly not all, of those cases in which notions of menstrual pollution are found. That is, it should explain those societies in which are found an idea both of menstrual pollution *and* of the menstrual constitution of the fetus. We hope future researchers will pursue this line of inquiry. They will need to take into account indigenous perceptions of biological processes. We turn now to a brief consideration of biological presuppositions in Western cultures and of their role in shaping analyses of the menstrual customs and beliefs of others.

BIOLOGY AND THE INTERPRETATION OF MENSTRUAL SYMBOLISM

Symbolic analyses of pollution have contributed much to a general understanding of cognitive structures. They have not, however, contributed significantly to an understanding of the actual menstrual experiences of the world's women. In part this is because the discourse that includes these analyses neglects physical and individual experience. Absorption in "social facts" has contributed to a disinterest among ethnographic field-workers in gathering data on women's menstrual periods per se. Then, too, the intimacy of the topic and the related difficulties of both cross- and same-gender interviewing may contribute to the dearth of data (Ardener 1972; Gregory 1984). Prudery among both field-workers and native informants has no doubt played a part, despite the fact that anthropologists are widely perceived as less squeamish about such matters than other social scientists (Wood 1981:712).

For all these reasons, the menstrual periods of mature women have received little anthropological attention (but see Snowden and Christian 1983). What is generally available in the literature is detail of a limited nature on the ritualization of a putatively normative menstrual period, ending with an implicit "and so on"—throughout the society and all of its women's reproductive careers. There are few comparative data on such apparently purely physical matters as the expected duration of women's fecundity, or on the expected or realized frequency of menstrual punctuation during it. "And so on" assumes an undemonstrated monthly round, despite the strong possibility that, in fact, menstruation itself has been a comparatively infrequent occurrence in many cultures for most of human history (see later discussion).

Our assumption of monthly repetition in interpreting menstrual rituals reflects a sureness in our own scientific model of menstruation as being applicable to all women at all times. Views of the physical actualities of menstruation other than those promulgated by science (such as the folk-theories of conception and gestation sketched earlier) tend to be received as representing "a curious blending of speculation and superstition, with very little foundation of real fact" (Novak 1916:270). With only a few notable exceptions (e.g., Shostak 1981:*passim;* Howell 1979:120–121, 177–179, 189–211), such unexamined certainty in our own scientific models has discouraged as unnecessary the gathering of detailed information on the physical actualities of menstruation in other cultures at the same time as it has mitigated against close scrutiny of folk-biological models. However, the biological models themselves are based in studies of modern Western populations; moreover, biology, whatever its empirical base, also of necessity has folk-biological components. The unexamined assumption of the pertinence of scientific biology to the study of menstruation in other cultures, then, comprises a species of ethnocentrism and, like all ethnocentrism, distorts cross-cultural understanding (see Bleier 1984; Ehrenreich and English 1974; Fausto-Sterling 1985; Koeske 1985; Sommer 1985).

SCIENCE AS FOLK THEORY

It has long been routine to insist upon a rigid distinction between, on the one hand, folk theories such as those of fetal composition outlined earlier, apparently based in "irrational belief," if not "superstition," and, on the other hand, scientific theories based in empirical observation and the experimental method and leading cumulatively to positive "knowledge."

Although the justice of such a distinction has been hotly debated (e.g., Horton and Finnegan 1973; B. Wilson 1977; Needham 1972; Geertz 1984), it is, in anthropological practice at least, more habitual than examined.

We recognize, of course, folk theories within scientific cultures. For instance, Snow and Johnson, in an article on menstrual "folklore" (1977), show that many poor Mexican-American, black, and white women in urban Michigan believe that

> the time that a woman is most likely to become pregnant . . . [is] immediately before menstruation when the uterus is beginning to open, during the menstrual period when it is fully open, and immediately after the cessation of the flow before it is tightly closed again. At other times, the women reasoned, the sperm would not be able to enter to allow conception to take place. (Snow and Johnson 1977:2737; compare Hanson 1970, 1975; Hunte 1985:53; Price 1984:22–23)

The beliefs of the Michigan women gain their meanings in academic discourse in part through their apparent contrasts with scientific "knowledge." Yet such contrast is not always as stark as it is presumed to be. After all, only within the past half-century has the most likely time for ovulation as roughly twelve to fourteen days after the onset of the flow been accepted by the scientific community (Laqueur 1986:3). As late as the 1960s some Western physicians themselves considered conception most likely to occur during menstruation (Burley 1979:836; also see Laqueur 1986 for a history of changing Western ideas regarding fertility).[9]

The point here is not to catalog, yet again, errors that have occurred along the route to scientific knowledge and thus "prove" the fallibility of science. Rather, we wish to argue that the rigid dichotomization of "folk" and "scientific" theories of menstruation, and the usually unexamined acceptance of the latter as more "truthful" than the former, has weakened the anthropological study of menstruation. We have tended to view our scientific biology as independent of historical context, and our own culturally constructed views of the human body as received from the laboratory on solid empirical grounds. We presume, then, to "know" what menstruation *really* is and turn our attention to nonscientific "belief" systems armed with this knowledge. In studying menstrual taboos we have tended to take the bodies of women as empirical givens, quite separate from the multiple cultural variables that are the subjects of our inquiries.

For example, Western culture has long had a tendency to dichotomize the life of the body and the life of the mind. A corollary in the medical field is the proclivity for assigning the causes of given diseases as lying in either the mind *or* the body but not in both. In the case of "female problems," this view has been particularly prominent. As Emily Martin shows in chapter 7, nineteenth-century physicians portrayed the gynecological complaints of women as originating either in hormonal changes over which they had no control or in the supposed unsteadiness of the "female mind" itself. Until recently, twentieth-century doctors have been likely to dismiss women's menstrual complaints as being "all in the head" and to leave it at that. Current medical thinking has now gone to the opposite extreme and increasingly views menstrual complaints as "all in the body," to be treated with drugs alone (New York Times 1986).

Yet this rigid dichotomy between "diseases of the body" and "diseases of the mind" may be at once "hard science" and a culturally contextualized and sophisticated folk belief system, as Martin argues for the "premenstrual syndrome" (PMS) in industrial societies. She accepts that hormonal changes in women during the paramenses may one day be established by science and that such changes perhaps physically affect women's consciousness. Martin argues, however, that what such putative "facts" *mean* to scientists and medical doctors, and how these people respond to the "facts" that they have reported, both theoretically and therapeutically, are very much culturally conditioned and biased (see also Koeske 1985; Sommer 1985). Such meanings and responses, rather than springing from empirical research, are the symbolic products of culture history.

To date, very few studies have investigated the extent of

PMS as a physical *and* psychological experience among non-Western women. What data are available, however, suggest that the severe PMS discomfort and psychological changes familiar to many women in industrialized societies are not universal experiences. As early as 1928, Margaret Mead wrote in her popular study of Samoan women that the extreme symptoms of menstrual discomfort found among Western women were absent among their Samoan counterparts (Mead 1928:113). More intensive studies of non-Western women's experiences are clearly needed. In the meantime, some writers on medicine have questioned the validity of all current scientific research into the physiological basis of paramenstrual symptoms (Sommer 1985; Harlow 1986).

That our scientific knowledge of menstruation is culturally constructed is further shown by our invention of the contraceptive pill, which was developed to "mimic the monthly menstrual cycle in the belief that this was more normal than amenorrhoea" (Anderson 1983:31). In his study of the effects of lactation on fertility, Peter Anderson points out that although monthly menstruation has been seen scientifically as normal and amenorrhoea as abnormal, there is a fair amount of evidence that regular menstrual periods are deleterious to women's health and, more certainly, that "many women would now welcome a form of contraception that mimicked the natural effect of breast-feeding and produced amenorrhoea" (Anderson 1983:31). The scientists who developed the contraceptive pill assumed both the normalcy and desirability of regular periods. Yet there is strong evidence that "normal" monthly periods are probably not that at all, historically and cross-culturally, but rather are most likely biologically anomalous products of particular cultural systems at specific historical conjunctions. Both Frisch (e.g., 1975, etc.) and Harrell (1981), among others, present arguments that put into question the unexamined assumption of universality in the menstrual patterns familiar to contemporary industrialized societies.

Frisch argues (e.g., 1975) that both historically and cross-culturally, there is ample evidence of far later menarche, earlier menopause, and greater frequency and duration of amen-orrhea than that to which we are now accustomed. She postulates that the causes of historically and culturally specific shifts in menstrual patterns are related to changes in diet and physical activity. The menstrual pattern most familiar to Westerners seems to be the result of high-fat diets together with a decline in rigorous exertion among women. This suggests that until we have far more data on menstrual patterns in nonindustrial societies, all general theories of menstrual symbolism may be skewed by mistaken assumptions of menstrual frequency and regularity and about the duration of female fecundity.

The point is reiterated and underscored by Harrell (1981). Basing her theories on the ethnography of a Taiwanese village, Harrell investigates the effects of lactation in suppressing menstruation. She suggests that the frequency and regularity of menstruation in contemporary industrial societies in which both low pregnancy rates and bottle feeding prevail may well have influenced our interpretations of menstrual symbolism in different types of societies. What we deal with as a frequent and regular phenomenon of long duration in a woman's life may be, in other cultures and at other times, a fairly rare occurrence, the rarity of which may indeed inform the great potency attributed to it and the stringency of ritual prohibitions by which it is so often surrounded. Diane Bell, for example, reports that the elderly Australian Aboriginal women with whom she worked could remember each menstrual period of their fertile lives and count them on their fingers (personal communication, 1983). Howell (1979) provides more formal data on the rarity of menstruation among !Kung San women in the Kalahari region of southern Africa.

Findings such as those of Martin, Frisch, and Harrell may have direct implications for the symbolic analysis of menstrual customs and beliefs in a variety of cultures, including those of the industrialized world. Harrell (1981) suggests that where the phenomenon of menstruation is biologically anomalous in people's experience, it may be construed as out of place in their symbolic schemes as well. In societies in which this is demonstrably the case, the physical extraordinariness of menstrual periods themselves, as well as the logic of their symbolic construction, must be considered. Although a structural theory of pollution such as Douglas's may be pertinent to analyzing the latter, a more processual one, such as Victor Turner's "anti-structural" theory of "liminality" (1969), may be more capable of reflecting the cultural response to the physically extraordinary. Analyses such as Marla Powers's (1980) of Oglala menstrual symbolism in light of Turner's theory make good sense when applied to societies in which the incidence of menstrual periods is low and where such periods, when they do occur, are granted the transformative powers of the physically anomalous (but compare Bynum 1984).

The implications of infrequent and irregular occurrences of menstruation for the symbolic analysis of menstrual customs have not yet received the full attention they clearly deserve, yet other recent findings regarding the physiology and biology of menstruation have been more fully addressed in the present volume. The relationship of menstrual periods to lunar cycles, while a perennial feature of folklore in both industrial and nonindustrial societies, received little scientific attention until the past three decades. Such a connection, when attended to at all, had customarily been deemed "absurd" (Novak 1916:274) because were it to exist, all women would menstruate at the same time—something viewed as "obviously untrue" (p. 274).

Beginning in the 1950s, however (Menaker and Menaker 1959; Hauenschild 1960; Dewan 1967; etc.), this "lunar connection" came under serious consideration by biologists, with results highly suggestive of both evolutionary and synchronic connections between lunar periodicity and the menstrual cycle. Concurrently the corollary that women tend to menstruate "at the same time" was substantiated by McClintock's 1971 report on menstrual synchrony and suppression among women in college dormitories. While the cultural-anthropological implications of new cross-cultural findings regarding menstrual anomaly and irregularity have yet to be fully investigated, three chapters (8–10) in the present volume do initiate anthropological consideration of the relationship between the "McClintock effect" and menstrual customs.

The authors of these chapters have not, however, fully reconciled their hypotheses with those of Frisch and Harrell, nor do those of the latter authors always accord with data that, in some cases at least, suggest regularly recurrent menstrual periods among certain nonindustrialized peoples.[10]

Clearly the cultural construction of reality depends upon the embodiment of minds in physical forms, and those forms must have *something* to do with the conceptual worlds that are (relatively) arbitrarily constructed. Conversely, the meanings that are culturally attributed to the human body and its processes, including menstruation, must have *something* to do with those processes—so-called psychosomatic illness and "voodoo death," as well as PMS, providing obvious examples. As ecologists have shown the land to be, so is the human body changed by people's culturally shaped conceptions of it.

Menstrual symbolism has been eloquently addressed as a mental product of social requisites, but the dialectical role of physical experience in such creativity has been virtually ignored. We are not suggesting that the culturally defined body shapes society, or that the reverse is true; rather, that body, culture, and society are all implicated cybernetically in a single system of highly complex origins and functions. It is our own cultural system, in which the (culturally defined) body is divorced from the mind that constructs it, that dictates a reading either from society to body or, in the sociobiologist's view, from body to society, rather than a dialectical relationship between the two terms.

CONCLUSION

Our effort throughout the foregoing has been to provide a context within which the explorations of menstrual customs and beliefs that are presented in the following essays might be better appreciated. These essays grow out of a venerable tradition in ethnological inquiry and, at the same time, break from that tradition. By looking critically at the dominant lines in earlier investigations of the topic, we have suggested why such a break has been necessary.

The various scholars who have contributed to this book have investigated a wide variety of ethnographic situations and theoretical possibilities. None has suggested single, general theoretical alternatives to received, universalistic approaches (although Knight, chapter 10, comes close in a way that we view as heuristically useful, though by no means definitive). Yet all do contribute cumulatively to the eventual construction of a comprehensive theoretical approach to the topic of menstruation, if in no other ways than by making clear the kinds of historical and ethnographic diversity and both symbolic and biological complexity that must be accommodated. And many do suggest specific new lines of inquiry that might next be pursued.

Finally, we hope that such new inquiries will continue to illuminate the practices and systems of knowledge not only of "exotic" societies but also of our own society. As we write, the issue of menstrual discomfort, both physiological and psychological, is very much in the news (e.g., Holden 1986). Indeed, PMS, understood as the involuntary and complex result of hormonal change, is today forwarded as a scientific explanation (and, now, justification) for periodic irrationality in women, excluding them from responsibility for, among other things, murder (Sommer 1984). One suspects that given the current fashionableness of PMS as a sort of revisionist feminist-inspired restatement of the hormonal onslaught thesis, a fresh supply of explanations of menstrual taboos as necessary to control "hormonal onslaught" is in the offing, to be rationalized somehow as in women's interests (but see Rome 1986). Yet before such an "anthropological" trend gets under way, we would urge that researchers acquire better knowledge of *both* hormonal changes throughout the menstrual cycle and of native perceptions of women's behavior during the paramenstruum as well as their own explanations for it. In the meantime, "hormonal onslaught" would seem the contemporary equivalent of "menotoxins": notions cast in a scientific idiom that are reflective of far broader symbolic complexes in the cultural construction of gender.

Obviously we agree with many others of our era that scientific knowledge is historically and culturally contextualized, relative rather than absolute. As Augé has written (1982:6), "Anthropology is produced and received by men [*sic*] of a particular epoch and society, in a determinate intellectual and political conjuncture."

The intellectual axis of the contributions that follow was provided by "the virtual explosion in anthropology" during the 1960s "of the idea that cultures were systems of symbols and meanings" (Singer 1980:486). Its political axis has been provided, directly or indirectly, by the modern restatement of feminism that began to emerge at about the same time. Twenty years have intervened, lending a certain perspective on the limitations as well as the strengths of both symbolic anthropology and the initial restatement of feminist ideology. It is from this latter-day perspective that the following chapters view the topic of menstruation.

The essays that follow are divided into three sections, the first two broad in range, the third concentrated on a single topic. The first of these sections, part II, "Menstrual Images, Meanings, and Values," offers three accounts that focus on the cosmologies and semantic categories of specific cultures as embedded contexts for understanding both those cultures' menstrual practices and the symbolic valuations of menstruation that underlie them. Part III, "The Sociology of Menstrual Meanings," comprises three chapters that concentrate on the social and political dimensions of menstrual customs, exploring in a variety of ways the basic issue of gender authority. In part IV, "Exploratory Directions: Menses, Culture, and Time," contributors investigate the relevance of "menstrual synchrony"—the fact that the periods of individual women who share close social space tend to occur at the same time— to an understanding of menstrual meaning and experience in diverse cultures. The contents of parts II and III are based in their authors' direct observations; those of the fourth section are in large part deductive, historically reconstructive, and heuristic.

The six essays of the two parts that follow make clear the fruitfulness of current explorations in the anthropology of menstruation. The more speculative essays in the final section suggest the possibilities that may ultimately be substantiated through continuing exploration. The specific chapters that make up the remainder of this volume are introduced in greater detail at the beginning of the part to which they belong.

PART II

MENSTRUAL IMAGES, MEANINGS, AND VALUES

The three essays of this part, by Alma Gottlieb, Carol Delaney, and Laura W. R. Appell, offer analyses of non-Western cultural systems in which menstruation is accorded positive, negative, and neutral valences, respectively. The section begins with Gottlieb's interpretation of menstrual taboos among the Beng of Ivory Coast. Addressing a set of proscriptions affecting Beng women and men, Gottlieb shows that whereas at first these proscriptions seem to exemplify a familiar set of negative beliefs regarding menstrual pollution, this is not the case. Rather than placing it in simple opposition to a native category of "pure" things, the Beng find menstruation meaningful through a far more complex system of signification revolving around worship of the Earth. Beng menstrual taboos cannot be understood independently of Beng cosmological, subsistence, and fertility symbolism. Within this context Beng menstrual practices reveal a central concern, not with absolute pollution but with respect for the processes of reproduction (which include menstruation) and of the Earth.

Through her Beng case study, Gottlieb demonstrates that the significance and value of menstruation in any given culture must be determined *in situ* and cannot be ascribed on the basis of an a priori scheme. Specifically, and contrary to received interpretations, the existence of menstrual taboos does not necessarily signify a general devaluation of women or the female sphere. Rather, Gottlieb shows that the significance and value of menstrual taboos do not exist in bounded isolation but occur within the context, especially, of religious symbolism and cannot be understood without accounting for such embeddedness. These two points are given further attention in the third chapter, Carol Delaney's "Mortal Flow."

Delaney investigates menstrual symbolism in a Muslim Turkish village. Like Gottlieb, she locates the significance of menstruation within the context of a religious cosmological system, and in relation to ideas about land and reproduction. Whereas Gottlieb demonstrates that the Beng do not view menstruation as polluting in any of the usual senses, Delaney analyzes the reasons that the Turkish villagers she has studied *do* view it in precisely this way, and how their view reflects and enhances the subordination of the interests of women to those of men.

In village Turkey, Delaney argues, the meaning and value of menstruation arise as parts of a larger web of Koranic ideology and indigenous agrarian belief. Within this multilayered context women's bodies are ambiguous loci of reproductive power as well as male fear and disgust. Menstrual blood stands as a prime symbol of women's nature, both physical and metaphysical, and menstrual taboos as a means through which men gain security in an ambiguous, culturally constituted world through affirming the values of an "other," equally culturally constituted, paradisical world of Islamic salvation.

While Gottlieb and Delaney both establish the significance of menstruation in terms of cosmology and reproductive ideology, Laura W. R. Appell, in chapter 4, establishes such significance—or, rather, a total lack thereof—among the Rungus of Borneo in terms of its social and sexual contexts. Whereas the Beng value menstruation and Turkish villagers abhor it, the Rungus seem to ignore it completely.

According to Appell, Rungus women treat their menstrual periods as simple processes of elimination, paying them as little attention as possible. This neglect, Appell argues, must be understood in light of Rungus attitudes toward other aspects of their sexual lives, for in their understanding of menstruation the Rungus emphasize sexuality rather than reproduction. The Rungus do not view menstruation as either polluting or pure, seeing in it only a manifestation of sexuality. Because all sexual matters are highly private and potential sources of public embarrassment, Rungus do not call attention to this dimension of their lives through articulated menstrual symbolism or elaborated menstrual practices. Importantly for Appell, this lack of menstrual symbolism is coherent with Rungus social organization and ideology, emphasizing as these do a balance of power between men and women. Given Rungus insistence on gender symmetry, the kinds of negative menstrual taboos found by Delaney in Turkey, with their grounding in a native theory of female pollution, are absent.

The three chapters of this section elucidate a full range of culturally specific codings of menstruation. In their methodological emphases, they also introduce three quite distinct approaches to menstrual meaning: Gottlieb stressing symbolic analysis; Delaney, cultural interpretation; and Appell, a sociological approach. Appell's contribution thus serves as a bridge into part III, in which sociological issues are central.

2

Menstrual Cosmology among the Beng of Ivory Coast

Alma Gottlieb

I seek in this chapter to relocate the topic of menstruation to a new framework at variance with much of the received literature on menstruation (see part I)—a framework not directly defined by gender at all and not restricted to the view that menstrual pollution and menstrual blood are by definition viewed negatively. Specifically, I explore Beng notions of menstruation as they relate to wider notions of pollution and of fertility. I argue that rather than indicating a concern with the general pollution of women and, hence, women's lower status, Beng menstrual taboos and notions of menstrual pollution address a larger concern with the spatiosymbolic pollution of human fertility when it is removed from its proper place. Moreover, rather than debasing women, menstruation among the Beng serves to give added value to a major aspect of women's labor—that of cooking.

THE BENG OF IVORY COAST

The Beng are a small ethnic group in Ivory Coast, having a population of about 10,000 in the prefecture of M'Bahiakro, and speaking a Southern Mande language. Traditionally the economy was a mixed one of hunting, gathering, and extensive horticulture; currently the introduction of cash crops (mostly coffee but also rice and cocoa) has meant that farming has taken precedence over hunting for men, though women continue to gather actively as well as to farm. Politically the

Beng are divided into two regions, the Savanna and Forest, each ruled by a king assisted by a queen (Gottlieb 1988). In addition, each village has its own male and female chief. The social system is based on double descent, with corporate matriclans and patriclans, each having its own functions. Only the matriclans are localized, the majority of members residing together in a section of a single village, whereas the members of the patriclans live dispersed throughout all the Beng villages (see Gottlieb 1983; 1986b).

As in several other West African societies, the main cult of traditional Beng religion is that of the Earth. There are several named Earths on which all the villages as well as the surrounding forest and fields are located. All autonomous villages have their own Earth shrines and priests ("Masters of the Earth") who regularly offer sacrifices and prayers to the Earth on behalf of individuals or groups. Women as well as men may offer animals to be sacrificed to the Earth (by the Master of the Earth), but only men may eat the meat from such sacrificed animals (*ba sòŋ,* "Earth meat"). The Earth holds wide-ranging powers over human life (see later discussion, note 10, and *passim*). In addition, ancestor and forest spirits are recognized and worshipped either individually or as part of various cults. Nowadays many Beng, especially in certain villages, have converted to Islam and a few, especially in one village, have become Catholics. Most aspects of the traditional religion remain intact, however, and many of the Muslim and Catholic converts participate in at least some of the older practices.

There is no initiation ritual to mark the passage of boys from childhood to adulthood. Teenage girls are initiated, but it is an individual ritual done singly for each girl. When her daughter reaches the age of about fifteen or sixteen years, a mother formally announces to her husband that the girl is of marriageable age. Depending on a complex set of marriage rules, the mother or father (with their kin) may arrange a husband for the daughter at this time (Gottlieb 1986a). If the parents do select a groom, the girl's initiation takes place up to one or two years later and constitutes the first day of her wedding. If, however, neither of the parents arranges a husband for the daughter at the time of the announcement of her eligibility, the girl is then initiated within a few weeks. In this case it is said that she is "married" by the initiation, despite the fact that she has neither a husband nor a fiancé. This is because there are certain consequences common to both initiation and marriage: most important, after she is initiated, as well as after she is married, a girl may no longer go into the forest while menstruating, and she must wash daily, every morning (see later discussion).

As in most of sub-Saharan Africa, polygyny is the male ideal for marriage, though by no means attained by all men. The Beng admit that most women do not like polygyny, though it is not unheard of for co-wives to get along. In polygynous marriages the husband establishes a rotational system: each wife sleeps three to five consecutive nights with him, during which time she cooks for him and brings him his bathwater.

MENSTRUAL TABOOS

Beng observe four taboos concerning menstruation:

1. No initiated, married, or previously married woman who is menstruating may set foot in the forest for any reason other than to defecate. In particular, she may not do any kind of work in the fields (which are located in the forest), nor chop wood or fetch water, both of which tasks are generally performed daily. (For this reason any premenopausal woman who does not have a daughter to help her with these tasks is wise to keep a sizable store of firewood and water at the house, in preparation for the days when she will be menstruating.)

2. A menstruating woman may not touch a corpse.

3. A man may not eat any food cooked by a menstruating woman if he has ever eaten meat from animals sacrificed to the "strongest" Earth of his village.[1] Significantly, this taboo is more relevant for old men than for young men (see later).

4. A menstruating woman may not touch the logs or live coals on the fire of a nonmenstruating woman, nor may the logs or live coals of her own fire be brought into the forest by another farmer for the purposes of cooking lunch.

When I first learned of these taboos I thought they indicated yet another case of the pollution of women through menstruation, and yet another instance of women's oppression. I therefore felt little curiosity about them and little need to explore them further. I did, however, ask a Master of the Earth one day exactly what it was about menstrual blood that was polluting to the Earth. His answer was unexpected:

> Menstrual blood is special because it carries in it a living being. It works like a tree. Before bearing fruit, a tree must first bear flowers. Menstrual blood is like the flower: it must emerge before the fruit—the baby—can be born. Childbirth is like a tree finally bearing its fruit, which the woman then gathers.

I was delighted with this poetic statement but saw no relevance to my original question. I repeated the question—Why is menstrual blood *polluting*?—and the Master of the Earth only shrugged, got bored, and soon left.[2]

PREGNANT SEX, MENSTRUAL SEX, AND POLLUTION OF THE EARTH

Ignoring my informant's lead, I started to look for the kinds of answers that anthropology leads us to expect, by seeking other ways in which menstrual blood and other female substances might be considered polluting. I was surprised to find that there seemed to be no other rules specifying what activities a woman should or should not pursue during menstruation: she might attend funerals and weddings, and dance and sing at both;[3] she might attend a childbirth, cook for the woman in labor, remove the placenta, and do other childbirth-related chores; sit in on trials and political meetings; spin cotton; bathe her small children; and so on. In short, she was by no means isolated from the flux of social life.

I was even more surprised to find that sexual activity seemed not to be affected by female substances as it often is in societies where these are considered polluting. Thus though not commonly done, it is not taboo (*sõ pɔ*) for a husband and wife to have intercourse during the wife's menstrual period. My informant giggled when I asked her about this: she said that generally the couple wouldn't want to have intercourse then "because it would be too bloody" but that if they did, there would be no negative consequences. No sacrifices or other ritual expiations would be required, as there was nothing spiritually wrong with the act. While it is not common for a menstruating woman to make love with her husband, it is common for them to sleep together, regardless of whether or not she has a co-wife.[4] This casual attitude toward menstrual blood on the part of men extends to another aspect of menstruation: a husband is not forbidden contact with his wife's menstrual cloth, which she washes every night (and at noon, if the flow is heavy) and stores in her room between periods.[5]

Just as there is no taboo on sex during menstruation, so there is none on sex during pregnancy. A couple may continue to have sexual intercourse so long as it is not uncomfortable for the pregnant woman, although it is not required for the formation of the fetus (which is held to require only a single act of intercourse to form properly). This lack of taboos relating to pregnancy and menstruation raises a number of intriguing questions. Since menstrual blood is considered polluting in one context—the Earth—why should it not be considered polluting in another, more commonly associated context—sex? Surely the mass of comparative ethnographic evidence has led us to seek out men as the first victims of pollution where menstrual and pregnant sex are concerned. And even more perplexing, why should eating food cooked by menstruating women be considered polluting although having intercourse with them is not? Comparative data indicate, again, that these two taboos are commonly found together. For instance, among the Mae Enga of the Papua New Guinea Highlands, men may neither copulate with nor eat food cooked by their menstruating wives (Meggitt 1964:207–208). Likewise, why is a menstruating Beng woman permitted to attend a funeral but forbidden to touch the corpse?

In seeking the usual explanations of menstrual pollution in the general pollution of women, I came across another fact that at first seemed to support this type of explanation: the Earth is male. Thus the fact that menstrual blood pollutes the Earth might at first glance seem to indicate a wider theme of women polluting men or objects that are classified as male. This explanation is invalidated, however, by the associated taboo on a man and a woman having sexual intercourse on the male Earth. This taboo, which affects both genders equally, seems to indicate that the Earth is not being polluted because of the male gender assigned to it but because of some other defining feature, as will be seen later.

To understand these perplexing issues, I began inquiring into related aspects of the life cycle. Why is it only married (or previously married) women who are forbidden to enter the forest while menstruating? Is it sexual contact with her husband (or lover) that makes her more polluting than a (presumably) virginal girl? I was told that one of the most important aspects of her daily routine that changes when a girl gets married (or initiated) is that she may no longer enter the forest when she has her menstrual period. Associated with this change is a sacrifice that is performed. If the girl is a virgin at marriage, her father provides the necessary sacrificial animals; if she is not a virgin, her previous lover(s) provide(s) them. In either case the ritual consists of chickens and/or goats being sacrificed to the Earth. The purpose is to apologize to the Earth for the girl having gone into the forest during her menstrual periods before her marriage (or initiation) and to promise that she will never again repeat the offense now that she is married. If this necessary sacrifice is not performed by the time she gets pregnant, the girl will have a very difficult childbirth. If the child that is born survives, it will become sickly. Concomitantly, should a married or previously married woman go into the forest during her menstrual period, she too will have a very difficult delivery during her next childbirth. There is another negative result of violating the taboo: the crops in the field she is working in while menstruating will die. In 1979 I recorded such a case:

> About a year ago a menstruating woman was in the forest to work in her husband's yam field. Two days later, all the leaves

of the yam plants in that part of the field fell off and the yams died. In addition, she herself developed bad stomach cramps. She consulted a diviner to discover the cause of her stomach cramps and he accused her of having been in the forest while menstruating. She confessed but explained that her period had come while she was in the fields and she didn't want to return to the village right away. However, as a result of her misjudgment the whole year's yam crop [the starch staple of the Beng diet] in that field was spoiled and the Earth was polluted [*e ba zozona:* she polluted the earth]. To rectify the latter condition, the woman's husband was required to sacrifice a female hairy goat.

While interesting in itself, this case did not seem to answer the question of *why* menstruation and the Earth were mutually inimical. I started on another tack: what are other substances or actions that, rather than being polluted *by women*, are considered polluting *to the Earth*? In other words, I switched from considering the crucial aspect of the problem as the inherent pollution of menstruation (or women) to considering the vulnerability of the Earth. In so doing I learned that there are many substances or actions that pollute the Earth, mostly related to illicit contact by people other than Masters of the Earth with various Earth shrines and with the Earth itself on sacred days.

For instance, the traditional six-day week of the Beng includes one day that is considered an "Earth Day" (called *Po Fẽ* in the Forest region and *Ba Fẽ* in the Savanna region). On this day no work is done in the fields (unless a sacrifice has been performed beforehand by the village chief to apologize to the Earth in advance for any future sins). Moreover during the evening and night hours of every Earth Day (the Beng day begins at sundown), no one is to make a noise in the village. Fights are taboo. Indeed, talking above a whisper was forbidden "in the old days," and because young children could not be relied on to carry out this rule they used to be stuffed into large ceramic pots to keep them quiet all evening. Finally, women may not pound yams or other foods in the large mortars whose pestles make a loud noise. The violation of any of these taboos results in the pollution of the Earth and requires any of a variety of animal sacrifices to the Earth on a later Earth Day.

In pursuing this theme I was told that there is one action considered to be the gravest of all the possible offenses to the Earth, causing it the severest form of pollution and in turn posing the gravest possible threat to humankind: the act of human sexual intercourse in the forest or in the fields. In order to distinguish between the social spaces for legitimately and illegitimately conducted sex, a Master of the Earth ritually plants in each village a kapok tree, which serves to make sexual activity in that village acceptable. Sex in the forest is forbidden because no kapok tree has been ritually planted there that would legitimate sexual activity (though kapok trees do grow wild in the forest). One informant described the village kapok tree as "the beginning of all things in the village." A forest camp, which is formed to shelter farmers whose fields are many miles from the village, is considered a "village"—a social and political space where sexual activity may take place—only when such a kapok tree is planted there by a Master of the Earth (Gottlieb 1983:53–55).

The consequences of violating the taboo against sexual activity in the forest/fields are various and grave. Not only may the woman involved have a difficult time in her next childbirth (and in ensuing ones as well, if the sin is not expiated), but the couple's children and any close or distant kinspeople (especially members of their matriclans) will be endangered. In one case I recorded, a married couple had slept together repeatedly in the forest for a year. Six of their relatives died or suffered acutely before the act was ritually punished, and these deaths and misfortunes were all attributed to the Earth as indirect punishment of the couple.[6] In addition to endangering the couple's own relatives, however, the man and woman who have sexual intercourse in the forest/fields also jeopardize the lives of the entire Beng people: a general drought will ensue that, if the Earth is not properly propitiated in time, will result in the ruin of the entire year's crop and, ultimately, the starvation of all the Beng.

During my fieldwork a minor drought in June 1980 was

blamed on two separate couples having had intercourse in the forest. In fact, such illicit acts seem to be common: an informant of about thirty-three years recalled at least five cases as having occurred within her recent memory for three Beng villages. Significantly, many of these forest sex cases also seem to be cases of rape. In these instances the rape is blamed on madness (which is itself caused by witchcraft). In one case I recorded a well-known healer was bewitched and attempted to rape his wife in the forest. She escaped, and when he "came out of it" within a few hours, he hanged himself in the forest from shame. Having sex in the forest is thus more shameful as one ages and presumably becomes more responsible for one's actions. This is borne out by another case. A middle-aged man was bewitched to have sexual intercourse in the forest (presumably with his wife), but other witches of his matriclan were able to protect him partly and change the "spell" so that it was the man's son (about twenty years old) who committed the offense with a girlfriend. Although the cosmological result was the same—the Earth was polluted—the boy's father, though deeply ashamed that his son had engaged in forest sex, was less ashamed than if he himself had polluted the Earth in this manner.

The punishment meted out to the guilty couple who have sexual intercourse in the forest or fields is considered drastic (*o grégré*). They must return to the spot where they copulated. There they repeat the act in front of a large, jeering audience of middle-aged and old men who brandish sticks and firebrands with which, respectively, they beat and burn the couple during the act of sex. This over, a cow is sacrificed by the Master of the Earth. The couple's clothes are then taken from them and later given to the king of their region, and they are given new clothes to wear back to the village.[7] This punishment was meted out to one of the two guilty couples during the minor drought that occurred during my fieldwork, and soon after the rains indeed came.

A variation of this ritual punishment is possible in extenuating circumstances. Thus in one case a man who raped his wife in the forest was sent to jail by the woman's relatives.

But since the Earth was still polluted and needed purification, the raped wife was required to perform the ritual in the forest and go through the motions of sex without her husband, all the while being beaten and burnt by the old men present. My informant couldn't recall any cases in which, for whatever reason, it was only the guilty man who was present without his partner at such a ritual punishment.

Related to the prohibition on sexual intercourse in the forest is a rule that all adults must bathe in the morning to "wash off" sex from the previous night (whether or not they actually had sexual relations the night before). Should a man or woman have sexual relations one night and go into the forest/fields the next day without having bathed in the morning, he or she runs a good risk of getting bitten by a snake while in the forest. In this case none of the usual snake remedies would be effective, and it is said the person would inevitably die. The logic is clear: sex must be washed off in the morning before "entering" the forest Earth during the day.

MENSTRUATION AND FERTILITY

How does the direness of sexual pollution of the Earth in both its forms (copulating in the forest/fields, and not washing off sexual substances before contacting the forest Earth) tie in with the pollution of menstruation? The beginning of an answer may be found if we note the consequences of each type of pollution. When the Earth is polluted by menstrual blood, the offending woman will have difficulty giving birth to a child; when it is polluted by sexual activity in the forest/fields, the whole area's crops will be ruined by lack of rain. The link between the two consequences is clear: they are both associated with aborted fertility. It is here that the explanation of "menstrual pollution" lies for the Beng.

Menstrual blood, as my informant articulately and poetically explained, embodies a symbolic principle that makes possible human fertility in the form of babies. Because of the Earth the Beng can survive (by eating), with the mediation of the rain which makes the crops grow. The essential aspect of this cosmology is that to the extent that human fertility and forest/field fertility are seen as parallel, to the same extent they must be separated. If human and subsistence fertility are inappropriately combined, the mediating force that makes each possible becomes in its own way aborted: the rain stops, the delivery of the child is impeded. Children and crops represent parallel but distinct realms of human and human-related fertility, as they in turn represent the conceptual distinction of the village and the forest/fields.[8]

It would be tempting to follow Lévi-Strauss here and equate "village" with "culture" and "forest/fields" with "nature." Thus one might surmise that the taboo against menstruating women entering the forest is representative of the distinction between culture and nature, as Lévi-Strauss (e.g., 1969, 1970, 1973, 1976a, 1978, 1981) defines those realms. Indeed, because Lévi-Strauss postulates that all societies make a basic distinction between what is natural and what is cultural, and, moreover, because he views this very distinction as the basis of all social life (e.g., Lévi-Strauss 1969), it would be especially tempting to apply his analysis to our data and suggest that the Beng taboo on menstruating women entering the forest is, as Lévi-Strauss says of the incest taboo, "the fundamental step because of which, by which, but above all in which, the transition from nature to culture is accomplished" (1969:24). From this perspective the Beng taboo could be said to create the distinction between "natural sex" (in the forest) and "cultural sex" (in the village). This interpretation, however, is not appropriate to Beng society precisely because the Beng themselves do not make a distinction between what we define as "nature" and what we define as "culture" (see Strathern 1980 for a similar case among the Mount Hageners of New Guinea).

Specifically, the Beng view the forest/fields as an orderly space, infinitely classified (they say, for example, that all the plants have names, regardless of whether or not the Beng know those names), and having intimate relations with the village through sacrifices in the forest to the Earth and to various forest spirits. Moreover for the Beng it is the Earth (whose ritual locus is in the forest) that has control over all human (village) affairs, whereas in Lévi-Strauss's scheme it would be the village ("culture") that should inevitably triumph over the forest ("nature"). So in the Beng world it is the Earth, in this instance, that is in control not only over forest fertility (the crops) but over human fertility as well.[9] Thus during his wife's pregnancy a husband should contribute an egg to the Master of the Earth, who will then "sacrifice" it in the forest to the Earth to ask that his wife's childbirth go well and she deliver the baby successfully. After the delivery the husband will sacrifice a chicken with which to thank the Earth. Ultimately, then, the two realms of human and forest/ field fertility are interconnected, as both are regulated by the Earth, and both babies and crops are here by the grace of the Earth.

But conceptually as well as spatially, the two realms of fertility must first be separated before they can be joined; hence the washing off of sex before entering the forest Earth. The actual creation of human life—the act of sex—and the symbolic principle representing human fertility—menstrual blood—must be separated from the creation of the Earth's fertility in the forest/fields. This is in keeping with the axiom, well developed in anthropology and originating in linguistics (see Lévi-Strauss 1963a, 1963b, 1963c), that realms must first be differentiated before they can be joined. Indeed, as Leach writes (1976:34), "all boundaries are artificial *interruptions* to what is naturally continuous" (emphasis in original). Human beings have taken the continuum of "nature" and segmented it by defining boundaries because, as Lévi-Strauss says (1963e:89), such boundaries are "good to think"; in other words, we derive intellectual satisfaction from classifying the world in terms of discrete entities. In postulating such discrete entities we create relationships between them, and it is such relationships that in turn create meaning. Thus in the Beng case, the realms of village and forest/fields, rather than being autonomous, are seen as discrete yet connected by their mutual dependence on the same Earth (imbuing both realms with meaning) for their reproduction via children and crops, respectively. The taboo on menstruating women entering the forest is a symbol of this complex, symbolically resonant relationship.[10]

MENSTRUATION AND DEATH

There is further confirmation of the interpretation offered here that the ban on menstruating women entering the forest is unrelated to any idea of the essential pollution of women or of menstrual blood. This has to do with the second taboo relating to menstruating women: the prohibition on touching a corpse. Unlike many other societies, Beng do not specifically forbid menstruating women contact with any objects (including men's tools) other than corpses, which would suggest that it is not a question of gender pollution but, rather, some other kind of pollution. It is well known that corpses themselves are often viewed as polluting (e.g., Douglas 1966), and in Beng thought this is certainly the case, as we will soon see. Thus it would not seem to be a menstruating woman who pollutes the corpse but instead the corpse that pollutes the menstruating woman.

Beng indeed view corpses as contaminating, lodging a disease called "Corpse" (*gale*), which is contagious, especially through touch. The symptoms, like the name of the disease, are also metonymic: the victim becomes listless, loses all appetite and energy—becomes, in a word, corpselike. The action of the disease is swift, and if untreated, the victim may die in a matter of a few days. The disease is both caused by and, in turn, causes death and is thus inimical to menstrual blood, which represents fertility, or potential life. Hence the taboo on menstruating women touching a corpse is clearly not explained by any natural state of female pollution but by the fertility symbolism inherent in menstruation.

A related set of funeral customs is found among the Ewe of Ghana, confirming my interpretation of the Beng data. At Ewe funerals, women regularly fan the corpse, yet menstruating women are prohibited from this activity. Again, as with the Beng, it is not a case of the menstruating woman polluting the corpse but of the corpse afflicting the women—in this case, with *perpetual* menstruation (Fiawoo 1974:272). I suggest a similar explanation to that for the Beng: the menstruating woman, symbolizing fertility, should not have close contact with a corpse, a symbol of death. The infraction of this rule results in a reversal. "Perpetual menstruation" represents a sort of hypersymbolization of fertility that, paradoxically, precludes real fertility. As in the Beng taboo prohibiting a menstruating woman from touching a corpse, the Ewe taboo emphasizes the vulnerability, rather than the threat, of the menstruous woman in relation to symbols of death.

THE CUISINE OF MENSTRUATION

We have seen how menstrual pollution of the Earth can be explained not by the naturally polluting state of women but, in the case of the Beng, by the religious principle of separation of the kind of fertility represented by women's menstrual blood from the kind of fertility represented by the Earth in the forest/fields. It remains to explain the associated taboos against certain men eating food cooked by menstruating women, and against menstruating women touching the logs and live coals of nonmenstruating women's fires, as well as against the live embers of a menstruating woman's fire being brought into the forest.

Like the taboo against menstruating women entering the forest, I propose that the taboo on some men eating food cooked by menstruating women may also be understood as deriving from notions of the Earth and its dually defined fertility (forest/village), rather than from a theory of the general pollution of women. A woman who is menstruating is, as we have seen, producing a symbol of human fertility. When she cooks she handles foods that have come from crops grown in the fields and that thus represent the complementary but opposed domain of forest fertility. It is precisely such a combination of these two realms, human and crop fertility, that Beng religion prohibits, as outlined earlier. A "cuisine of menstruation" thus seems a contradiction, as defined by Beng religion.

The reason that certain men but not women are prohibited from consuming such dishes relates, in the Beng view, to the specific way that the Earth is worshipped. Particularly relevant is the kind of sacrificial food that is seen as the "strongest" kind of "Earth meat" that men on occasion eat—"strongest" because it has been sacrificed to what is viewed as the "strongest" named Earth that is associated with a particular village (see note 1). I suggest that there is a symbolic contrast between this "strongest" type of Earth meat, on the one hand, and food cooked by a menstruating woman, on the other. The latter represents the combination of symbols of human fertility (the woman's menstrual discharge) and forest fertility (the crops she is cooking), and should thereby constitute a forbidden entity. In contrast, Earth meat (and, *a fortiori*, "strong" Earth meat) is associated with only one domain, the forest. This is so because it comes from domesticated animals that are offered to the Earth at a forest shrine. Although they are raised in the village, these animals are nevertheless said to "belong to" the Earth, as localized in the forest shrine, and they are thus associated with forest fertility. Therefore the association of both menstrual cooking (which combines human and forest fertility) and "strong" Earth meat (which represents only forest fertility) should be considered taboo to the Earth, and men—who on occasion do consume "strong" Earth meat—should be prohibited from consuming the products of a menstrual cuisine.

Why, then, may women themselves eat food prepared by menstruating women—cooked either by themselves or by someone else (a sister, co-wife, etc.)? The Beng answer is that it is because women have no direct ritual contact with the Earth and its shrines and abstain from eating sacrificial meat from animals dedicated to the "strongest" Earth. Thus women may consume, on their own, a "forbidden" item because they do not mix this consumption with the consumption of the "strongest" Earth meat associated with forest fertility.

The taboo against the burning embers of a menstruating

woman's fire being taken into the forest, for cooking lunch in the fields, is related to the previous taboo. Having had contact with the village fertility that menstruation represents, such embers should not contact the forest Earth, with its associated forest (crop) fertility.

The symbolic value of heat and cold should also be considered. The last taboo—against menstruous women touching the fires of nonmenstruating women—is further explained not by a concept of essential female pollution but by a system of hot-cold symbolism that is central to Beng religion. In essence, cold is associated with fertility, health, and life, whereas heat is associated with sterility, sickness, and death. For example, regarding the association of cold with fertility, remedies for a woman's barrenness (termed *nǒ bàtú*, "hot stomach"), as well as for breast milk that is not flowing properly in a nursing mother, always require "raw" treatment with unheated leaves (unlike cures for other illnesses, which involve leaves that are simmered). Regarding the more general association of heat with disease, a village in which there is an excessive amount of illness is referred to as "hot" and may be abandoned if it does not "cool down." In the same vein, the last part of daily conversational greetings involves an exchange that translates loosely as:

–I stayed over there [i.e., what's new over here]?
–Here, it's cool [i.e., no deaths or other untoward events have occurred].

Other cures for specific diseases make use of variations on this set of relationships (see Gottlieb forthcoming for further examples and discussion of hot-cold symbolism).

As with the two products of the Earth, forest fertility and village fertility, for the Beng the two polarities of heat and cold should generally be kept apart.[11] In keeping with this, items that are classified as "hot" may even be used in cures to treat diseases that are associated with heat, on the principle that "two negatives equal a positive" (for an example, see Gottlieb forthcoming). On occasion, however, the two polar principles of heat and cold may be combined in cures. Thus amenorrhea, which, like barrenness, is seen as caused by a "hot womb/stomach" (*nǒ bàtú*), is cured by a "raw" remedy using uncooked leaves.

In line with the foregoing, I suggest that menstrual blood, which represents fertility, is associated with cold. Therefore the cold of a woman's menstrual period is incompatible with the heat of fire. In this case it is the cold of the menstrual cycle that appears symbolically "stronger" than the fire and thus nullifies the heat of the fire, thereby "ruining" it. The taboo against menstruating women touching the fire of non-menstruous women does not derive, then, from a conception of the intrinsic pollution of females. Rather, it is part of a specific aspect of Beng religious ideology that defines certain objects and states of being as "hot" and others as "cold" and (with a few specific exceptions) seeks to keep such items apart. This explains further why a menstruating woman's fire —representing the contradictory principles of cold fertility and hot sterility—should not be brought into the forest to contact the Earth.

The lack of a religious taboo against sex during menstruation no longer seems problematic. Sex during menstruation combines two versions of the same type of fertility (human and village), whereas a man eating food cooked by a menstruating woman combines symbols of two different types of fertility that should remain apart (human and forest/fields).[12]

There is one final noteworthy point about menstruation and cooking which goes along with the taboo on some men eating such food. Women themselves are said to enjoy food cooked during their menstrual periods immensely and for a specific reason: women cook best when they are menstruating. In particular, there is one dish, a sauce made from palm nuts (*sì béŋ dǒ*), that is supposed to be most delicious when prepared by a menstruating woman. This is because the sauce gets better and better (i.e., thicker and thicker) as it cooks longer and longer—up to four or five hours for optimum flavor. Usually a woman does not have the time to cook a sauce for so many hours because she is busy working in the fields. While she is menstruating and confined to the village, however, she has the leisure to cook the sauce properly—virtually all day—and she and her friends and close female kin with whom she exchanges food[13] have the exquisite pleasure usually denied to men of eating palm-nut sauce as it was meant to be eaten. It might also be added that although no Beng ever said so, palm-nut sauce may be seen to resemble blood. As it cooks for hours its color develops into a rich, deep red, not unlike the color of menstrual blood.[14] If Beng culture has an *haute cuisine*, it is this rich, red, thick palm-nut sauce—a cuisine of menstruation.

Indeed, many men may forgo eating the sacrificial meat dedicated to the strongest Earth precisely because they do not want to give up forever the possibility of eating menstrually cooked palm-nut sauce. For this reason the de facto situation is that it is mostly *old* men who refrain from eating the cuisine of menstruation so as to be able to consume the "strongest" of Earth meats, whereas many young and middle-aged men have not yet made this commitment.

These data concerning the high value placed by men and women alike on food cooked during a woman's menstrual period are theoretically significant in two ways. First, it has been postulated (Ortner 1974:80) that where societies have developed traditions of *haute cuisine* it is generally men who take it over and leave the daily, boring cooking to women. This hypothesis has been adduced to support the more general theory that societies universally accord higher status to men and men's activities than to women and women's activities (Ortner 1974). In the case of the Beng, however, both men and women acknowledge that the *haute cuisine*—especially long-simmered palm-nut sauce—is cooked (and sometimes consumed) by women alone. Second, the facts of Beng menstrual cuisine should serve to convince us that despite the existence of menstrual taboos, the activities of menstruating women may be granted positive value by men as well as by women.

CONCLUSION

Until recently most anthropological explanations of comparative menstruation beliefs have focused on the polluting nature of menstrual blood and inferred from that the polluting nature of women in general. I have tried to show how such a theory does not apply to the Beng data. In the Beng case the fact that it is only working in the forest (and not other activities) that is prohibited to menstruating women reveals that menstruation is not viewed categorically as dangerous to men or as polluting in general. Rather, menstrual blood is viewed as a symbol of human fertility. For this reason it is not allowed to touch the forest/fields, which are viewed as a form of Earth fertility; for forest/fields fertility and village fertility (which is symbolized by the menstrual flow of women) must be conceptually kept apart, according to the Beng view of the world.

Many older Beng men may not eat food cooked by menstruating women for a related reason. Menstruating women who cook are handling crops produced in the forest/fields, and old men, who may consume "strong" Earth meat, must therefore avoid contact with such food lest the two realms of forest fertility (embodied by the crops) and village fertility (symbolized by menstrual blood) be mixed. Moreover, far from being considered disgusting, food (especially palm-nut sauce) cooked by menstruating women is agreed among Beng to be the most delicious of all food, giving positive value to an activity of menstruating women.

We have discovered, then, that a rule that seems to impose a restriction on women, and thus to reflect their general polluting character—the taboo on their entering the forest while menstruating—is instead part of a wider system of symbolic classification of space and fertility; and that a rule that also seems to indicate the polluting nature of menstrual blood—the taboo on men eating food cooked by menstruating women—is rather part of that same complex symbolic system. This cosmology revolves around Beng notions of fertility in two separate but related spheres. Furthermore, the taboo against menstruating women touching the fires of nonmenstruating women emerges as part of a wider system that associates cold with fertility and heat with sterility.

Other anthropologists have previously noted a connection between culturally specific ideas about menstruation and fertility (compare p'Bitek 1966:99). For example, Novak (1916: 273) writes of the Germanic countries that

> the function of menstruation was commonly designated by some term equivalent to "flowers," indicating, perhaps, that it is a species of blossoming, with the possibility of bearing fruit. German peasant women, for example, according to Schurig, speak of menstruation as the "Rosencrantz," or rose wreath.

Despite such statements, anthropologists have repeatedly stressed the polluting power of menstrual blood rather than its potential as a symbol of fertility, or life. As the other chapters in this collection show, however, the specific meanings of menstruation in a given culture can by no means be presupposed, even in the presence of menstrual taboos. They can be determined only through sustained and particularistic analysis of the case at hand.

3

Mortal Flow: Menstruation in Turkish Village Society

Carol Delaney

As an introduction to the taboo nature of menstruation in Turkish society, which is predominantly Muslim, I relate the history of my initial fieldwork goals. In order to conduct ethnographic research in Turkey a proposal outlining the topics to be investigated is required by the government. Before submitting my proposal I consulted with a Turkish colleague who advised me to omit the section on menstruation. Birth, circumcision, marriage, and kinship are recognizable and acceptable topics, but menstruation is unmentionable. He also suggested that some of the young unmarried men processing my permission to conduct research might not know what I was referring to. The veil of silence is drawn over the ethnographic literature on Turkey,[1] lifted only rarely to reveal that menstruation may be a reason for proscribing certain activities.

The official silence may be a result of specific cultural notions of propriety. But taboo, rather than repelling anthropologists, has generally attracted them. Their silence on this matter demands some explanation. That is not the purpose of this chapter; nevertheless I suspect this ethnographic silence is related to researchers' own perceptions of menstruation as a "natural"—that is, physiological—process having to do only with women and therefore not of significance culturally.

Yet despite the fact that it is a universal physiological process among women, perceptions, meanings, and practices related to menstruation are not universal. In order to understand the meanings and practices of menstruation in a particular society, certain crucial questions need to be raised and answered: What is menstruation? How is it perceived? What is its function? Why do women menstruate? In other words, how is menstruation culturally defined, how is it viewed, what are the attitudes toward it? What is the cultural understanding of its function? This is related but not identical to reasons given for why women menstruate. Perhaps because the questions have seemed so obvious and the answers self-evident, they have rarely been asked. Yet the answers take one immediately to more general beliefs about the body, sexuality, and procreation. These in turn are inextricably intertwined with the set of cosmological beliefs about the nature of the world and the place of humankind in it (see Delaney 1987*a* for the relationship between theories of procreation and cosmology).

In Muslim Turkish village society, I suggest, menstruation is a fecund symbol for both condensing and expressing a complex set of notions about women, life, and the world. As an index of fertility, it heralds the possibility of life in "this world" (*bu dünya*), as seen in Islam. But earthly life, as the earth itself, is characterized by its mutability and susceptibility to corruption, decay, and death. Existence in this world is juxtaposed to that in the "other world" (*öbür dünya*), considered to be one's original home and the one to which all true Muslims will return.[2]

The other world is a potent reality to villagers, heightening the contrast to life in this world. In the other world there is said to be food and drink of an ambrosial sort. However, metabolic processes do not occur: the "body" is incorruptible and self-contained. As we shall see, that is the ideal image of the self, and it is associated with and can be approximated in this world only by men. Women, on the other hand, are associated with the physical and perishable aspects of life—that is, with corporeality.

Like Mary Douglas (1970), I believe that the body is a rich source of "natural symbols" that are, however, neither universal nor equally distributed between the sexes. But unlike

Douglas, I do not believe that the "body is a model which can stand for any bounded system" (1966:115); in Turkish village perception the female body is relatively unbounded—or, more accurately, the boundaries fluctuate, are diffuse and permeable. In other words, although both men and women have bodies, male and female bodies mean different things and are differentially associated with notions of corporeality.

In the other world, voluptuous pleasures for the satisfaction of men are believed to exist, but there is no sweat and no issue. Sex in the other world is recreational; in this world it is for the purpose of procreation. Indeed, procreation is what this world is all about. Procreation is felt to be an intimation of Creation and is the locus for the articulation of intimate and ultimate concerns. Contemplation of the process of procreation is felt to reveal the deeper meanings of gender and of the distinction between this world and the other world.

In cosmological perspective, menstruation pertains only to this world and is an ambivalent symbol. In both its positive and negative aspects, it represents carnal existence. Menstruation opens the way for the possibility of life in this world and is an apt symbol for the messy flux or mortal flow of life. Menstrual taboos, on the other hand, express the incommensurability of this world and the other world. Rather than an insignificant outpost on the cultural map, menstruation may well lead directly into some of its major arteries. This chapter is a preliminary attempt to chart some of these connections. My implicit aim is to argue for the central role of symbols as motivational factors in society (Geertz 1973). In the concluding remarks I contrast this approach with that of Mary Douglas as a contemporary representative of sociological determinism.

SETTING

The research on which this chapter is based was conducted from August 1980 through June 1982 in a central Anatolian village. There are more than 30,000 villages in Turkey, some extremely remote and isolated, others more or less so. Many have been debilitated by emigration of men or families to urban centers or to Europe. In the village in which I worked, however, this is not the case. While there has been gradual migration to urban areas, no one has emigrated directly to Europe. A fair percentage of young people have married relatives or fellow villagers living outside the village, but more than half of the newlyweds have chosen to remain in the village. There are approximately 850 people evenly divided by sex and between adults and children, and all profess to be Sunni Muslims. The village is a viable one and survives by a combined economy of wheat cultivation and animal husbandry. Wheat provides the flour for bread, which is the most important ingredient in the village diet. The surplus is sold for profit. Sheep and goats are raised primarily for their wool and world-famous Angora hair, and to be sold as meat. Along with cows they provide villagers with occasional meat but are valued especially for their milk to be used in the form of yoghurt, butter, and cheese. Milk products form the second major component of the villagers' diet.

The village boasts both a primary and a middle school, although the latter is not well attended and very few girls are sent. In addition to about eight nonlocal but resident teachers there was, during my time in the village, a government-trained and appointed midwife. She has since left. Many villages are rarely visited by a doctor or midwife, others only occasionally; thus in the villagers' own estimation their village is a "modern" one. Nevertheless, in spite of her training, the midwife's knowledge about human physiology, the mechanics of reproduction, and the function of menstruation was not modern, if by that we mean scientific.[3] Her views did not differ significantly from those of the villagers. In any case, the educational function she performed or could perform was restricted to married women.

BELIEFS AND PRACTICES RELATING TO
PUBERTY AND GENDER

Silence on the topic of menstruation is kept until a girl has begun to menstruate. While I cannot say with certainty that this is true throughout village society in Turkey, or more generally in the Muslim world,[4] the few published sources do appear to confirm it. For example, Saadawi, an Egyptian physician, laments that "ignorance about the body and its functions in girls and women is considered a sign of honor and purity" (1980:45). She recalls her own shock at menarche. Thinking there was something terribly wrong with her, she took to her bed for several days before confiding in her mother. Similar reactions were recounted by village women. The response of Saadawi's mother led her "to understand that in me there was something degrading which appeared regularly in the form of this impure blood, and that it was something to be ashamed of, to hide from others" (1980:45). Especially it is to be hidden from men, including one's father and brothers, but even older sisters do not necessarily share information with their younger sisters. It is not a topic of conversation in mixed-sex groups, and if Turkish men speak about it among themselves, I do not know. What I do know of men's attitudes about menstruation comes partly from a few private conversations with men, but more generally from their elliptical remarks. Women, however, once they cross the threshold to womanhood, talk quite openly about "blood and babies" (Good 1980).

According to village women, and as confirmed by men, menstruation is believed to have been given to women because of Hawa's (Eve) act of disobedience against Allah in Cennet (Garden/Paradise). Her susceptibility to the persuasions of Satan that led her to eat the forbidden fruit is a sign of her moral weakness and thus provides the rationale for women's being under the protection of men. But there were more serious consequences.

Hawa's transgression against the command of Allah is also responsible for bringing *pislik* (dirtiness) into existence. Referred to here are the creaturely functions of defecation, urination, and sweating which characterize metabolic process and change but also transgress bodily boundaries. The "definition of dirt as matter out of place" (Douglas 1966:35) is apposite here since these functions contravene the ideal of the contained self.

In addition, women were singled out by menstruation, which contributes further to their closer identification with carnal existence. The closest physical ties, constituted by women's blood, are those that exist between siblings—those nurtured in the same womb by the same blood. As will become clear later, however, these physical bonds are superseded by the "spiritual" bond incorporated in seed (semen) which provides specific identity and transcends time. Blood, almost a universal symbol of life, is also in Turkish worldview a symbol of mortality, for the primary opposition is not between life and death but between earthly existence and that in the other world.

Procreation and birth are utilized symbolically in the conception of the "spiritual" birth for which this life is only a prelude. In Islam the end of life is conceived as a return to the beginning (compare Meier 1971), giving the impression that earthly life is not only an exile from the divine realm but is also only a temporary condition, as is life in the womb. At the same time, there is no concept of original sin in Islam, and children are considered sinless until puberty. Children who die before puberty are thought to go directly to Cennet. They have not yet reached the age of reason, which is why it is said one cannot reason with them. Sin begins to accumulate with the onset of puberty, described as the production of semen in boys and menstruation in girls. After puberty one is held accountable for one's sins. The attainment of reason—that is, the ability to distinguish right from wrong—is thus intimately related to the attainment of adult sexuality, signified by the production of different sexual substances. Consequently sin lies in the improper use of sexuality and the lack of understanding about the function and meaning of these substances.

Menstrual blood and semen are both powerful and potentially polluting substances (compare Dwyer 1978), and great care is taken to avoid contamination. They are different, however. By tracing the logic of the different ways they pollute and the rituals attached to them, a deeper understanding of sexuality and of the different nature of men and women is obtained.

Semen released in nocturnal emission is polluting, and a man must perform an *aptes* (ritual ablution) afterwards. Semen accumulated under the foreskin is felt to be extremely unclean and is the reason given that *sünnet* (circumcision) is performed at some time between the ages of seven and twelve, before the first seminal emission occurs. Yet if cleanliness were the only issue, there would be nothing to prevent *sünnet* being done at birth, but it is not. To experience and survive this ordeal is the first test of manliness (compare Erdentuğ 1959:40) and a matter of pride, for male pride is focused on the penis. This one-time, permanent operation renders a man invulnerable and self-contained, approximating the ideal of self.

Women, on the contrary, controvert this ideal and constitute a threat to the social order. Only in childhood and old age do women approximate the ideal. Between menarche and menopause women's bodily boundaries are periodically transgressed. The most general terms used to refer to menstruation express this periodicity: *adet* (habit, custom) or *aybaşı* (beginning of the moon or month). Because this periodic flow is not under her control, she cannot be self-contained. She is "naturally" open (*açık*). It is important to point out that "naturally" or "by nature" does not have quite the same sense in Turkish as it does in English. The Turkish word in this context is *yaradılış*, which, although translated as "nature" or "temperament," means "by creation" or "created nature." It is related to *Yaradan* (Creator) and *yaratmak* (to create). All created things have a divine purpose: they are created for the purpose of instruction. In this case the lesson to be learned is that women are created differently from men, and their differences reflect and express the order and ordering of Creation. The fact that a woman is not self-contained and self-controlled but is instead open is interpreted as a sign that she must be socially controlled and closed, or covered.

Neither *sünnet* nor its analogue for girls coincides with the actual physical event of puberty but rather marks the social recognition of its imminence (Van Gennep 1960); however, they are differentially marked. The honor and pride of male sexuality is revealed by the removal of a covering (foreskin), whereas female sexuality must be hidden by covering. Like Saadawi, a Turkish girl learns that "the female body is an obscenity that must be carefully hidden" (1980:46).

Female genitals, unlike the male's, are not a source of pride but a reminder of her shame and are unmentionable. The meaning of female shame will be taken up later in the section on procreation, but I note here that it is because of this shame that the focus of attention of female sexuality is displaced from the genitals to the head.

Like flowers of the field, a young girl's hair grows freely, representing the rampant fertility, beauty, and seductiveness of the world, as well as the entanglements by which men are ensnared. Around the time of menarche, when a girl's sexuality ripens, it must be enclosed; it is not free for the plucking. The hair and the girl must be domesticated. At the end of primary school (when children are about twelve years old) a girl must put on the headscarf. The headscarf binds and covers her hair and symbolically binds her sexuality, which is henceforth under the cover of her father and brothers until stewardship is transferred to her husband upon marriage. The term used to describe a woman who wears the headscarf is *kapalı* ("closed," "covered"); an uncovered woman is referred to as *açık* ("open," "uncovered"). A woman who walks around *açık* is open to sexual advances from men. It is as if she were exhibiting her private parts in the open.

The uncontrolled mixing of the sexes, like the mixture of sexual fluids during intercourse, is felt to be *bulaşık*. *Bulaşık* means soiled, tainted, contagious, and is the word used to describe both dirty dishes and contagious diseases. The city (as well as Europe and America), in which this kind of mixing takes place, is considered *bulaşık*, unlike the village, which is *temiz* (clean). The village, where the sexes are relatively segregated, is clean because it is *kapalı*, as are its women.

Particularly, pubescent girls and boys before marriage are kept strictly apart. This applies even to brothers and sisters outside, but not inside, the home. Social intercourse between unmarried men and women is practically equivalent to sexual intercourse; however, the shame of dishonor falls mainly on the woman. A woman's chastity is compromised by even a glance or casual conversation with an unrelated male. More serious, of course, is the loss of virginity to a man other than her husband, and absence of a hymen at marriage is reason for repudiation. Such repudiation is warranted not only because the bride has given to another man what it is the husband's right to possess but also because she is irreparably soiled by contact with another man's semen. Semen is a powerful and polluting substance that is mitigated only by marriage, but its polluting potential is different from that of menstrual blood. As we shall see, semen (seed) carries a person's essential identity. Since sex is said to take place inside the woman but outside the man, some indelible imprint is left within the woman during intercourse. After intercourse both partners should perform *aptes* (ritual ablution), but it is recognized that the *cünüb* (ritual uncleanness) comes off the man more easily than the woman. No matter how careful she is, residues are bound to remain, leaving her permanently defiled.

That is why not only an unmarried girl is defiled by intercourse but a married woman who has intercourse with any man other than her husband is permanently defiled as well. Such a woman is considered *pis* (dirty, defiled). A series of miscarriages or the birth of a deformed child sometimes gives rise to the suspicion that the woman had been so defiled. A woman's sexual life is restricted to intercourse with one man unless she wishes to invite serious consequences; a man is not so restricted. Because a man is invulnerable, he is not susceptible to defilement by women, not even by a defiled woman (Engelbrektsson 1978:137).

While generally true, this statement must be qualified. A man can never be permanently defiled as a woman can, but he can be temporarily defiled by intercourse with a menstruating woman. Sexual intercourse is forbidden during menstruation:

> They question thee (O Muhammed) concerning menstruation. Say: It is an illness, so let women alone at such times and go not unto them till they are cleansed. (Koran 2:222)

This directive is given to men, telling them how to view women. Menstruation is to be viewed as a female illness and as a powerful reminder of women's constitutional infirmity, rather than as a normal function. Menstrual blood, like other exudates, is unclean. It is *kirli* (soiled, blemished, canonically unclean) or *lekeli* (spotted, stained, dishonored) for it is believed to be saturated with impurities accumulated in the course of the month. What these impurities are is never specified.

When asked whether men have such constitutional impurities, the immediate response of both men and women is that they do not and therefore they have no need to rid themselves of them. Deeper inspection revealed a different view, however. A few men made reference to the fact that with age their blood becomes increasingly *zayif* (weak, thin). Despite the fact that many women are anemic, the normative view is that women's blood is *gümrah* (rich, abundant, luxuriant) and *bol* (full), for it is periodically renewed and refreshed. Like all processes subject to taboos, menstruation arouses ambivalent attitudes and provides an intimation of an underlying contradiction in the system. In general the system of beliefs expresses the notion that menstruation is a sign of women's weakness, but implied in men's statements is a certain amount of jealousy at women's power of revitalization. Women are considered naturally—that is, by creation—physically stronger. This is exemplified by the practice of nursing boy babies longer than girls, for it is felt that boys are weaker at birth and need the additional sustenance. Women, because of their strength, are also expected to shoulder the heaviest burdens, to do the most backbreaking work in the fields, and to haul heavy containers of water from the fountain as well as huge bags of animal fodder, wood, and dung fuel. When visiting in town or city, women carry all the baggage. Indeed, it became clear that the weakness of women is to be understood in moral, not physical, terms.

Women appear to accept the view that menstruation is a sign of their moral weakness and susceptibility to sin, but they also consider it beneficial. It is a source of renewal that leaves the *döl yatağı* (womb; lit. "seedbed") an immaculate ground or virgin soil for the reception of seed (*döl* or *tohum*).

PROCREATION

The theory of procreation in the Turkish village (as in Western society until relatively recently) is monogenetic. *Tohum'dan çoçuk gelir*—the child comes from the seed. The woman is perceived as a *tarla* (field) in which the seed is planted.[5] "Women are given to you as fields, go therein and sow your seed" (Koran 2:223). The woman's womb, like soil, is a generalized medium of nurture that contributes to the growth and development of the fetus but in no way establishes its specific identity. As a Turkish villager put it:

> If you plant wheat, you get wheat. If you plant barley, you get barley. It is the seed which determines the kind (variety) of plant which will grow, while the field nourishes the plant but does not determine the kind. The man gives the seed and the woman is like the soil (Meeker 1970:157)

The Turkish word *döllenmek* (to inseminate) incorporates the word *döl*, which means "seed," "fetus," "child." As the etymology of the English word also implies, *döllenmek* does not entail merely fertilization of the ovum, or provision of half the genetic material; it includes the entire process. That the theory is monogenetic is also conveyed by the words *gebe kalmak*, usually glossed as "to be pregnant." *Kalmak* means "to stay" or "remain"; *olmak* is the verb "to be" and is not used in this context. What is implied is that the seed remained in the womb and therefore the woman is pregnant. The fact that this is not the way the process of conception takes place physiologically but rather is the way the process is imaged should give pause to those who do not recognize the symbolic dimension and its power to structure belief, action, and institutions in the world.

Procreation is felt to teach the lesson of Creation. Hawa was taken out of Adam; thereafter, men have had the power of creation or self-perpetuation within them. Woman's creation is also intended to show that women are subordinate to and dependent on men, implying that they should be *muslim*, or obedient, to the will of their husbands as the world is to Allah.

In this construction of procreation it is men who give life; women merely give birth. Although children, especially sons, are greatly desired, birth itself is somewhat shameful for it is by means of the female genitals that life is made manifest. Primary identity, however, is transmitted by seed. By means of seed men give the spark of life, which is theoretically eternal, provided they continue to produce sons to carry it down the generations; hence the tremendous importance attached to producing sons.[6] *Sulale,* the Turkish word for patriline, is, according to Rahman (1980:17), derived from the Arabic meaning "reproductive semen." If a man has no son it is said that *ocağı sonmuş,* his hearth is extinguished: the name and the flame of the patriline have died out.

The creative self-perpetuating essence concentrated in seed allies men with Allah. As Allah is author of the world, so too are men authors of children, and upon this their authority rests. Indeed, villagers say the husband-father is the second god after Allah.

The female body is perceived as life-supporting and sustaining like the earth; it is not life-generating. The rich and luxuriant climate or fertile ground of the womb supports the growth of the seed-child and provides for its nurture with blood; but this is something any woman can provide. A woman's value lies not so much in her fertility, given that all women are presumed fertile until proven otherwise, but in her ability to assure the legitimacy of a man's seed. It is here that the complex of honor and shame, about which there is a vast but unsatisfactory literature, becomes relevant. According to Meeker (1976:264), male honor is essentially concerned with the legitimacy of paternity, yet he does not explore the relationship of male honor to the pertinent Turkish theory of procreation. In order to guarantee that a child is his own—that is, from his own seed—a man must have possession and control of the field. Women's shame, as I have argued elsewhere (Delaney 1987*b*), is related to the view that she does not contain the power of creation within her. Her fertility is basically a kind of indiscriminate fecundity that is redeemed only by being "enclosed" and "covered" by a man.[7]

The guarantee of paternity is more easily assured if the girl is married before any contact with men may have occurred, and indeed most village girls are married young. Today this means between the ages of fifteen and eighteen, but in the near past it was even earlier. A number of women confided to me that they had been married before menarche. The custom of *beşik kertme* (cradle engagement) also occasionally obtains. Given the foregoing, I would object that "menarche does *not* represent the earliest point in the life cycle at which bargaining over rights to a girl's fertility becomes critical," to both paraphrase and argue against Paige and Paige (1981:79). Again, such practices underscore the fact that meanings of gender and marriage strategies are constructed not from universal physiological facts but from the ways these are interpreted in light of a particular logic of procreation.

Villagers recognize that a girl cannot become pregnant before menarche, but they have no knowledge about ovulation and its relation to menstruation and no knowledge of the relation of both to conception. Although cessation of menses is generally taken as a sign of pregnancy, it is not always.[8] All women, however, were insistent that the blood the fetus suckles in the womb is clean blood and is not the same as the blood that flows out in menstruation. This contrasts with beliefs of certain Iranian women who, according to Good (1980:150), believe that "the dirty blood (*kasif qan*) of the menses is consumed by the fetus, thus ridding the mother of her natural pollutant." Women in the Turkish village were shocked by such an implication. The source of the blood is the same but it has two quite distinct destinations and valences. On the one hand, it constitutes the physical substance (as opposed to the spiritual essence) of the growing fetus and sustains it; on the other hand, when the blood flows out in menstruation it carries the impurities resulting from the processes of life. It cleanses the body periodically but is itself unclean. As a general capacity, then, menstruation signals the possibility of life, but menstrual blood in the specific is impure and serves as a reminder of life's corruptibility. The periodic flow of blood exemplifies the waxing and waning of earthly existence, its temporality and ultimate perishability. Menstruation condenses the conceptual cluster having to do with corporeality, time, and decay—unlike seed, which carries meanings of creativity, spirituality, and the eternal.

MENSTRUAL TABOOS

With the foregoing as background we can now approach the Anatolian villagers' menstrual proscriptions. Those directly related to the practice of Islam are most easily comprehended.

During the menstrual period a woman may not touch the Koran, enter the *cami* (mosque), or keep the fast of Ramazan (Ramadan).

To touch the sacred Book or to enter the sacred precinct while menstruating would introduce an element of the profane where it does not belong; it would besmirch the spiritual domain. Especially during the sacred month of Ramazan, when one's mind and body should be devoted to Allah and concentrated on the other world, the juxtaposition is too obvious. While menstruants are listed along with others exempt from keeping *oruç* (fast) during Ramazan (i.e., pregnant and nursing women, people on a journey, the old and the sick), there is a great difference that is often overlooked. The exemption of the latter is in recognition of hardship. They may keep the fast if they so desire and often do, for it is felt to bring even greater *sevap* (blessings). Even though Ramazan fell in August and July, respectively, during the two years I was in the village, many pregnant and nursing women kept the eighteen-hour fast from dawn to dusk for the full month. Menstruants *must* be exempted, for menstruation by itself makes the fast *bozulmuş* (ruined). Because menstruation is unmentionable, women must eat secretly when they have their periods during Ramazan. Regardless of the reprieve it offers, their eating and drinking is considered shameful. On occasion my house became something of a "menstrual hut." Because I lived alone and people knew I was not keeping the fast, a few of my close female neighbors came to my house when they were menstruating to share a cup of tea. Ironically, they signaled what they were doing by drawing the curtains. Normally this kind of menstrual commensality would not occur during Ramazan and it was actively discouraged by the men.

The belief that a menstruating woman can ruin a sacred ritual applies also to the *Hac* (Hajj), or pilgrimage to Mecca. For the few days before Kurban Bayram (Festival of Sacrifice), hundreds of thousands of pilgrims gather in this most sacred city. Every precaution is taken to ensure that the minds and bodies of the faithful are purified. A menstruating woman may not perform any of the rituals or enter the sacred precinct. But not to be able to perform the rituals is, in effect, not to have made the *Hac*. No doubt this is one reason that most women who go on the *Hac* are postmenopausal. There is a coherent logic behind these proscriptions. Menstruation as a symbol of fertility, process, and change has no place in unchanging ritual directed toward the eternal.

There are, however, other taboos that do not relate specifically to religious ritual but do highlight the notion of creativity/generativity, which is a primary attribute of Allah. Intercourse, the act of procreating, is forbidden during menstruation. Recalling that the seed carries the spiritual, generative essence relating men to Allah, and that the act of procreation is the earthly equivalent of Creation, it becomes clear that intercourse during menstruation would constitute a most flagrant mixing of the two domains. Menstrual blood, contaminated with impurities, would impede the creative and essentially spiritual process of conception. This creative act must be performed in a pure environment. After menstruation, an *aptes* (ritual ablution) is made with the purpose of *"cemi bedeni bütünce pak yapmak"*—to make "the earthly body totally clean and holy."

The period of incubation of the seed (pregnancy) is a precarious time, for the new seed of life is taking root. A woman who is pregnant should not be approached by one who is menstruating. Menstrual blood is laden with impurities, as evidenced by its noxious odor. This blood is not contained in the body but flows from inside to outside, transgressing the bodily boundaries. Implicit in this menstrual prohibition is the belief that the noxious elements in menstrual blood are released into the air, where they have the power to penetrate bodily boundaries and bring about a miscarriage or deform the fetus.[9] The first forty days after birth are analogous to the first forty days of gestation. It is a creative and precarious time when life is held in the balance, and thus precautions against the deleterious effects of menstrual blood are also taken during this time.

This logic, never entirely explicit, is transferred to bread making, which, in the village imagination, is metaphorically similar to the process of procreation. Both sons and bread are needed to *coğalamak* (increase and multiply) the family. Unlike cooking, which comprises daily reiteration, bread is reproduced. In order for bread to increase and multiply, sourdough or *maya* (yeast, root, origin, essence) from the previous batch must be introjected into the inert flour and water of the next batch, in which it incubates overnight. The *maya* is the live germ transmitted from batch to batch as seed from generation to generation; thus is bread self-perpetuated. Bread is the staff of life, it is the quintessential food; all else is considered *katik* (additional). Bread is regarded as almost holy. It should not be thrown out, and if it is found on the ground it is picked up. Although bread making is not a sacred activity, the creative, engendering process is. The rising of dough is a mysterious and creative process similar to pregnancy, and it is feared that the powerful impurities in menstrual blood may inhibit the process.[10]

One more prohibition must be mentioned which relates not only to the times women menstruate but to the entire period of a woman's life during which menstruation occurs. During a woman's reproductive years, until menopause, she may not "cut"—that is, slaughter—an animal. Generally this has been perceived as a menstrual taboo, but if so, why is it not restricted only to the specific days a woman is menstruating? Once the flow has stopped and an *aptes* performed, what prevents a woman from "cutting" an animal?

Behind the idea that men give life lurks the corollary that they therefore have the right to take it. Indeed, this was the essence of the ancient Roman *patria potestas*. In rural Turkey this power has been mitigated but at the same time symbolically reaffirmed. In Islam, and vividly in the village mind, this is expressed in the story of Abraham. "In ancient times we used to cut our sons. Allah gave Abraham a ram, now we don't cut our children." This story is central to Islam, as well as to Judaism and Christianity (Delaney 1977), and is reenacted every year on the most sacred day of the Islamic calendar, Kurban Bayram (Festival of Sacrifice).

Men in performance of the Kurban ritually reproduce this metaphor of power over life and death. Women's exclusion from this rite cannot be adequately accounted for in terms of pollution by menstrual blood, for women are forbidden to slaughter not only when menstruating but throughout their entire reproductive lives.

To focus narrowly only on the physical event of menstruation misses the point that menstruation also indexes fertility—that is, the capacity to bring forth life and sustain it. Nevertheless, as we have seen, menstruation in both its positive and negative aspects symbolizes mortality. Women, whose blood forms the closest physical ties, also represent the eventual dissolution of life and thus stand in stark contrast to those who share an enduring spiritual bond. Undoubtedly the notion of pollution is operating here, but it is not simply pollution by menstrual blood; instead it refers more to the contamination of the spiritual realm by the physical. Women's exclusion, I suggest, expresses the incommensurability of eternal life and earthly life.

CONCLUSION

As earthly life is bounded by birth and death, so is the possibility of this life bounded by menarche and menopause.[11]

Menstruation represents both the potential and the limits of life and symbolizes carnal existence. In the villagers' theory of procreation, however, life is not the result of the union of male and female but an unstable mixture that persists for a short time and upon death is resolved again into its elements—the physical dross and the eternal soul-body. Burial, the placing of the seed-body into the earth, is thought to be analogous to insemination. Understandably burial is a male ritual at which women are not present. The body buried in the earth's soil is the symbolic equivalent of the seed in the womb; after a brief period of incubation, it is reborn into the other world.

But the promise of another life in the other world implies a devaluation and sacrifice, at least emotionally, of the only life and only world we know. The entire system could be interpreted as an elaborate denial of the awesome power of women to bring forth life and a response to and a prophylactic against the mess, fluidity, and change that are its inherent characteristics. It could also be viewed as a projection of the ideal of invulnerability and incorruptibility. Instead of affirmation there is a fear of the mutability of life and a desire to keep it under bounds and under control.

The female body as a source of this fear becomes the focus and object of control. Since the female body is symbolically associated with the material and unregenerate aspects of existence, it is appropriated as the conceptual framework for configuring the structures and contours of lived space. As the woman's body encloses the seed-child in the womb, a house encloses the family, the village encloses a group of interrelated families, and the nation encloses all those born upon and nurtured by its soil. Men "cover" these entities. The notion of cover, of being *kapalı* (covered, closed), is not restricted to women but applies equally to the house, the village, and the nation. Attitudes and responses evoked by one are applicable to the others. In order to preserve the integrity and honor of these entities they must be kept distinct and separate. Access to and between similar units at the same level of structure or between different levels of structure should be limited and controlled by men. Boundaries thus become a focus of anxiety, and exits and entrances are controlled and under surveillance. This is true no matter whether the point of reference is the boundary of the nation, the village, the house, or the bodily boundaries of women.

Mary Douglas, in her now classic study of pollution beliefs, has written that "to understand body pollution we should try to argue back from the known dangers of society to the known selection of bodily themes" (1966:121), but in this chapter I have argued the converse: that a particular cultural understanding of the body may generate the anxieties or dangers felt to be impinging on the society. In other words, notions of the body and corporeality are neither universal nor gender-neutral but change according to specific cultures. It is not enough to look only at specific pollutants, for one must understand them in relation to the entire cultural corpus of beliefs. In the case of Turkish menstrual pollution, this includes beliefs about the body, gender, procreation, and the place of humankind in the world. In place of a simple cause-and-effect equation, regardless of the direction, I have tried to show how the perceived dangers and bodily pollutants in Turkish village culture are both expressions of the same worldview. A full description of this Turkish village worldview must take into account the important realm that Islam designates the "other world." To ignore the invisible but omnipresent reality of the other world is to miss the deeper ontological meaning of menstruation.

4

Menstruation among the Rungus of Borneo: An Unmarked Category

Laura W. R. Appell

Menstruation among the Rungus is an unmarked category, both socially and culturally. A menstruating woman is neither polluting nor propitious. There are no restraints, no forms of social separation regarding menstruating women.

One explanation that has been put forth for the existence of taboos on menstruating women is the dominant role occupied by men. Thus the lack of a focus on menstruation in Rungus society might be associated with what I term *gender symmetry*. Rungus women occupy a position of high regard and share equivalent status with men.

However, an alternative explanation for menstruation as an unmarked category among the Rungus may be found in the basic value premise of Rungus society: sexual relations, if entered into illicitly, are dangerous and deleterious to the whole society. As a result sexual matters, particularly among unmarried females, are seldom discussed (see Appell 1965). In this chapter I explore both of these explanations by, on the one hand, examining the structures of power and authority in Rungus society and, on the other, considering the nature and extent of Rungus reticence in sexual matters. I suggest that together these considerations go a long way toward accounting for the absence of taboos or other emphases on menstruation among the Rungus.

THE RUNGUS

The Rungus are an ethnic group inhabiting the Kudat District of Sabah, Malaysia. They speak an isoglot of the Dusunic

language family (Appell 1968). The Rungus are swidden agri-
culturalists planting rice, maize, cassava, and a variety of
vegetables. They raise chickens, pigs, and water buffalo.
Agricultural surpluses are converted into durable property
consisting of brassware, gongs, and various types of ceramic
ware, principally old jars. This property also forms the major
portion of the bride-price that is required for each marriage.[1]

The Rungus believe in a variety of localized spirits that are
easily angered and can cause illness and bad fortune in
human activities. These spirits are placated with sacrifices of
pigs and chickens to promote human fertility and the productivity of swiddens and domestic animals, to cure illness, and
to provide success in the accumulation of property. Communication with these potentially malevolent spirits is managed
by female spirit mediums who enter into trance and, with the
help of their spirit familiars, determine the source of the
offense. Sacrifices to the rice spirits, however, are generally
handled by men.

Their social organization is cognatic, and the kinship ter-
minology is primarily of the Eskimo type. Residence following
marriage is with the bride's family until the next agricultural
year. Then a separate family apartment is built by the bridegroom onto the longhouse of the bride's family (Appell 1966,
1967, 1976a, 1978).

Each domestic family has its own apartment in the longhouse consisting of a closed compartment, *ongkob*, and an
open verandah, *apad* (see figure 4.1). The enclosed compartment is divided into a raised sleeping area, the *tingkang;* the
eating and cooking area, the *lansang;* the hearth, *ropuhan;* and
a small entryway, *salow*. The verandah is composed of three
sections. Immediately outside the compartment is an aisleway, *lansang*, which is used by all members of the longhouse
to pass from the entry ladders, located at either end of the
longhouse, to the various apartments. The pounding of rice
also takes place along this aisleway. Though communally
used, this aisleway consists of sections built and owned by
each domestic family. A narrow section of the verandah,
salow, is used for storage of rice-pounding blocks when not
in use. The largest area of the verandah is the *tingkang*, where

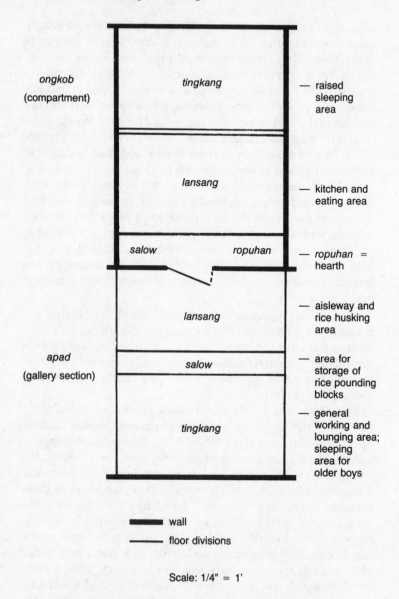

Fig. 4.1. Floor plan of apartment of domestic family.

all the daily activities take place. Here the women prepare food, weave, tend their babies, and so on during the day. In the evenings it is the gathering place for social intercourse. Men make baskets, sharpen knives, tell myths and stories; women rock children to sleep before putting them into the *ongkob* for the night; and the young boys and girls play their musical instruments and flirt. When the longhouse is settled down for the night, this is where all young unmarried boys and visiting males sleep.

The domestic family is the major unit of production, consumption, and asset accumulation in Rungus society (Appell 1976a, 1976b).

RUNGUS FEMALE ROLES

One of the basic tenets of a good marriage is that the husband and wife should *mitimbang*—balance each other—in almost every phase of life. This symmetry of roles is symbolized in there being only one term, *savo*, to refer to both husband and wife.

Bride-price is required, which is an expression of the cultural value of the female role. The size of a girl's bride-price is dependent primarily on the wealth of the suitor's family but also on the qualities of the girl. If she is accomplished in the study of ritual, a hard worker, and comely, her parents can expect a larger price for her hand. Uxorilocal residence, bride-price, and the prohibition against premarital sexual relations are all indicators of the high value of the female role.

Male and female roles are not explicitly marked as asymmetrical, and the status attributed to each is generally equivalent. In the domestic realm female roles are considered complementary to those of males. For each skill exhibited by a male, there is an equally important one possessed by the female (see table 4.1). This applies to household tasks, agricultural activities, hunting and gathering techniques, child-rearing, and so on.

Although the accumulation of family property and the settlement of disputes in the village moot lie in the hands of

TABLE 4.1
RUNGUS MALE AND FEMALE ACTIVITIES

Male Activities	Female Activities

Agricultural

Clearing and burning for swiddens	Help in clearing up small debris prior to planting
Planting swiddens	Planting swiddens
Weeding swiddens	Weeding swiddens
Harvesting swiddens	Harvesting swiddens

Care and Raising of Domestic Animals

Dogs	Pigs
Water buffalo	Chickens

Hunting and Gathering

Hunting with spears for large game	Gathering snails and shellfish
Fishing with traps and nets for large fish	Fishing with scoops for small fish and prawns
Gathering honey and orchard fruits	Gathering wild roots, nuts, berries, and vegetables

Domestic

Collecting firewood	Husking the family's rice supplies
	Carrying water
Tending children	Tending children
Making knives, rope, fish traps, carrying baskets	Weaving, dyeing, sewing, making rice-winnowing baskets

Property Accumulation

Marketing of agricultural surpluses	
Bargaining for purchase of property	

Birthing and Child-Rearing

Midwifery	Ritual aspects of birth
Child-rearing and nurture	Child-rearing and nurture

TABLE 4.1 (*Continued*)

Male Activities	Female Activities
	Ritual
	Communication with spirit world through spirit familiars
Ceremonies for swiddens	Ceremonies for health and illness of domestic family
Minor ceremonies for longhouse	Major ceremonies for longhouse
Ceremonies for property	Ceremonies for village
	Political Activities
Participation in village moot	
Headmanship	

men, the complementary role Rungus women occupy is that of religion. It is only the *bobolizan*—the female spirit medium—who has spirit familiars. Through these, during trance she can pose questions to members of the spirit world and receive answers from them with regard to the relations between them and community members. The health and spiritual well-being of the domestic family as well as of the whole Rungus community lies in the hands of women. Thus because of her preeminence in the fields of health, religion, child-rearing and domestic activities, a woman more than fulfills her side of the balance in the male-female dichotomy. She enjoys considerable prestige because of these roles. Men do participate in those forms of ritual dealing with the swidden, handling most of the ceremonies for the rice spirits. They do not go into trance, however, nor do they have spirit familiars or converse with the spirit world.[2]

With regard to relations between the sexes, in general there appear to be few of the tensions that exist in male-dominated societies, and there are few ambiguities in expectations of gender role fulfillment. There are, however, two minor conflicts that arise from time to time. Because the preferred form of postnuptial residence is uxorilocal, in intervillage marriages (which occur less than thirty percent of the time), an occasional man misses his natal family, and his desire to spend more time visiting them may create tensions. If this tension becomes irreconcilable, divorce may result. We know of one such case that ended in divorce.

Another conflict between men and women is over the use of domestic animals raised by the family. Men may want to use these to exchange for brassware and gongs, and women may want to retain them for sacrifice if there is a threat of illness to the family. Such conflict is only episodic, however, and occurs only within the confines of the domestic family, and so does not constitute a major source of tension in defining male-female roles in Rungus society.

BASIC VALUE PREMISE ON RELATIONS BETWEEN THE SEXES

Menstruation as a socially unmarked category may be related to the major value premise in Rungus society:

> all sexual relations are potentially deleterious for the partici-
> pants, as well as the rest of the society, the domestic animals,
> the crops, and the land itself, unless properly entered into
> through marriage. (Appell 1976a:71)

Any illicit sexual relationship causes "heat" to radiate outward from the offending couple. This heat angers the spirits, who then cause illness and crop failure. Thus an act of fornication or adultery will affect the health of the offending couple, their families, the longhouse members, the village, and the world at large. Not only is the health of humans involved, but the productivity of the swiddens, success in raising livestock, and accumulating assets are all affected.

In order to "cool" this heat, chickens or pigs must be killed, and those affected by the act are marked with blood. A feather is dipped into the blood of the sacrifice and "painted" on the ankles of those people who have been affected. Blood is also sprinkled on the swiddens and on family property.

This value premise regarding the potential deleteriousness of sexual relations finds expression in the developmental cycle of a Rungus female.

GROWTH STAGES OF RUNGUS CHILDREN

The growth and maturation of males and females are divided into labeled stages. For examples, after birth the first stage is "smiling," followed by "rolling over," "crawling," and "walking." These stages cover the period from birth to approximately one year or eighteen months of age. While not yet self-conscious about running around nude, boys and girls are still referred to with one term, *amupo ilo ikum*—"do not yet know enough to be ashamed." As soon as they start to wear clothes (about three or four years old for girls, a bit older for boys) a girl is referred to as *manintapi* ("wearing a skirt") and a boy as *maninsuval* ("wearing pants"). Before her breasts begin to enlarge, a girl starts wearing a sarong, and by about the age of ten a girl will be referred to as *maninsukalab* ("wearing a sarong"). When breast development is apparent, a girl is called *samuni*, which roughly translates as "maiden." A girl is *samuni* until she is contracted for marriage. It is important to note that menarche does not constitute a labeled stage in a girl's development.

There are no institutionalized rites of passage for either males or females upon reaching puberty or sexual maturity. In an effort to make themselves attractive to the opposite sex, however, both males and females at the age of approximately twelve to fifteen years will have their teeth filed and blackened. This is an individual act with no community ritual accompanying it. And it illustrates again the emphasis on gender symmetry among the Rungus.

Early childhood

Young girls are taught at a very early age to start imitating their mothers in almost every aspect of daily life. As soon as a young girl is able—at the age of about three years—she has her own miniature pounding pole for husking rice and miniature trays for winnowing. She will sit beside her mother, at first practicing with chaff only, and when she is accomplished enough she is entrusted with a small amount of "real" rice to pound and winnow. Her father makes her a small water-carrying tube of one joint of bamboo, and she goes to the river to fill it, carrying it on her shoulder in imitation of the older girls. By the age of about five years she will feed chickens and pigs, calling them to her and chasing away those that do not belong to her family. At five she has her own weeding knife and accompanies her mother and older sisters to the swidden. If there is a younger sibling, a five-year-old girl is also capable of staying in the longhouse to babysit in the presence of other women so that her mother is free to go unencumbered to the swiddens for short spells. In short, a young girl is brought up to imitate her female elders in almost all aspects of Rungus life. As she gets older she is entrusted with more and more responsibility until, at the age of eleven or twelve years, she is an accomplished housekeeper and can be considered a suitable wife. In one instance a man, when his wife died in childbirth, was left with the motherless infant. He turned over his newborn to his eldest child, a girl of about seven, to feed and tend. The baby thrived and grew to adulthood.

Young boys, on the other hand, engage in play of various sorts which are mainly nonconstructive and not specifically in preparation for adult activities. Boys do not incorporate the imitation of adult tasks into their play. Although capable of collecting small fagots for starting fires on the hearth, young boys will resist strongly when asked to do so. Instead, young boys spend endless amounts of time playing in the water or running around on the ground near the longhouse. While a girl can demonstrate a high degree of competence and responsibility in female tasks at the age of about twelve, a boy at this age is just beginning to learn how to help in the swiddens. By the time he is in his mid-teens, however, he is fully competent in the swiddens and other male tasks, such as housebuilding, and is equal with a girl in his ability to start a family.

This difference in male and female socialization is a function of the adult tasks and their locations. Men work in the swiddens all day, unaccompanied by their wives and families while there are small children to be reared. Young boys, because the swiddens are potentially hazardous—the cutting of the jungle can anger the indwelling malevolent spirits that cause illness—are left to play around the longhouse with other boys. The young girls, however, are with their mothers and start helping with the household tasks in the longhouse. When a young girl starts to wear a skirt she is perceived as old enough to take care of her younger siblings and run the household while her mother accompanies her husband to the fields. As a result of this exposure to adult female tasks and the expectation that the young girls will help, they become active in learning adult tasks at an earlier age than do boys, whose fathers are largely absent from the longhouse during the day in the early years of their sons' lives.

Adolescence

Where the environment might facilitate sexual contact, Rungus males and females are required to remain apart. Both male and female children under the age of nine or ten years sleep with their parents in the enclosed family living area of the longhouse apartment. Boys beyond this age must sleep on the verandah, or open area of the longhouse, however, while unmarried girls continue to sleep with their parents. Male visitors also sleep on the verandah; their wives sleep in the compartment.

Young boys and girls must not be found alone together unless in the presence of a number of adults, and intentional physical contact with a girl on the part of an unmarried boy will be cause for litigation. The father of the girl who has been fondled by a boy can sue for compensation from the father of the boy.

A young girl will find herself fully prepared for marriage insofar as she has all the skills to keep house, raise children, and work in the swiddens. She is ignorant about sexual matters, however. All she knows is that if she were to engage in sex prior to marriage it would have disastrous consequences. A Rungus mother does not give her daughter any instruction in sexual matters, and this includes menstruation. The following account given to me by my major informant represents the norm.

Itulina was married at the age of about twelve. Her periods had not started and did not start until she had been married almost two years. When this happened, she was very frightened. Fearing she had contracted some dread disease, she ran to her mother only to be brushed off and told not to worry about it as it was perfectly normal for girls to have this happen to them. In a similar fashion, she was equally worried when her periods ceased upon conceiving her first child. She bore ten children, and after the first two or three she deduced the pattern and realized the connection between conception and cessation of her periods. She added that she rarely experienced more than one or two periods between pregnancies.

PRELUDE TO MARRIAGE

Although young Rungus males and females are enjoined from any activities that could lead to sexual contact, there are accepted forms of flirting and courtship. Mixed work groups are formed whenever there is a sizable job to be done. When a ceremony is held or there are major agricultural tasks to be performed, work groups of young boys and girls gather to help. During such group work, and also in the evenings when longhouse members relax and engage in light work, young unmarried boys and girls engage in verbal games, somewhat like riddles, which involve special vocabularies and poetic forms. And there are times in the evenings when boys play a stringed guitar-like instrument and the girls answer with nose flutes. Through these formalized verbal and musical patterns of communication, a boy can indicate to a girl that he is interested in her, and she can indicate her acceptance or rejection of his advances. However, this is as far as any pairing off is permitted prior to marriage.

When a boy decides upon a certain girl as the one he wants to marry, he says nothing explicitly to her about it. Before bride-price negotiations can begin, he must make his intentions known to her parents. This he does by arriving one evening on the verandah of their longhouse apartment and offering first her father, then her mother, his brass box containing betel chewing supplies. No words are exchanged. But if they accept his proffered box, it is an indication that they are willing to have his parents open bride-wealth negotiations. The young man then returns to his family's apartment. Although she is most likely aware of what has transpired, the girl he intends to negotiate for must not display her awareness or show any interest in marriage. For a girl to express any interest in marriage is tantamount to saying she actually desires sexual relations, which is considered to be immoral.

BRIDE-PRICE NEGOTIATIONS

Bride-price consists of gongs, brassware, and ceramics. A very high value is placed on the services of a young Rungus girl as a wife, and elaborate negotiations take place between her parents and the parents of the prospective bridegroom to arrive at the size of her bride-price. During these negotiations the father of the bride-to-be will tally all the attributes of his daughter in order to increase the value of the bride-price as much as possible. These attributes include her virtue, beauty, and comeliness, skills in household tasks, in the swiddens, at sewing and weaving, and so on. An especially high bride-price will be asked for a girl who is learning the ritual chants necessary to become a priestess, as it is in the hands of these skilled spirit mediums, all of whom are female, that the health of the community and its members lies. A woman who becomes an effective healer receives a considerable amount of goods in payment for her services.

However, as a result of the value premise in Rungus society that all sexual relations are potentially dangerous unless properly entered into, "the explicit and acknowledged purpose of the bride-price is the purchase of rights to the enjoyment of these services as well as the reproductive services of the female" (Appell 1976a:71).

Bride-price among the Rungus also contributes to ensuring stable relations between husband and wife. If a woman is abused by her husband, she can walk out of the marriage, and the bride-price will not be returned. The bride-price thus serves to protect the female. A man, on the other hand, can ask for dissolution of his marriage and the return of part of the bride-price if no children result from the union. The same is true if his wife leaves without cause. If the marriage is not consummated because of refusal on the part of the bride to engage in coitus, all but a few basic pieces of the bride-price will be returned.

THE WEDDING

A girl is not supposed to acknowledge that she knows anything about the bride-price negotiations. As elaborate preparations for the wedding festivities are begun, she is given devious answers by her friends and family if she should ask what is going on. Many people must be fed as friends and relatives arrive from distant villages. Rice wine is prepared, a process that takes several weeks, and large amounts of rice are winnowed ahead of time. The bride observes all of these preparations and even participates but still must not give any indication that she knows it is for her own nuptials. Of course she most likely knows, but it would be undecorous of her to let on or to discuss it with anyone. All references to her as bride are surreptitious. When the date of the wedding has arrived, the bride is referred to as the *valangan*—"the one to be told a secret."

At about sunset on the first day of the wedding the groom, his family, and his attendants arrive at the longhouse of the bride. Some time before their arrival the bride is approached by a number of the young married girls in the longhouse who "capture" her with a ceremonial sleeping robe, pull it over her head, and at the same time tell her she is to be married. This is the first "official" notification a girl receives from anybody that she is to be wed. She immediately tries to fight off her captors, falling on the floor, kicking and screaming while they restrain her and carry her bodily to a neighboring apartment. Here she will be guarded by these young married women until daybreak the next morning, at which time she will be prepared for the marriage ceremony.

All night she carries on ritualized wailing about her desire to run away into the jungle to escape her fate. She must struggle and object enough so that she does not appear to desire marriage and the concomitant sexual relationship, but not so much that she will embarrass her groom and her family. This period of struggle can last from a few minutes to several hours. In extreme cases, when a girl is genuinely frightened of going through the marriage ceremony or not certain she wants to marry her suitor, she will carry on all night, and girls have actually been known to break free and run into the jungle to hide. But this is considered bad form, just as it is considered bad form for a bride not to show a struggle but to giggle and appear to be enjoying her fate. Even up to this point the mother of the bride has not herself communicated anything to her about her impending marriage.

While she struggles, wails, and declares her humiliation and embarrassment at the thought of being married, the bride is admonished by her companions. The bride makes statements such as "I will kill my mother for doing this to me"; "Doesn't she feel sorry for me?";[3] "I won't go through with this"; "Let's run away."

In response to these outbursts her "captors" and the friends assigned to tend her through the night admonish her: "Don't thrash too much, you'll get hot, you'll break your beads and lose your skirt"; "You'll embarrass your fiancé"; "It is the fate of young boys and girls of every race in the world to get married. Raising a family of children is fun, would you rather have a baby in the jungle, a bastard?"

On the morning of the second day the bride is led to her own family apartment with her head still covered and still objecting to the proceedings. Here she is readied for the actual ceremony by her attendants. She sits completely passive while being dressed and adorned, not actively resisting but not cooperating with her attendants.

This passive resistance is sustained through every phase of the wedding—when bride and groom must feed each other cooked rice, address their in-laws by the proper term of address for the first time, and so on. Although the bride knows what is expected of her because she herself has witnessed many previous weddings, she "plays dumb" so that her attendants must physically take her hands and move them in the correct direction for her. All of this resistance is to indicate her reluctance to being married because a virtuous woman should not be desirous of sexual relations.

MARITAL RELATIONS

When at last the formal wedding ceremony is over, the newly married couple returns to the apartment of the bride's family where they will reside until at least the next swidden harvest. Having been enjoined against all sexual relations for her entire life, and knowing of the dire consequences that will ensue if she should stray, the young bride is now expected to submit completely to the advances of her new husband. Moreover she is expected to do so while sleeping next to her parents and younger siblings. This sometimes produces severe psychological discontinuity, and some girls may reject their husbands completely. It is said of these girls that they *amu tumutun*—"do not turn toward" their husbands. The refusal to consummate the marriage brings shame on the groom and embarrasses the family of the bride.

A family, because of their embarrassment over having a daughter who rejects her husband, will take measures to ensure consummation of the marriage. At first they will start by vacating the apartment for a night or two, taking the younger children out onto the verandah to sleep, leaving the young couple alone. If this fails, they will move to their swidden house for a week or so, hoping their absence will encourage the girl to shed her self-consciousness.

Despite the fact that a mother observes her daughter going through this period of trauma, she will not offer her any advice or give her any verbal guidance. These topics are simply not discussed.

The roles of fiancé and affianced, and the relationship of newly married husband and wife, may not appear consistent with the symmetry I have reported for Rungus gender roles in other arenas. For example, there is concern that a new husband might physically abuse his wife. But if the female is abused, she may divorce, and the bride-price is not returned. Divorce is as accessible to the female as it is to the male.

THE MANAGEMENT OF MENSTRUATION AMONG THE RUNGUS

Because of Rungus attitudes toward sexual matters, even I as a female had difficulty eliciting information on the observance of menstrual customs. It was not a topic one discussed with young girls around the swimming hole in the river, nor could one sit on the verandah of the longhouse, always within earshot of others, and interview on such a subject. There are no explicit proscriptions against discussing menstruation. Rather, it simply is not considered a matter for discussion.

My chief informant and closest friend was a priestess of high standing whom I interviewed on religion and ritual in her swidden house. Our conversations were in the Rungus dialect and also involved a complex special lexicon used only for ritual purposes and not understood by the layperson. We were accompanied by a young Rungus man who was my husband's linguistic informant. He was familiar with our research and was himself very insightful into his own culture. In the beginning he would paraphrase any difficult questions and help elucidate for me the responses of my informant. His presence precluded my doing any interviewing on sexual topics, however, as a woman could not discuss such a topic with a male, especially an unmarried one, present. It was therefore close to the end of our field stay, when I was thoroughly competent in the language and intimate enough with my informant to ask her, one day when my assistant was absent, whether she would be willing to tell me a bit about *adat ondu*—"women's customs." To my relief she not only consented but showed none of the traditional embarrassment and answered all of my questions openly.

She informed me that a Rungus woman observes no taboos when menstruating. She is not prohibited to work in the gardens, at the hearth, or in any other household tasks. She does not observe any special method of hygiene, except perhaps to bathe more frequently, and she employs no napkins or tampons. During the time of heaviest flow a woman chooses less strenuous tasks which can be performed while sitting on the longhouse verandah. She sits with her skirt discreetly pulled up and her legs covered with a cloth. (In outward appearance, this is not different from the position frequently taken by women while tending babies or working at their daily tasks in the longhouse.) If she gets up to move about she simply flushes the floor of bamboo slats with water from a bamboo tube which is kept handy to clean up after all messes, including puddling babies, and spills.

A menstruating woman is not considered unclean or polluting by any member of the society. This is evidenced by the fact that a menstruating priestess can effectively communicate with her spirit familiar, although spirit familiars are angered by priestesses whom they consider unclean and will refuse to communicate with them. Thus a priestess may not go under the longhouse where she may come into contact with human or animal feces. Even mud is considered filth by spirit familiars. For example, a spirit familiar of my informant suddenly ceased "talking" with her while she was attempting to cure a sick grandchild. When she was able the next day to make contact again with her familiar and asked why he stopped talking so suddenly, she learned that he was angry because she was *asakau*—"filthy"—since she had touched cat vomitus. And he told her what she must do to purify herself.

It is all the more striking, then, that menstrual blood does not pollute priestesses or spirit familiars.

Another illustration of the nonexistence of menstrual taboos can be seen when one examines Rungus sanctions regarding blood and bleeding. Human blood is believed to attract or summon malevolent spirits who will cause illness. If a man cuts himself with his machete while working in the jungle or swidden, he may not cross a stream or river until the bleeding stops. If he does cross and the blood is carried on the water, the indwelling spirits of the water will be angered. A menstruating woman is not enjoined from bathing in the river, however.

CONCLUSION

Menstruation among the Rungus is both a socially and culturally unmarked category. Girls are not formally enculturated in dealing with it. There are no taboos connected with it, and it is considered neither polluting nor purifying, propitious nor dangerous. There are no Rungus myths or rituals connected with menstruation. Even where other body by-products such as feces and vomitus are considered ritually filthy, menstrual discharge is not. While blood from an injury is considered dangerous, in that it will anger malevolent spirits, menstrual discharge is not. In fact, one may say that menstruation and menstrual blood are socially ignored. The Rungus view of menstruation is thus in sharp contrast to most other societies described in the anthropological literature.[4]

Various explanations have been advanced to account for menstruation being a marked symbolic category in other societies. These include female solidarity (Lawrence, this volume); differences in power relations and contradictory gender norms (Douglas 1966); and the separate and conflicting economic activities of male and female (Friedl 1975).

With regard to female solidarity, in Rungus society females maintain solidarity through the custom of uxorilocal residence; yet menstruation is unmarked.

With regard to differences in power between roles, I argue

that the Rungus have gender symmetry. Gender roles among the Rungus are not stratified but are complementary. Does this mean that they are also equal? In general, yes. There is but one term of reference for both husband and wife, and one of the prime requisites for a couple to be considered suitable for marriage is that they *mitimbang*—balance each other. Though their tasks are not the same, equal value is placed on the contributions made by both sexes. But these economic activites are not completely independent. They are complementary. Focused on the swidden and the domestic economy, the tasks do not occur in different physical or social environments.

The payment of bride-price, which is for the female's sexual and reproductive services, and uxorilocal residence are both indicators of the high value of the female role. The reluctance of the bride, in some cases, to engage in coitus immediately after marriage appears to suggest an imbalance. Yet women use this reluctance to maintain control, and there are sound psychological reasons for it in their early training in modesty and morality. Furthermore, it must be realized that illicit sexual intercourse has the same ritual consequences for both males and females.

It would appear from the foregoing that part of the explanation for the lack of menstrual taboos among the Rungus might be found in the social complementary of male and female roles, which I have termed *gender symmetry*, in turn a reflection of Rungus economic organization. Another part of the explanation, however, lies in the value premises of the Rungus cultural system itself. The lack of menstrual taboos seems clearly related to Rungus reticence about all sexual matters, for fear of supernatural sanctions.

PART III

THE SOCIOLOGY OF MENSTRUAL MEANINGS

The focus of this section is on the implications of economic, political, and overarching social structures in the shaping of menstrual experience, meaning, and practice. In chapter 5, Denise L. Lawrence presents a clear case of menstrual taboos. In strong contrast to Delaney's analysis of seemingly parallel Turkish taboos (chapter 3), Lawrence argues that in rural Portugal it is women themselves who actively maintain menstrual prohibitions because these taboos are in individual women's interests rather than means toward their suppression. The Portuguese housewives in Lawrence's study use their menstrual periods and the customs that surround them as means for achieving economic and political ascendancy within their neighborhoods.

The raising and slaughter of pigs by Portuguese families and, particularly, women's overseeing of the manufacture of pork sausage comprise both necessary subsistence activities and a way to accumulate influence. Sausage making is a communal activity in which neighbors and relatives assist one another by turn, forming economic and political networks through such mutual assistance. Although participation in this activity is governed by stringent menstrual taboos, women use the taboos creatively, manipulating them to control the flow of reciprocity and the formation of exchange networks as they vie for ascendancy with other women and their households. It is for this reason, Lawrence argues, that rural Portuguese women themselves choose to maintain the old taboos, despite the fact that they are recognized as anachronisms in rapidly urbanizing and industrialized contemporary Portugal. The case stands in stark contrast both to that reported by Delaney for village Turkey and to that reported by Vieda Skultans for Wales in chapter 6.

Skultans details the varieties of meanings ascribed by women themselves to menstruation and related aspects of their reproductive lives. In earlier chapters the relevant contexts within which contributors have found menstrual symbols meaningful have been broadly shared by members of given societies. Skultans demonstrates that although certain cultural and social contexts remain significant in the Welsh mining village that she studied, those created by individual women's life histories, particularly their marital histories, are profoundly relevant as well. The diversity of such histories is systematically correlated with the diverse meanings that women attribute to their own menstrual periods and to the climacteric. Thus within a single society there can be a variety of personal factors that create different symbolic codings and valuations of menstrual experience.

In their personal constructions of menstruation and menopause, Skultans's Welsh women do not seem to reflect the influences of social organization as usually understood. Yet as in Turkey, the Welsh macrostructures of asymmetrical gender relations *do* deeply condition menstrual meanings. Potentially at least, these meanings are oppressive of women. Such oppression is not, however, a *direct* effect of male domination but, rather, occurs through some women's own turning of menstrual meanings against themselves. Given the diversity of the meanings available, the resulting self-deprecation serves to isolate these women from others within the community who value their own reproductive functions more highly.

Skultans shows that these intricacies in Welsh menstrual semantics do turn on shared structures of intergender relations. These structures surface in the lives of individual women in diverse and even contradictory ways, and yet profound issues of inequality and alienation from power are deeply implicated in all cases.

Skultans argues that Welsh menstrual symbolism varies between women who find fulfillment in traditional gender roles and those who have failed at or rejected them. In the final essay of this section, Emily Martin concentrates on the second group, which she argues is prevalent in the United States. She analyzes how a specific constellation of cultural ideas has come to be associated with a range of frustrations with the role of women as defined in contemporary North

America. She argues that menstrual meaning in the United States was subverted in the nineteenth century by the culturally constructed requisites of an industrial economy. The weight of such meaning, Martin suggests, has shifted today from menstruation itself and come to rest most firmly on "the premenstrual syndrome," or PMS. This interim of heightened hormonal activity and (possibly) of increased emotional volatility has been cast negatively because, Martin argues, some women's biopsychic condition immediately preceding the onset of menstruation is antithetical to participation, through labor, in the dominant system of economic productivity. Scientific biology has been in collusion with this subversion of meaning, according to Martin.

Biologists have supported a cultural coding of the premenstrual interim as one of abnormality and dysfunction, upholding a disease model of periodic emotional volatility, because of the social and economic contexts within which biological "facts" are currently being determined. In Martin's analysis, PMS as currently understood is evidence not so much of an inherent weakness in female physiology as of the subtle and pervasive oppression of women in industrial and postindustrial state societies, which are rooted in economic structures supported by a scientific establishment. Thus the solution to perceived PMS "pathology" does not lie in the further dosing of women with medicines formulated to repress hormonal symptoms; these can only support the negative impact of current menstrual meanings on women's self-esteem, as well as supporting an alienating economic system. Rather, the solution lies in a radical reexamination of the presuppositions underlying present socioeconomic structures and women's expected behavior within those structures. Finally, PMS is not a women's disease but a social one, according to Emily Martin.

5

Menstrual Politics:
Women and Pigs in Rural Portugal

Denise L. Lawrence

Traditionally, discussions of menstrual taboos have focused on men's reactions of fear to menstrual blood and menstruating women. Occasionally women's opinions and views have been described, but only rarely have they been considered in the explanation of behavior that ultimately concerns them (see Buckley and Gottlieb's chapter in the introductory section).

This chapter describes avoidance behavior exhibited by some Portuguese women during menstruation at the time of the annual pig-killing. I argue that women's behavior can be explained not by reference to assumptions of male dominance over women but to women's conscious choice of modes of behavior reflecting strategic goals important to their own perceived self-interest. Women are the principal actors in maintaining the menstrual taboo because it allows them to control certain social interactions within and outside the household and affords them a rationale for protecting the economic privacy of their homes, for which they hold primary responsibility. Ultimately, my approach views women's behavior related to menstruation as embedded within the complexity of the social relations and values that surround them rather than as a simple function of pollution concepts.

It is often implied, but not specified, that both males and females in a particular culture hold equally to the same beliefs (Hoebel 1960:95). Occasionally male opinions of the menstrual taboo are discussed whereas female attitudes are ignored or left underreported (M. Wilson 1951:219). Women's views of menstruation may be only superficially explored, or discussed in an anecdotal fashion as an aside not central to the main issue. Finally, some evidence of women's views may be given a doubtful interpretation. Lowie, for example, argues that it is difficult to obtain information from women on their beliefs about the polluting effects of menstrual blood. Yet he apparently takes women's "disinclination to speak" as proof of their feelings of "dread of menstrual blood and of its contaminating sacred objects by contact or proximity" (1963:90).

Older theories purporting to explain the origins and maintenance of the menstrual taboo tend to emphasize cross-sexual pollution. This may be a result of the fact that ethnographic data are already androcentrically oriented. These theories often assume that males are instrumental in limiting the behavior of menstruating women, presumably because they fear menstrual pollution and have the power to do so (see the editors' introductory chapter).

Women's views of menstruation and taboo customs have not been totally ignored, but descriptions are scant and few anthropologists in the past considered women actors in their own right in discussing menstrual taboos. Kaberry, however, noted that Australian Aboriginal women occasionally broke the taboo, an act intended to evoke fear in others in order to retaliate against someone for a perceived personal abuse (1939:240). M. Strathern reiterates this theme in her discussion of New Guinea women (1972:166). These two accounts suggest that women may have accepted the dangerously powerful conception of themselves as menstruators but utilize the fears associated with menstruation to achieve their own ends.

The line of argument developed here assumes that women are actors in their own right who actively choose among cultural alternatives in pursuing goals. Women, like men, manipulate valued resources, cultural norms, and social relationships to maintain positions of relative power (Bailey 1969). But because men monopolize decision-making powers and positions of authority in most societies, women often must work through or around men to achieve their goals. Thus women most frequently operate within an arena of informal power relations (Friedl 1967; Riegelhaupt 1967). Furthermore, as the primary childbearer/child carers, women are often primarily associated with a domestic sphere of influence (Rosaldo 1974).[1] As such, their goals and strategies vary according to their position within the family as well as in extradomestic social structures (Lamphere 1974). Social structure and family form, then, influence the way in which women may be drawn into competitive or cooperative relations with men as well as with other women.

In societies in which nuclear families predominate, women are not forced to overcome a male hierarchy within the household to achieve their domestic goals. This is not to say that a woman is easily able to assume an equal or dominant position in relation to her husband at home. Rather, her relationship to her spouse is conditioned in large part by the extent to which his position of authority in the home is supported by forces beyond the household. Thus in many societies, most notably class-stratified states, weak male control at home is seen to be a function of men's lack of power in the community (Lamphere 1974:111; Reiter 1975:272). Lower-class women, then, may be in a better bargaining position within the household than their upper-class counterparts.

Many of these class societies also exhibit a marked polarization of public and domestic spheres, with males associated primarily with the former and females with the latter (Rosaldo 1974). For example, in southern France as in much of the Mediterranean, Reiter notes that a community often gives the appearance that men and women occupy and operate within sexually distinct but relatively equal autonomous spheres (1975:272). Although males hold ultimate societal power and authority, within the local community women's relations seem to parallel men's as they link individual households through relations with other women; these ties they may manipulate for their own purposes. Thus women's strategic positions involve their relationship with the husband in the household and with other women within the community at large.

Southern Portuguese community and family structures parallel those generally characterized in the Mediterranean. Rural life, and in particular that of the community described here, is marked by the presence of nuclear family organization and, traditionally, a highly class-stratified social structure.[2] Women's social networks appear to exist somewhat autonomously from those of men. Women hold relatively equal power with males within the household even though some men hold formal authority outside. In this respect the menstrual taboo is one of those elements women manipulate to maintain their positions within the household and to control relations that link households in the larger context of the community. Although women interact in patterned ways with other households, they do so at the expense of forming large, cohesive all-female groups. Ultimately the nuclear family as a corporate unit predominates in women's conceptualizing strategic goals. It is the upward social and economic mobility of the family unit that women seek to further, and to that end women see themselves as in league with their husbands.

ETHNOGRAPHIC BACKGROUND

Vila Branca (a pseudonym) is a small town of about six hundred permanent residents located in the Alto Alentejo in southern Portugal.[3] The primary economic activity, agriculture, was traditionally organized in the latifundist pattern typical of southern Iberia. The majority of the population was poor and landless and worked on the estates of a few wealthy landowners as laborers or in various sharecropping arrangements. Community life was characterized by rigid class stratification, the upper class dominating all economic, political, educational, and religious institutions. Once an important social, economic, and governmental center, the town is now a mere shadow of its former self.

Since the 1960s changes in the regional and national economies have altered Vila Branca's class and community structures. Massive outmigration of most of the wealthy and many of the poor to the urban-industrial belt near Lisbon has reduced the local population. A drastic decline in the number of traditional agricultural jobs was brought about by the introduction of commercial farming techniques. Today only half the active adult male population is engaged in regular agricultural employment; the other half finds work in the building trades, state-subsidized public works projects, government jobs, and small businesses. Guaranteed minimum wages established during the regime of Marcel Caetano and increased after the 1974 revolution have significantly improved the standard of living.

In Vila Branca women have been affected greatly by the changes in agricultural production, but they have generally not moved into other forms of employment. A few have found jobs in a small local factory, and many continue to participate in the annual winter olive harvest. The majority of women, however, do not work outside the home and consider themselves "housewives." Most families are now able to subsist on a husband's earnings alone.

Although they are at a decided disadvantage in the job market, women are not necessarily in an inferior position at home. Indeed, women may be said to have considerable power in the household despite the fact that Portugal is considered a patriarchal culture in the Latin tradition (Pescatello 1976; Riegelhaupt 1967). Households are almost exclusively organized on the nuclear family model, and family size is kept small. Women are often the primary managers of the household, making a majority of the day-to-day decisions regarding the control of the family budget. Although they have strong positions at home, women ensure their domestic positions by formally deferring to their husbands in public.

Most southern European communities are characterized by the spatial separation of spheres of activities by sex (Campbell 1964; Freeman 1970; Harding 1975). The validity of this assertion can be supported by even the most casual observation of spatial patterns of social interaction in Vila Branca. For example, men tend to congregate in the town or church square, in outside shops, in cafes and along the thoroughfares, where they discuss the presumably more important political issues of the day or conduct business negotiations. Men are largely identified with formal community organizations and institutions with the "public" sphere. Women, however, are loath to identify themselves with such institutions or activities and prefer to concern themselves with activities associated with the household and family. Women remain close to home and neighborhood and rarely venture beyond them except to visit kin or to perform tasks ostensibly associated with the home such as marketing, laundry, and the like. When females work in the fields, they are usually segregated from males, or their tasks are differentiated from those of males. Women shop quickly in public areas where men congregate; they rarely stop to talk in public but hurry from shop to home. When women do congregate it is always with other women, inside the shop itself or within the confines of the neighborhood. Men typically have no place at home; a man sleeps and takes his meals there but spends most of his free time elsewhere.

PIGS, WOMEN, AND MENSTRUATION

In Vila Branca men as well as women are preoccupied with the purported malevolent effects of menstruating women on curing pork. Preoccupation with this belief is evident during the cool winter months when most households conduct an annual pig-killing (*matança*). A taboo restriction is observed at this time by menstruating women, who avoid preparing pork into sausages or entering a room where this is being done, because the presence of a menstruous woman is said to cause the pork to spoil.

Almost every household kills at least one pig annually to provide meat for sausages. Household members consume the sausages and distribute them as gifts to fulfill ritual obligations. Pigs are purchased and raised as a form of savings and represent a major household investment. If the animal should sicken or die or if the meat should spoil, the loss incurred would be considerable since, in addition to losing the invested money, other sources of protein would have to be acquired.

Each family calculates how much it has "earned" when it kills its pigs by comparing the amount of money invested with the amount the fully grown pig would fetch on the market at the time of slaughter. Household members within the neighborhood often compare their matança "earnings" during this season. The comparisons are used by neighbors informally to rank the households. If, as occasionally happens, a household cannot afford to purchase, raise, and slaughter a pig during a particular year, the family's ranking in the neighborhood drops. Household pig-killings are important social status indicators and are used as a semipublic measure of familial well-being.

At the matança, the greatest threat to a household's economic well-being is posed by the purported destructive effects of menstruation on processing pork. Women argue that during her menstrual period a woman is "ill with menstruation" (*Anda mal com a menstruação*). They liken this natural, regularly occurring event to a disease, albeit a temporary one, which affects a woman's entire body. Women observe certain health and hygiene practices during their monthly periods.[4] Furthermore they are thought to have special powers over which they have little or no control. Contact with or the presence of a menstruating woman is believed to cause plants to wilt or objects to move inexplicably. A woman can bring chaos to her immediate physical environment. Cross-sexual pollution is feared during a woman's menstrual period, and for this reason sexual intercourse between husband and wife is avoided. Although this cross-sexual pollution is not a primary concern overtly expressed by the residents of Vila Branca, women have elaborated upon this avoidance by perpetuating a myth that has local importance and serves to underwrite their claims to menstrual power vis-à-vis men.

The myth concerns a Catholic saint, São Bras (St. Blas), whose image is the only one of a male saint carried in the town's annual *festa* ("feast day") celebration. São Bras is always portrayed in local paintings and shrine images with red hands. The women of Vila Branca claim that the saint got his red hands before achieving sainthood by committing a certain indiscretion with a young menstruating woman. Apparently, in the heat of sexual passion the young man began to explore beneath the young woman's skirts. Little did he know that she was menstruating, for when he pulled out his hands they were covered with blood. In order to "teach him a lesson," God permanently stained São Bras' hands red as a reminder to him and others of his lack of discretion. According to the women of Vila Branca, this incident was the turning point for São Bras after which he reformed his ways and later achieved sainthood by devoting himself to doing good works in the name of the church.

The power of menstruating women is thought to interfere directly with the successful preparation of pork sausages. Only pork is believed to be affected; when it spoils it turns blue in color and must be discarded. Two reasons are given to explain why only pork is affected. First, residents say pork is the only meat preserved through marinating, salting, and smoking. It is the curing process that is thought to be endangered by the presence of a menstruating woman. Since *toucinho* ("fat back") and bones are also salted to preserve them, they likewise are believed to be endangered by menstrual pollution. Fresh pork, or any other kind of meat that is cooked and eaten immediately, is in no danger of spoilage from this influence. The curing process is a "dangerous" time fraught with the fullest potentiality of failure from menstrual contamination.

A second reason that menstruating women spoil pork, according to Vila Branca residents, derives from their notion of a contagious influence based on parallel anatomical structures of humans and pigs. The internal arrangement of the organs in pigs and humans is argued to be similar enough that curiosity about the workings of the human body can be satisfied by examining the innards of a pig. Because of this anatomical similarity, menstruating women are thought to be able to contaminate the pig with their own "illness." That is, menstrual illness is contagious in analogous physiological structures. Live pigs are not generally thought to be affected; the only exception is in the castration of male pigs to encourage fattening before the slaughter. At this time menstruating women are banned from observing the operation because of the same fears associated with the contamination of slaughtered pork.

The facts of matança taboo observances illuminate further the theory of menstrual contamination maintained in Vila Branca. A menstruating woman is believed to be able to cause the pork to spoil simply by looking at it; her sight is the means by which contamination is communicated from her body to the meat. But it is not her casual glance that is feared. Rather, it is the fixed gaze (*olho fixo*), or stare, that is believed to cause the pork to spoil. Women say that a menstruating woman does not always intend to spoil the pork when she looks at it, but because she is menstruating she has little control over the potentially destructive effects of her condition. Furthermore, they argue that a woman does not know exactly when or for how long during her period she presents a danger; it may be at any hour, for a few hours, or several days. These beliefs reinforce the argument that menstruating women should always be banned from the matança and related activities to prevent accidents.

Informants also acknowledge the influence of other factors on the safe preparation of sausages. Residents argue that a pig should not be killed, the meat seasoned, or sausages stuffed when the moon is changing phase lest the meat spoil. An almanac is consulted to determine the date when the matança can be held in order to avoid this danger. It is also believed that if moonlight falls directly on the pork while it is marinating it will cause spoilage. Any windows giving onto the room where pork is being prepared are carefully covered to prevent "lunar" contamination.[5] Finally, flies and other insects (*bichos*) are believed to carry diseases that can contaminate the meat; thus the meat is carefully covered while marinating.

ORGANIZATION OF MATANÇA ACTIVITIES

The nature of the beliefs surrounding menstruation presents some interesting problems for arranging women's labor for the matança. The matança is organized by the husband and wife as the principal members of a nuclear family household. Because the labor required to carry out the necessary tasks normally involves more adults than those who live in the household itself, outside assistance must be arranged. The process of recruiting labor for the matança is a complex affair and takes into consideration factors concerned with task performance and preferences for certain social relationships. Only one of the factors influencing recruitment patterns concerns the preoccupation with the menstrual taboo, but it effectively underwrites women's implicit claim to control labor recruitment. Because menstruating women are potentially dangerous to the preparation of pork, great care is taken in organizing their labor and allowing them entry into the household where the matança is taking place.

Performance of the various matança tasks requires the participation of both males and females. Males are primarily responsible for slaughtering and butchering the animal; women process the pork and prepare the sausages. Men's activities most often take place out of doors and are usually completed by the end of the first day of the matança. These activities often attract the attention of neighbors and friends, who observe and offer help if needed. Women's tasks, by contrast, require the greater part of a week to complete and take place indoors. Long days are spent around giant bowls filled with chopped marinating meat while a group of women stuff sausages and gossip about family, neighbors, and friends. While women claim that they can use as much help as possible in preparing sausages, their work groups are usually quite small.

Residents say that a minimum of three men and two women is required to complete the matança tasks; however, more than these are usually involved (an average of four men and three women). Husbands and wives share the responsibility of inviting guests from among family members, neighbors, and friends living in Vila Branca and elsewhere. Many households use the matança as an occasion to bring family together for a *festa de familia*. Assistance obtained locally is usually reciprocated by exchanging labor with the guest at his matança, or by exchanging other kinds of favors. Inviting a guest is considered a request for a favor; therefore the request should not be refused. Occasionally the matador or an old widow who specializes in sausage-making may be paid for his or her services. All guests, however, are given some portions of the kill as a gift for their assistance.

Although hosting the matança is the joint responsibility of husband and wife, wives ultimately make most of the advance preparations for the event. In fact, 65 percent of the guests invited to thirty pig-killings during the winter of 1976–1977 in Vila Branca were invited by women.[6] Although there is a tendency for men and women to recruit members of their own sex to the matança, women cross sex lines more often than do men in lists of invited guests. In the study a total of six women, just 10 percent of all female guests,[7] were invited by men, whereas thirty-seven men, or 46 percent of all men invited, were recruited by women.

Matança recruitment across sex lines is not made easy in Vila Branca. Residents acknowledge a general restriction on extended social intercourse between unrelated men and women. Public encounters of this kind are awkward for participants and invite suspicion, censure, and gossip from the community. In daily life people avoid such situations by quickly extending a courteous greeting, never letting the eyes meet, and moving along. Informants claim this restriction does not apply to kin (who constitute 85 percent of the help recruited), although it may have some effect on the recruitment of distant relations. If this effect were present, however, one would expect the influence to be equal on both sexes, other things being equal—that men would invite kinswomen in numbers proportionate to women inviting kinsmen. This, however, is definitely not the case.

Although the matança is defined as a household activity with which women are primarily associated, the asymmetry in recruitment patterns is reinforced by the menstrual taboo and the avoidances it engenders between the sexes. Menstruation is not a topic that women and men discuss together in public or private, although women may discuss it freely among themselves. Not even husband and wife talk about menstruation; a wife simply says she doesn't feel well (*Ando mal*) to warn her husband about her period. Because planning around menstrual periods is so critical to the success of the matança, women are more easily able than men to recruit other women to the matança.

Early seeking of assistance by women leads to their recruiting more helpers, many of whom are men. Women often begin recruiting a month or more before the scheduled event. A woman arranges labor with other women for the day of the matança and the week following when several women are required to prepare sausage. Commitments are secured from these women, and backups are casually arranged in case of "illness" among some of the participants. Women may also tentatively recruit men (husbands or sons) through the women they contact directly. In fact, the matança labor resources of each household are largely controlled by the women. When the help one household receives from another is reciprocated by a labor exchange, a wife may send her husband or children, or may go herself, as a representative of the entire household to work at the matança. Husbands, by contrast, do not commit their wives' labor to the matanças of others, not only because they are less involved in recruitment but because of the menstrual taboo. Women, therefore, are the primary creators and managers of the networks of exchange of matança assistance between households.

Women also control much of the social activity connected with the matança, starting the first day and continuing until all the sausages are stuffed. Once the pig's innards are exposed, the danger from menstrual contamination is believed to begin. For this reason the carcass is moved from the street, out of the sight of curious neighbors, into the interior of the house for butchering. Women take charge of regulating the entry of the guests they have invited, as well as that of uninvited visitors, into the household. Husbands become quite nervous while the butchering is taking place because almost any woman could represent a danger to the pork. Often men are not aware of all the helpers their wives have invited to the matança and must defer to their wives, whose judgment regarding the entrance of various individuals constitutes the final authority.

During the matança a woman asks all female visitors who come to her door: *"Pode ver?"* (lit., "Are you able to see?"). The question underscores the basic belief that menstrual contamination is achieved through a fixed gaze. If a woman is not menstruating, she may answer *"Posso"* ("I can see"). Many women, however, take the query to mean that their presence is not altogether welcome. Ana, an eighteen-year-old student, once explained that she would never enter the house of anyone, family member or friend, if she were asked this question at the door unless she had been previously invited. The risk to her relationship with the members of the household, as well as to her own reputation, if the pork spoiled was too great to chance a visit. Indeed, uninvited women are reluctant to enter any matança household during this season because if the pork spoils at any time before smoking, they fear they will be suspected of intentionally causing it through menstrual contamination.

Fear of being accused of having malicious intentions not only prevents many women from asking entry into a household but also inhibits offers of assistance. One Saturday a young woman and I watched her neighbor's pig-killing taking place in the street. I suggested that we offer to help once the carcass was moved inside the house. She flatly refused, saying that she feared her neighbor would think she was purposely trying to bring misfortune to the pig-killing activities. Women rarely offer assistance at matanças or, if they do, they are often past menopause.

It would be incorrect to say that residents of Vila Branca are patently uncooperative. Within the neighborhood residents strive to assist one another in resolving the problems of daily life. An offer of assistance cannot be easily turned down, in the same way that a favor must be granted if at all possible. Yet favors and offers must be reciprocated. No one, however, wants to lose control over the numbers and kinds of people to whom one is obligated to reciprocate. Furthermore as offers of assistance are reciprocated with food gifts in the same way that invited guests are thanked, too many guests may drain household resources. By maintaining the menstrual taboo women can promote a neighborly coopera- tive ideal without actually having to act on it.

THE EVIL EYE, ENVY, AND COMPETITION

Ultimately women's behavior is more crucial than men's in maintaining the menstrual taboo in Vila Branca. The taboo prevents women from forming cooperative groups that could add to their power and control beyond the household, in the community. Women, in fact, seem purposely to keep their work groups small, barely above the stated minimum of two required to perform the tasks, and certainly below the num- bers they claim they would welcome. Yet women's reluctance to add more participants, which would increase gift outlays and reciprocal obligations, is understandable.

Why the regulation of matança labor should be expressed in the menstrual taboo is an important issue. Maintenance of the taboo appears motivated by a strong undercurrent of fear: Not the fears men have of women but women's fears of each other. These fears, and the form the taboo itself takes, struc- turally parallel the belief in the evil eye and its pervasive association with envy found throughout the Mediterranean (see Maloney 1976). In fact, one Vila Branca informant, who openly doubted the purported effects of menstruation on pork, suggested that the reason women clung so tenaciously to the taboo was related to their fears of envy.[8] The connection of the evil eye and envy with upward economic mobility in ideally egalitarian small communities has been documented elsewhere (Foster 1967). Similarly, economic mobility and competition seem to underlie the presence of the menstrual taboo in Vila Branca.

Belief in the evil eye assumes that the desirous stare of an individual thought to be motivated by envy can bring illness or misfortune to the object or person envied. The feature characterizing both the evil eye and the menstrual taboo is belief in the powerful influence of the fixed gaze: Whatever harm is thought to be communicated is transmitted through the eyes. The folk theory underlying the belief is based on the notion that staring, or even paying a compliment, implies desire. Unsatisfied want or frustrated desire are thought to lead to envy, jealousy, and ill feelings.

In Vila Branca the fear of being envied gives rise to two contradictory behaviors: (1) the appearance of generosity and selflessness in daily actions, and (2) secretiveness and the public masking of wealth differences by an outward appearance of poverty. Often the mere mention of a lack of some needed item such as matches or potatoes results in their appearance as a neighbor or friend responds with the unobtainable item. To hold back is one thing, but to hold back and be discovered, given that privacy is difficult to maintain, is feared to endanger one's reputation and social relationships. Similarly the display of new acquisitions and home improvements results in a public recognition of possible asymmetry in social relations and invites envy and discord. Thus residents are inclined to hide, or at least refrain from exhibiting, new possessions to avoid these antisocial feelings. Although many young residents of Vila Branca do not readily admit belief in the efficacy of the evil eye, largely because they seemingly do not wish to be thought "backward," the continued influence of these ideas is evident in other practices usually associated with evil-eye beliefs.[9]

According to informants there is a difference between intentionally casting the evil eye (*Mau olhado*) and casting it unintentionally (*quebranto*).[10] Menstruation puts a woman in an uncertain state of control: She does not know when during her period she may endanger others, and even if she did know, she would not be able to control her period's influence. By virtue of her condition a menstruating woman is classified as able to cause misfortune through quebranto, especially at the matança. This classification, however, does not rule out the possibility that such a woman may consciously desire to cause misfortune. Because there is no way for others to really know if a woman is menstruating or to know a menstruating woman's intentions (because she might lie in order to deceive others whom she wants to injure), every woman is suspect. A woman (regardless of whether she is menstruating) must comport herself in a manner that is above reproach in order to avoid suspicion. A menstruating woman who sincerely professes her innocence of harboring malicious intentions when a misfortune does occur can, however, be excused from blame by reference to quebranto.

DISCUSSION

Women's interest in maintaining the menstrual taboo might easily be explained by arguments that connect menstruation symbolically with social order. For example, Turner argues that a Ndembu woman, "in wasting her menstrual blood and failing to bear children, is actively renouncing her expected role as a mature married female" (1967c:42). The appearance of menstrual blood signifies the failure to conceive, a woman's most important purpose in society; menstruation and menopause symbolize death (Friedl 1975:29). If children are highly valued, as is the case in many if not most societies, it can be argued that the failure to become pregnant is likely to make a woman envious of other women and their children. Indeed, this kind of envy has been offered as the folk explanation for casting the evil eye in much of the literature on Europe, and has also been associated with witchcraft, especially in post-menopausal women (Chadwick 1932).

On a parallel symbolic level, just as menstruation is an indicator that conception has failed to occur and pregnancy will not follow, the spoilage of pork represents the failure of the curing process. In a sense, food-processing activities such as sausage preparation might be taken as a metaphor for reproduction.[11] The gestation period necessary between conception and birth is like the period of time between slaughter and consumption of sausages, when marinating, stuffing, and smoking must occur for successful preservation to take effect. In both cases, the "conception-gestation" period is fraught with danger and the risk of loss.

Although this argument constitutes a plausible causal explanation in cultures where many children are desired, it seems to be no longer applicable to the residents of Vila Branca. Large families were traditionally preferred until about twenty years ago; children were put to work as additional laborers in the majority of households. Children, like pigs, represented an economic investment and resource for the household. Today changes in the economy, law, and social values have led most parents to regard children more as an expensive liability than an economic asset. Most young and middle-aged couples prefer only two children for whom they can provide more advantages, and birth control is practiced in order to keep families small. Parents urge their children to attend school, which is now compulsory through the sixth grade. Education is costly but manageable for the poor, who see it as an important means of upward economic and social mobility.

The relationships between reproductive activities and food preservation are suggestive and may provide some clues to the origins of the menstrual taboo within the context of the matança.[12] Indeed, the unconscious influence of these belief structures might easily continue to affect the maintenance of the taboo itself. Women's consciousness in manipulating the taboo for their own purposes, however, is a more obvious factor in explaining their behavior. Clearly what is thought to be envied by the menstruous woman, or what a woman fears other women will envy, is not the child but the pig—the representation of a family's main economic investment and savings which it risks each year. The pig now occupies a more prominent position than children as a symbol of relative wealth and economic well-being.

The current focus on the pig and the matança as symbols of household status is emphasized by informants who say that in Vila Branca twenty years ago only the rich killed pigs. The poor never killed their own but worked at the matanças of the landowners and in return received a small portion of pork. Today changes in the local economy allow almost every household to participate in this custom. The spread of the household matança was one of the first obvious indicators of economic change in Vila Branca; it constitutes a powerful symbol of upward economic and social mobility and of competition in the local community.

The neighborhood is the main arena of household competition as well as the setting in which expectations of mutual aid are expressed. Residents are aware of gaining slight advantages over their neighbors or of being left behind in the struggle to raise their standard of living. To a large extent the failure to make expensive purchases for a refrigerator or television or to install a bathroom can be ignored, but the purchase of a pig, because it requires only a small initial investment, cannot. If a household does not slaughter a pig each year, it indicates that it is strapped and may be falling behind. Conversely, competition among neighbors is tempered by the expectations of neighborly generosity. A willingness to assist, to exchange favors, to take an interest in the welfare of one's neighbor forms the basis of the commitment. Although each household sees itself in competition with its neighbors, it also strives to participate in good neighborly relations by recognizing mutual obligations of assistance.

The neighborhood is also the focus of women's activities, as women are seen as the principal sources and conveyers of information and gossip. During the pig-killing a woman and her household are potentially vulnerable to outsiders, in particular to neighbors who, attracted by the noise and activity, may be tempted to offer help. What a woman fears from her neighbors during the matança is the information they may transmit to others over which she has no control. One woman at whose matança I assisted asked me not to tell anyone that her sausages occasionally came untied and slipped off the pole onto the floor. She was afraid that her neighbors would think her incompetent at her *serviço da casa* (housework).[13] Although women often compare openly the size of the pigs they have killed or discuss new possessions they have recently acquired, they usually limit it to a verbal report. Thus a woman may exaggerate the truth or hide it, or she may lie outright in order to control public impressions (Goffman

1959). The privacy that the menstrual taboo helps a woman secure at the matança allows her to represent herself in accordance with her own self-image. In addition, by legitimizing a woman's selectivity in recruiting assistance, the taboo allows her fuller control over the numbers and kinds of people she permits into her house and to whom she is obliged to reciprocate. Thus it contributes to a woman's control of her own and her household's social networks as well as to household privacy.

The fact that the menstrual taboo is the expressive medium through which women regulate matança social relations is important. According to Douglas (1966), it is not unusual to find taboos operating within spheres of intensely conflicting norms and desires: "When moral principles come into conflict, a pollution rule can reduce confusion by giving a simple focus for concern" (1966:133). Women's desire to control information, prevent envy, and regulate social relations beyond the household are directly related to their role in protecting the interest of the family. These interests are often antithetical to the sentiments of good neighborly relations. Yet the necessity of maintaining cordial social relations in the face of potential socioeconomic asymmetry within the neighborhood is paramount to understanding the taboo and its focus on women. Thus if Douglas is correct, the conflict between family interest and neighborliness is resolved through the pollution rule, the menstrual taboo, which inhibits and clarifies the behavior of the most active participants in this sphere: women.

CONCLUSION

The annual matança in Vila Branca being the major household activity requiring outside cooperative labor, women's control of recruitment and access to their homes is not insignificant. Although women's participation in these activities may be taken as a necessary extension of their domestic responsibilities, the important role played by the menstrual taboo underwrites and reinforces women's claims to that pivotal position. By consciously maintaining the beliefs, they are able to manipulate social relations, both within and beyond the household itself, and thereby perpetuate a custom the original causes of which seem to have lost influence. Nevertheless, the maintenance of the menstrual taboo is clearly linked to other concerns as women seek to protect and promote the upward mobility of their own nuclear families. And although women fail to form cohesive work groups with one another, they do collude in a competitive socioeconomic struggle within the community.

Previous accounts of the menstrual taboo have often reduced the ethnographic complexity and variability of expression to a simple pollution concept. By ignoring or underrepresenting women's roles in maintaining the taboo, our analyses have traditionally failed to take into account the views of a significant portion of the population that these customs affect. It cannot be denied that Portuguese women appear to have accepted an image of themselves as being occasionally polluted, but they have also managed to use this image to their own advantage. In light of this example it seems reasonable to assume that women in other cultures may play a more active role in customs that purportedly act to restrict their behavior. Women's comparable control elsewhere, however, may depend on factors beyond the taboo expression itself. Certainly the variability in family form (nuclear, extended, or polygynous) provides some clues to social contexts in which the taboo might be expressed elsewhere. As the other examples in this collection demonstrate, it seems prudent to refrain from further simplistic interpretations of the meaning and use of the menstrual taboo until more data become available.

6

Menstrual Symbolism in South Wales
Vieda Skultans

In 1970 and 1971 I conducted research on the symbolism of
female fertility and traditional femininity in a South Wales
mining village. An early, incomplete presentation of the findings was published while the research was still in progress
(Skultans 1970). This chapter gives a fuller discussion of the
symbolism of menstruation and its relation to femininity. My
general premise is that notions of menstruation are strongly
correlated with the overall structure of gender roles. In particular I found that there were two attitudes concerning
menstruation in the village: some women had developed an
elaborate set of ideas concerning menstrual blood loss, which
they viewed as beneficial, while other women were at best
indifferent to their menstrual periods. In this chapter I
analyze these two contrasting attitudes and show them to be
correlated with structural differences within and attitudes
toward the female social role.

THE VILLAGE

I carried out my research in a village I shall call "Abergwyn,"
some miles north of Port Talbot. The village is "blind" in the
sense that the road stops there. Its "blindness" and the effect
on communication is perhaps one of the most significant features of the village, particularly for women: the insularity
resulting from Abergwyn's geography is a more marked feature in the lives of women than in those of men.

Abergwyn has a population of about seventeen hundred.
The oldest houses in the village date from 1854. They are

one-story terraced cottages built on a steep incline beside the railway line, which was laid out in the same year. Both houses and railway line were built in response to the many surface mines or "levels" that had been opened. However, the greatest number of the houses in the village were built between 1905 and 1912, when the deep pits were opened. Fluctuations in village population have been related to pit closures: "When a pit closes we always lose some people, but then others come back." Despite such difficulties in employment, the village has had a relatively stable population. (Almost half the people in Abergwyn in 1970 were born there and had never moved away.) Currently, however, there are thought to be a great many strangers in the village.

There is a distinction between "good" and "bad" families in the minds of many villagers. "Good" families are usually those long established in the village, although newcomers are not automatically "bad." "Good" or respectable families are well organized. Their time and money are spent in approved ways involving long-term planning. Their children are well fed, well clothed, and well disciplined. The wives are faithful and home-centered. "Bad" families possess the opposite characteristics in varying degrees. I found that whenever I mentioned a woman I had interviewed to Madge, my hostess who worked at the village health center, she immediately brought these categories into play, classifying the woman in question as belonging either to a "good" or a "bad" family.

The exception of Madge and a very few other women notwithstanding, Abergwyn may be unusual, even for South Wales, in that there are virtually no employment opportunities for women. In part this is a result of the fact that the village is blind. Because the road from Port Talbot stops there, the village has no north exit. Recently there was an advertisement for three hundred women factory workers in a nearby town. Were there a road running north from Abergwyn, the factory would have been accessible in fifteen minutes. As it is, public transportation is so slow and awkward that work in the factory is impractical for Abergwyn women.

Most of these women spend their lives within the confines

of the village. Although they deplore the lack of work in a general way, few actually express the desire to work. Rather, they express aversion to outside work in terms of a lack of confidence: many women, when asked if they would like to do simple manual jobs, said they would lack the confidence. Bad communications and lack of work have combined to produce in the village an emphasis on women's traditional housewife role and an ill-preparedness for any other kind of role. Given this, it is perhaps not surprising that the categorization of families as "good" or "bad" depends in large measure on the perceived quality of the adult women as wives and mothers in those families.

I suggest that because of the isolation of women from the outside world, the village is especially conducive to the symbolic elaboration of all aspects of the traditional female role. In Abergwyn I found that menstruation and menopause were described in highly figurative language and that aspects of these processes were elaborated upon verbally to a high degree. Female bodily processes seem to serve in Abergwyn as a source of metaphors for making statements about women's place in the social structure.

THE PROBLEM

My hypothesis is that in Abergwyn women are using a biological given—the loss of menstrual blood—not only to assert their anatomical femaleness but also as a source of symbols for communicating their own perceptions of their social roles. Analysis of the connection between menstruation and role must also include a consideration of the menopause, or "change," as a symbolic passage from one kind of social role to another.

My hypothesis that women identify their own reproductive processes with their particular perceptions of their social roles arises in part from my experience of women in Abergwyn speaking of hysterectomies. Some, like my friend Madge, strongly related her reproductive capacities and her identity, saying about her own hysterectomy, "I remember being upset because I was to have it. It's a queer thing isn't it? I realized that something had been taken away from me that was going to decide a fact of me, you know." Yet although women such as Madge seem to voice regret for their loss, doctors are frequently confronted with such bald statements by women as, "I want to have it all out" and "I want to get rid of the lot" (compare Miller 1946; Doyle 1952). It would seem that although women often related reproductive capacity and social identity, not all women do so with the same feelings about that identity symbolized for them by their uteruses. In Abergwyn, with its particular geography and history, such identity is largely bound up with social role, which in turn conditions women's perceptions of their reproductive organs and processes.

To an extent my thinking on this is based in a connection that Mary Douglas has drawn between pollution concepts and social boundaries. Citing Woodburn's work on menstrual pollution among the Hadza, Douglas remarks (1970:99–102) that Hadza pollution concepts divide their society into "two hostile classes," male and female, and that "This extraordinary intense consciousness of sexual difference is the only permanent level of organization that the Hadza ever achieve" (p. 101). Yet the social boundaries created by Hadza menstrual concepts are not simply those between men and women but are more complex and fragmenting:

> the rule, which in its general form sets all women apart from all men and treats them as dangerous, in its particular incidence sets each woman apart from other women, but not apart from her husband; he, in his turn, is, in virtue of his married state, set apart from other men. Thus the pollution rule draws very precise lines of incorporation and exclusion. (Douglas 1970:101)

Although the idea of "menstrual pollution" per se is not found among the women of Abergwyn, the general connection that Douglas draws between menstruation, social boundaries, and defined social roles would seem to be relevant. Moreover Douglas's point that the functioning of Hadza menstrual symbolization cannot be fully understood outside the contexts both of the experience of individual women and of the wife-husband unit has a certain resonance in the present case, as we will see.

In Abergwyn the women whom I interviewed expressed two distinct attitudes toward menstruation and menopause, quite as Madge and other women expressed distinct attitudes about hysterectomies. In the remainder of this essay I explore the relationships between such attitudes, the terms in which they are expressed, social roles, and expressed identity.

THE INTERVIEWS

I interviewed mature women about their experience of menstruation and about their feelings regarding menopause. The sample of responses with which I must work is a small one, for a variety of reasons.

First, the population of Abergwyn itself is small, and the number of mature women is smaller yet. I also encountered considerable reticence among these women to speak with me, a reticence that perhaps increased as my stay in the village lengthened. Of the ninety-one women whom I asked, thirty-six were willing to be interviewed. Responses to requests for interviews differed widely according to age group, as is evident in table 6.1.

TABLE 6.1.
REQUESTS FOR INTERVIEWS

Order Asked	Age of Women	Number Asked	Number Agreeing
1	49–51	31	18
2	69–71	10	8
3	39–41	20	4
4	29–31	30	6
	Totals:	91	36

As may be seen in this table, the two youngest age groups, which were also the ones contacted later during my study in the village, were the most reluctant to be interviewed. Reluctance to discuss menstruation and menopause might, then, have been a function of age and/or of increasing suspicions aroused by my questioning. Whatever the sources of women's reticence, only the two older age groups, comprising "menopausal" and older women, provided me with enough material to merit analysis and discussion. Thus the following observations are based on the testimony of twenty-six women between the ages of forty-nine and seventy-one. This is a small and age-limited sample, and my findings are offered as suggestive rather than definitive.

TWO ATTITUDES TOWARD
MENSTRUAL LOSS

As interviewing progressed I found that women's attitudes toward their own menstrual periods fell into one of two distinct categories. Some women wished to avoid the loss of menstrual blood, whereas others desired it as being beneficial to them. The women in the second category tended to elaborate more expansively on the symbolic attributes of menstrual blood. I explore both attitudes in turn, focusing particularly on the second group of women.

Women in the first category saw menstruation as an unwanted occurrence that, rather than contributing to their overall sense of well-being, instead detracted from it. These women tended to express their thoughts about menstruation in brief commonsensical or quasi-scientific terms. They said that they did not "make a fuss about periods"; "I just carry on as usual" was an oft-repeated phrase. They had an attitude of tolerant, or perhaps stoical, acceptance of its actual occurrence; nevertheless they saw menstruation as physically damaging and as leading to a condition of pathological weakness—they were fearful of "losing their life's blood." Hence these women were eager to reach menopause as soon as possible and, while not elaborating on menstruation to any extent, had a good deal more to say about menopause (see later discussion).

In contrast, women in the second category, those who desired menstrual loss, regarded menstruation as a vital contribution to their physical and emotional well-being. They saw it as a corrective device in a biological system that would otherwise tend increasingly toward debility and inefficiency. These women wished menstrual loss to be copious. They said that they felt "huge," "bloated," "slow," and "sluggish" if they did not have a period or if they did not lose enough menstrual blood. One woman said that she felt "really great" after a heavy period, this time not using "great" in the sense of "huge." Most of these women insisted on the value of a "good clearance," especially in the ability to get on with housework. A few postmenopausal women said they used to find it much easier to do the cleaning while they were still menstruating regularly than they did in their present state.

In short, these women wanted to "lose" and to "see" a large quantity of menstrual blood over an extended period of time, believing this to be a rejuvenating process, to contribute to their general health, and to facilitate the performance of household tasks and family duties. But they also regarded menstruation as a time when they were particularly vulnerable and exposed to dangers. These dangers are most easily identified through the themes of "excess" and of "bad blood."

Women experience such excess and badness as slowing down their activities and making them feel not only huge and bloated but "poisoned" as well; some women think that unexpelled menstrual blood becomes poisonous and, rising to the head, causes migraine.

Surrounding such ideas of badness and the consequent need for purging are a number of prohibitions aimed at ensuring that the body does, indeed, succeed in ridding itself of the "bad." Women stated that they would not have a bath for fear the period might "go away," although they hastened to add that they would, of course, wash. Many would not wash their hair for fear they might go "funny." One woman was more explicit, saying that she had once tried to wash her hair while menstruating, but afterwards she "fancied I was not losing as much." The emphasis in such accounts is on purging oneself of menstrual blood, because this is "natural" and is a means whereby "the system rights itself." The women who regard menstruation as beneficial to their health and as "natural" do so within a context that includes what we might call mystical dangers.[1]

MARRIAGE AND ATTITUDES TOWARD MENSTRUATION

Having discovered two distinct sets of attitudes held by women concerning menstruation, I tried to ascertain if there were other features associated with the attitudes held by the women in each category, those who wished to avoid menstrual loss and those who desired it.

In the process of interviewing a woman, I frequently asked Madge and others at the health center what they knew of her. In conversation it became evident that these people used clearly defined, shared standards to evaluate women as "happy" or "unhappy." Such conversations enabled me to construct a limited cultural model of a satisfactory woman's life in Abergwyn. The model, while not altogether clear-cut in regard to what constitues feminine happiness, is nevertheless quite clear regarding the conditions that make "happiness" *un*attainable: spinsterhood, widowhood, childlessness, and extremes of sexual disharmony. When I mentioned a woman who met one or more of these conditions, people at the health center immediately emphasized the fact.

"Happiness," then, refers largely to conjugal condition, and the conditions for a satisfactory conjugal relationship can be readily identified. The minimum requisites for feminine happiness are satisfied when there is a regular sexual relationship between husband and wife that produces at least one child. Conversely, "unhappiness"is defined as a dislocation from the regular reaffirmation of that sexuality understood to be at the core of feminine identity and role.

In light of this cultural model, it is significant that the way women described their own conjugal relationships emerged, in interviews, as directly related to the way they described their experience of menstruation.

I did not find any immediate correlations between attitudes toward menstruation and medical or sociological factors.[2] The most direct and clear association was between the perceived need for purging through menstruation—the attitude of my second category of women—and these women's descriptions of their conjugal relationships as relatively undisturbed, happy ones in terms of the village model. In the following I illustrate this correlation through a selection of six case studies from among the eighteen women whom I interviewed in the 49–50-year age group. I start with my first category of women, those who attach no positive significance to menstruation. As we will see, they are also women who are unhappy in village terms.

WOMEN WISHING TO AVOID MENSTRUATION

Mrs. Elizabeth Richard was fifty years old at the time of the interview. She had three children, the youngest of whom was still at home. Her husband had died five years before. Her marriage had been a very unstable one. Her husband was an alcoholic and their life together went through extremes of disharmony. Asked if she thought men understand women, she said definitely not. "Men get away with murder." Her husband, apparently, was no exception to the rule.

Mrs. Richard was less than forthcoming on the matter of menstruation. At first, when I raised the topic, she said that her periods had been "no trouble." She never suffered from painful periods or had heavy bleeding or backache: "I don't know what it's like." She felt, however, that her general health was much better after her periods stopped and said that she had not been ill since menopause. Although she originally dismissed the importance of menstruation, later, while speaking of menopause, she said that while menstruating she could not cope as well.

Asked what her attitude toward a hysterectomy would be, she said, "You can have my uterus tomorrow."

In her talks with me, Mrs. Richard did not consider menstruation a topic of any real concern, and her attitudes toward it, when I elicited them, tended toward contradiction. Indeed, this element of contradiction ran through most of her self-revelations. She said she had not been ill since menopause and had never felt better. However, she also thought that she had been a "very keen person" once but now tired easily and could not concentrate. In fact the number of complaints to which she admitted was considerable, and her medical records revealed a variety of problems over the ten previous years: constipation, vaginal discharge, varicose veins, epigastric and low back pain, fits of unconsciousness, and a suspected tumor that turned out to be benign. The list is formidable, but it is significant that there is no mention of menopausal complaints.

My second example of an unhappy woman who wished to avoid menstruation is Mrs. Catherine Lawrence. Mrs. Lawrence was born in the village in 1919. At the age of twenty-one she married a miner, with whom she had three children. It was obvious that Mrs. Lawrence felt a very deep and persistent dissatisfaction with her marriage. Her view of relationships between men and women reflected attitudes that had become familiar through other interviews: men take women for granted; men lack feeling for women, especially when a woman is ill; when a man marries a woman, "he thinks she's in the home and has got to do everything." She described her husband as being "very grisly," for whom nothing seemed to go right: "How shall I put it? He's not a happy man then. We've got a boy of thirteen at home. We should be really happy but we're not happy."

Mrs. Lawrence showed marked indifference to the subject of menstruation, at the same time clearly indicating that she thought me a fool for having raised the subject. She had never had any trouble at all with her periods and she now felt well without them. They had "no effect at all" on her. Her medical record revealed a number of complaints that had not yielded a clear diagnosis. In it she was described as "a tense, nervous individual." She had suffered from prolonged epigastric pain, although no ulcer was found, as well as from a "bearing down pain," although examination revealed a healthy cervix. Nonetheless in 1969 she was admitted to hospital for dilation and curettage and "full anterior repairs."

My last example of an unhappy woman is Mrs. Leah Thomas. Mrs. Thomas was also born in the village in 1919. She was the daughter of a blacksmith and, like the two previous women, both she and her husband were brought up in the village. With her husband, a bus driver, Mrs. Thomas had five children, four of whom were still living. Her marriage had been highly unstable. Although she was still legally married and had been for over thirty years, her marriage had been punctuated by the regular disappearance of her husband, whom she described, somewhat euphemistically, as "not a very domestic sort of man." At the time of my research she had been separated from him for four years, during which he had been living with the matron of a small private hospital in the Midlands.

As with the two previous women, Mrs. Thomas placed no significance on menstrual blood or on the value of menstruation. She said she could not wait to stop menstruating because she was "losing such a lot." Of her periods she said, "I'm sure I'm no better in health by seeing them." Menstruation, to Mrs. Thomas, was an unmitigated source of annoyance and discomfort. Prior to and during menstruation, she said, she felt extremely weak and suffered from sick headaches, dizziness, and vaginal irritation. A hysterectomy would not have worried her in the least; in fact she thought it would provide a welcomed relief.

In contrast to the lack of value she placed on menstruation and her wish for its absence, Mrs. Thomas attached great importance to other bodily ailments. Her complaints were numerous, and she described them at length and in detail. According to her own account and to her medical records, she suffered from high blood pressure, headaches, dizzy spells, palpitations, backache, indigestion, nervous rashes, sleeplessness, and depression. (Recently her troubles reached a sad pitch when she suffered a stroke.)

The women in these three examples share certain features with each other and with the group of unhappy women that they represent. In each the dislocations within marriage were such that appearances could no longer be kept up, and failure to conform to expected norms had to be acknowledged. These women were reluctant to discuss menstruation in any but the briefest terms. Yet this reticence was due neither to a disinclination to "somatize" problems nor to a reluctance to discuss their bodies and their health: all experienced an ample share of physical complaints and were willing to speak about them, sometimes at length. This combination of culturally defined conjugal unhappiness, disinterest in one's menstrual periods, and history of self-reported medical complaints appears as a strong correlation among the women I studied.

I turn now to my second group, the women who had regular conjugal relationships—"happy" women by their own description—and to charting their attitudes toward menstruation. Together with their different experience of marriage, they present a very different set of attitudes toward menstruation than did the first group.

WOMEN DESIRING MENSTRUAL LOSS

As with the women in the first category, I will use materials from three interviews to illustrate characteristics of village women in the second category, those desiring menstrual loss. Again, as in the first group, all three representative women were between forty-nine and fifty at the time of my interviews with them, facilitating comparison.

Mrs. Megan Brown was born in 1919, the youngest of three children. She was married to the colliery undermanager. She admitted to feeling lonely and "cut off" in the village. Mrs. Brown showed a very deferential and dependent attitude toward her husband. The Browns lived outside and overlooking the village in a large somber house surrounded by a wall, and no doubt her dependency was accentuated by her isolation. Still, Mrs. Brown's attitude toward marriage contrasted with those of the unhappy women, and the quality of her marriage was also different; it altogether lacked the dramatic turmoil of, for example, Mrs. Thomas's and Mrs. Richard's marriages, as well as any other components that would have made her unhappy in terms of the village model.

When questioned, Mrs. Brown showed a fairly unconcerned attitude about her general health. In contrast, her attitude toward menstruation was far more anxious. She described her periods as being decidedly uncomfortable and very heavy. Even though she had been sterilized, however, she reacted with horror to the suggestion of a hysterectomy: "If you had sexual intercourse, like, there would be nothing there. Also, there would be no periods. It may be an old-fashioned idea, but I think all the badness comes away then. For instance, I now feel huge and bloated. If I had a period this would all come away." Even though when I spoke with her she had not had a period for several months, she thought it was better to carry on "losing," because it was "nature, really."

Although Mrs. Brown spoke little of illness, her medical report was full of past complaints. During her last pregnancy, in 1944, she developed an abscess on the right kidney that had to be removed. Following the birth she was sterilized. During the past few years she had suffered from hypertension and hot flushes. The following report was made: "I thought her actual symptoms were probably mainly menopausal. . . . But I think there is a clear indication here for treatment of her hypertension and it does seem possible that there might be a renal cause." Despite these several conditions, and although given the opportunity, Mrs. Brown hardly spoke of her hypertension or of menopause. Instead, her own medical preoccupation seemed to be with the menstrual cycle.

My second example of a happy woman is Mrs. Phylis Howard. She is the younger sister by two years of Mrs. Leah Thomas, introduced earlier. Although Mrs. Howard seemed to enjoy talking about reproductive matters in a rather coy way, she often repeated, "My husband believes in privacy," during our conversations. She described her husband as being very thoughtful and considerate and said she got on "wonderfully" with him.

On the subject of menstruation, Mrs. Howard said that her

periods were regular but not excessive. In fact, her periods were very "scanty" although she had recently "picked up." In other words, Mrs. Howard thought a small loss of blood to be a failing. She also spoke of the advantages of "clearing the system." Her medical report did not record many difficulties or complaints: a miscarriage in 1963, complaints of persistent tiredness, and an iron deficiency confirmed in 1969. She herself downplayed nonmenstrual medical symptoms that were themselves relatively insignificant.

My final example of a happy woman is Mrs. Olwen Jones. Mrs. Jones, aged fifty, had lived in the village all her life. She had been married for twenty-five years and had two children. She described herself as a happily married woman who was devoted to her husband, Fred, a coal merchant.

Although Mrs. Jones described her marriage as a happy one and herself as a "happy woman" in terms of the village's criteria, her speech was permeated with an undercurrent of dissatisfaction that was never fully identified. She said she was always depressed, especially since her children had grown up and her husband had taken to going out in the evening and leaving her at home by herself. She "felt sorry" for herself. She had come to see the world as bisected by an insurmountable communication barrier: Men can "never in this world of God" understand women. They are like animals, she thought, Fred excluded. Amplifying on this verdict, she said, "I'm not very fond of my sex life." She considered sex ridiculous at her age. Asked why, she said it was "just ridiculous." This did not prevent her from acceding to her husband's demands in bed, however, ridiculous and frustrating though she found them to be.

Contrasting with these scornful references to her sexual life, Mrs. Jones had very emphatic views about the importance and value of menstruation in her life. She said that she would feel very old and frustrated without her periods: frustrated, because she would not be able to get rid of blood and she would feel unclean; frustrated, also, because she would not feel like doing anything about the house, and the washing and cleaning would be left undone. For the same reasons, Mrs. Jones dreaded any gynecological operation, fearing that it might disturb her menstrual flow. By comparison to the other women discussed, Olwen Jones's medical complaints and record were meager: she complained of headaches, which she attributed to high blood pressure and to depression.

DISCUSSION

The three cases that I have selected, though each is obviously unique, illustrate my analysis. Those women who describe themselves in accordance with the village model for happiness have relatively undisturbed, though by no means problem-free, married lives. In speaking to me they emphasized the positive effects of the loss of menstrual blood and stressed that they wish to continue menstruating. They are sensitive to bodily changes at menstruation and regard such processes as essential in producing and maintaining healthy equilibrium. In contrast, women who are clearly unhappy, in terms both of the model and of their actual marital situations, although they often have many other medical complaints, minimize the impact of menstruation on their lives and would not or do not miss it.

There are two theoretical perspectives that, I believe, begin to make sense of these findings. The first derives from the psychoanalytic study of menstruation and the second from the anthropological study of ritual.

Freud (1930:36), Horney (1931), Deutsch (1950:308–311), and other psychoanalytic writers have all, in different ways, interpreted women's difficulties in menstruation as stemming from women's identification of their menstrual processes with their own femininity (a quality differently constructed by the different analysts), about which they have deeply ambivalent feelings. The theory of feminine ambivalence has also entered the ethnographic literature. For example, Grace Harris (1957) argues that in Taita women's "possession hysteria," women undergo a symbolic destruction of their inferior status as females in Taita society, the experience leaving them better prepared to *accept* the vicissitudes and constraints of marriage (compare Turner 1969).

Certainly happy women like Mrs. Brown and Mrs. Jones

evidence considerable ambivalence regarding their roles as dutiful wives, and I suggest that they have used their menstrual periods to resolve it. It may be that, like Taita women's "possession hysteria," the set of beliefs concerning menstruation found among my group of "happily" married women— "bad blood," "excess," the need for "good clearance," and so on—are ways of reaffirming and maintaining the intactness of bodily boundaries and thereby the social boundaries that define male and female (see Harris 1957; Douglas 1970, and the foregoing). It is because they are ambivalent about the roles demarcated by these boundaries, I am suggesting, that these women need to reaffirm them, as Taita women apparently need from time to time to reaccept roles experienced as inferior.

My comparison of Taita and South Welsh women in terms of their respective "rituals" is not spurious. The symbolic elaboration of menstruation by Abergwyn women desiring menstrual loss is striking when compared to the reticence and plain rhetoric of the village women who wish to avoid menstruation. Much of this symbolization itself suggests ritual, and especially ideas about purification and fears of mystical dangers.[3] Perhaps the "ritual" that these women are engaged in may be tentatively viewed, in a broadly metaphorical way, as a form of "blood sacrifice," understood in terms defined by Hubert and Mauss (1898). Following Durkheim, Hubert and Mauss equated "the gods" with the ideal representation of society and saw renunciation in sacrifice as a means of upholding and conferring strength upon social values. I am suggesting, then, that menstrual blood is used by happy women as a kind of "sacrificial nourishment" for the demands of the traditional feminine role in a South Wales village: nourishment that they feel is *necessary* precisely on account of their own ambivalence. However ambivalently, the women in my second category, those desiring menstrual loss, wish to nourish this role, whereas those in the first, who wish to avoid menstruation, seek to avoid the role, as well as their periods, to deny the pertinence of both to their identity.

I return now to the subject of ritual and its place in gaining an understanding of these happy and unhappy women. First, however, I take up the topic of menopause, for in Abergwyn I found that beliefs about menstruation could not usefully be studied without also studying beliefs about menopause. Attitudes concerning the cessation of menstruation further illuminate the significance and value assigned by women to the menstrual process itself.

MENOPAUSE

In my investigation of menopause in Abergwyn, I was not concerned so much with the clinical condition per se as with women's use of medical terms and medical symptoms, and with the symbolic attributes they attached to these. Thus "menopause" as I use the term refers to the popularly accepted syndrome of hot flushes, depression, "nerves," and tiredness, as well as any other symptoms a woman *herself* claims to be part of the syndrome (see Crawford 1970). In the following I explore the relationship between perceived menopausal symptoms and women's happiness and unhappiness as described earlier.

RITES OF PASSAGE

The language that many women in the village use in discussing menopause suggests that for them "the change" constitutes a true passage from one condition to another. This passage is spoken of in highly symbolic terms that imply both standardized modes of experience and a shared pattern of beliefs. Such qualities of language and conception again raise the matter of ritualization, and indeed I think that menopause in the lives of these women shares certain features with the classic *rites de passage* of non-Western peoples (e.g., Turner 1969).

Many of the premenopausal and menopausal village women whom I interviewed expected unknown dangers to be endured during menopause, and they emphasized the uncertain nature of these dangers: "I'm keeping my fingers crossed." These dangers were often given intrinsic value. Some women, for example, expressed the belief that it was good to experience hot flushes as frequently as possible; otherwise there was a chance of even more dangerous complications arising. Flushes were thought to "carry you through the change more quickly and safely." Some women who were "on the change" even voiced regret that they did not flush often enough: they admitted to what they thought was a failure, saying, "No, I'm not very good." For these women flushes were thought to be the result of menstrual blood rushing to the head, so that an absence of flushes implied a deficiency of menstrual blood (see note 3).

Some menopausal women emphasized prohibitions that incorporated magical elements. These women avoided touching red meat for fear it should "go off." They said they should not attempt to make bread because the dough would not rise, and should neither touch salt nor put their hands in anything cold.

Women envisioned "the change" as a time when actual, though ill-defined, anatomical or structural changes were taking place within their bodies. (This was the reason most often given in answer to the question of why menopause was called "the change.") One seventy-year-old woman said that at menopause, women turn into men "inside." She herself had been aware of this process taking place and experienced it as a "turning and tightening" of the thigh muscles. This last example of symbolic elaboration is of particular interest. In this instance women seem to be experiencing, in physical change, a change in social status as well, quite in keeping both with theories of rites of passage and with those, introduced earlier, that associate the body physical and physical boundaries with the body social and its symbolic boundaries.

I note that not all women stressed these types of ritualistic elements in discussing menopause with me. Some women dramatized menopause through stressing the importance of a culturally accepted, symbolically elaborated syndrome of symptoms, but others did not. My interest is in analyzing just who emphasized such elaborate elements in their descriptions of their own experience, and probably in that experience itself, and who did not, and why.

CORRELATIONS

Briefly, the correlations that I found are as follows. The unhappy women of my first category, who had failed to live up to village norms of femininity and who downplayed the effects of their menstrual periods, put a marked emphasis on the changes they went through during menopause. Conversely, the happy women of the second category, who described themselves as more or less content in the roles expected of them and who desired menstrual blood loss, elaborating on the theme in striking ways, *de*emphasized their experience of menopausal symptoms. In short, happy women who dramatized the menstrual process made light of menopause, whereas unhappy women who dismissed menstruation stressed the disturbance caused by menopause.

It would seem that dramatization of the climacteric involves public and private recognition of a transition in roles— figuratively, of a passage. Specifically, acknowledgment of "the change" involves acceptance of a postmenopausal role that is not determined by feminine reproductive function. By the same token, denial or underplaying of menopausal symptoms seems to be associated with *rejection* of the transition to a postmenopausal role and that role's culturally defeminized basis.

Given these equations, the unhappy and happy women are respectively more and less likely to emphasize the climacteric. My first group of women, those who have been unable to conform to the culturally dictated premenopausal role— who, especially, are not "happily" married—are pleased to celebrate the end of social expectations regarding this role and therefore welcome the climacteric. Seeing themselves as social failures, they may welcome the opportunity to conform to a new postmenopausal role that, though ill-defined, is perceived as less demanding than the more exacting pre-menopausal one, in which the risks of failure and stigma are greater.

Conversely, the women who have apparently conformed with relative ease to their expected role of "happily" married wife have learned to expect their rewards from that role and have little incentive to abandon it for another, less well-defined one with uncertain rewards. Thus in Abergwyn they wish to continue menstruating and deny the symptoms of menopause.

Ernest Becker accounts for the psychological dimension of what I observed in the village. Although his article (Becker 1963) deals with menopausal depression, its implications are far broader. He asks, "Why does a woman who to all appearances has led a satisfying life, suddenly break down at the menopause and decide that her life is not worth living?" (p. 355). He answers:

> Women become depressed at the menopause . . . they do not have enough reasons for satisfying action, and when they lose the one apparent reason upon which they predicated their lives—their femininity—their whole action world caves in. Let us be brutally direct: Menopausal depression is the consequence of confining women to a too narrow phenomenon. . . . We create menopausal depression by not seeing to it that women in their forties are armed with more than one justification for their lives. (Becker 1963:358–359)[4]

EXAMPLES

Although Mrs. Brown's and most especially Mrs. Jones's cases in the earlier samples from interviews with eight "happy" menopausal women illustrate Becker's central point, all three cases also point up the broader implications of his argument. In the three happy women's cases presented, as in four of the other five, the women all were resisting menopause, hoping to maintain the menstrual periods that they so valued: Mrs. Howard, who was relieved that her "scanty" periods had "picked up" again; Mrs. Brown, who was reluctant to discuss physical symptoms that a doctor had diagnosed as menopausal; Mrs. Jones, who openly feared the loss of menstruation because it would leave her "frustrated." The vehemence with which all three reacted to the possibility of hysterectomy might also be taken as resistance to the inevitability of menopause.

Yet, and in accordance with my hypothesis, perhaps some of the most significant evidence lies in what these women did *not* say: overall they were reluctant to speak about menopause.

By contrast, the ten menopausal women whom I interviewed who fell into the "unhappy" category tended to elaborate upon the topic, not only in their descriptions of their own symptoms but in their experiences as well. Again referring to the sample cases presented earlier, this time to those of women who wished to avoid menstruation, we find that Mrs. Richard was quite willing to discuss menopause and her belief that hot flushes took a woman through it "quickly and safely." She had first spoken to the doctor about hot flushes at the age of thirty-eight, and placed her "change" firmly between 1959 and 1963. In 1963 she had visited the doctor for swollen hands, flatulence, a burning in the breasts, and burning dysphagia, all of which she connected with menopause.

Mrs. Lawrence and Mrs. Thomas's readiness to "welcome" a hysterectomy suggest their equal readiness to welcome menopause. Further attitudes among these unhappy women are illustrated through a fourth sample case, that of Mrs. Beryl Dickens.

When she was twenty-two Mrs. Dickens married a bank clerk some twenty years her senior. She had two sons with him, both of whom were attending university at the time of my research. Her husband was retired. It seemed that the evening classes that she avidly supported and the difference between her and her husband's ages were the two most significant features of her life. She was deeply dissatisfied with her marriage.

Mrs. Dickens expressed a lack of concern for menstruation in a manner familiar through the cases of other unhappy women. She told me that she was very glad to reach menopause because she thought that it would help her anemia (which was self-diagnosed and unconfirmed). She attached no importance to the uterus and claimed that a hysterectomy would have about the same impact on her life as the removal of her appendix. However, although otherwise nonbody oriented, she had clearly conceptualized a particular portion of her life, from age forty to forty-six, as the time when "the change" had occurred.

My questions about the physical symptoms of the climacteric did not entirely please Mrs. Dickens. She felt I had not really tackled "the main problem of the menopause," and wanted more depth to things. She said that until she read Simone de Beauvoir's *The Second Sex*, she thought herself alone in her dissatisfaction and had assumed that all other women were satisfied with their married lives. After a period of depression and sleeplessness during menopause, she had finally realized that there was another person, "a me" inside her, one that had nothing to do with being a wife and mother. Women, she thought, especially those of her generation, had missed out on education.

While not dramatizing her menopause through presenting a range of symptoms as, for instance, Mrs. Richard did, like Mrs. Richard and unlike the "happy" women, Mrs. Dickens put emphasis on a clearly conceptualized, protracted period of transition. Most significant in terms of my argument, however, is Mrs. Dickens's association of her feelings of dissatisfaction with her family life, particularly with her marriage, and her discovery of a nonwifely "me" at menopause.

CONCLUSION

The most significant outcome of my interviews in Abergwyn was the discovery that the symbolic elaboration of one or the other of two major aspects of female reproductive life—menstruation and menopause—was correlated with the degree of conformity to the appearances (at least) of village gender-role expectations. The constellation of attitudes held by the women whom I interviewed were clearly delineated.

Of the eighteen menopausal women with whom I spoke, eight had irregular marital situations that involved either gross disharmony, a flagrant infidelity, or no conjugal relationship at all. Insofar as these women did not conform to local models for happy women, I have characterized them as unhappy. All eight of these unhappy women had a matter-of-fact attitude toward menstruation yet saw it as detracting from their general health. Seven of them had eagerly awaited or were awaiting menopause. These women emphasized, and often dramatized, the physical symptoms that they associated with "the change" and the passage that this change afforded them to a different way of life.

Conversely, the ten women with regular conjugal relationships, who described themselves in terms of the village model of a "happy woman," elaborated strikingly upon the physical experience and symbolic—even ritual—aspects of menstruation. In contrast to the first group, they saw menstruation as necessary to their overall health. I have suggested that these women's marked emphasis on the desirability of copious blood loss during menstruation might be viewed metaphorically as indicating their (ambivalent) need to offer a regular "blood sacrifice" at the "altar" of society: to nourish their perhaps shaky commitment to the culturally defined roles that they played with apparent success. For these women "the change" appeared as a threat to feminine identity. Therefore they deemphasized symptoms of menopause as a means, I suggest, of postponing the inevitable shift in status that accompanies these physiological changes.

One seventy-year-old woman with whom I talked in Abergwyn recalled how, when she reached menarche, her mother had sent her without comment to a married sister living five miles away. When she arrived at her sister's home, tired, bewildered, and bleeding, she was greeted with the terse statement, "You have arrived at your rightful place."

Considering village women's menopausal experience as a social as well as physical passage enables us to describe their situation at the climacteric in a way that makes sense of the correlations I have discussed. The hitherto happy women are caught in a state of suspension, about to lose their "rightful place," which they have richly symbolized through menstruation. The unhappy women, on the other hand, are able to make a long-awaited transition, out of a "place" that has been deeply unsatisfying to them (and which they have deemphasized through relative indifference to menstruation) and into a new, less clearly defined—and hence potentially liberating—"place."

The older woman's experience at menarche has other useful implications. The mother's silence on the matter of her daughter's menses was typical of the experience of most women in South Wales. In most cases the women I interviewed claimed that the onset of their menarche was passed over in silence: what information they did receive as girls was gleaned from gossip with their contemporaries. Unlike menstruation itself, there is an absence of shared beliefs and symbols regarding menarche in South Wales. The same curious absence of shared belief occurs at the other end of women's reproductive lives. Although shared symbolic means for experiencing menopause are readily available for women in villages like Abergwyn, shared models for the role that women might play *after* menopause are absent. It is here that the analogy with a rite of passage breaks down, for there is no demarcation of the end of the menopause available, nothing analogous to the rituals of reincorporation that follow the transitional phase of classic rites of passage.

The happy women who present themselves as approximating a culturally defined feminine role model elaborated on a biological process, menstruation, and invested their menstrual experiences with particular symbolic importance. The unhappy women who emphasized the symptoms of menopause used a different physical process to make a symbolic statement about their changed role and their dissociation from the norms for femininity, which they failed to meet. The lack of menopausal "rituals of incorporation" suggests, however, that despite the appearance of choice, there is an absence of clearly defined and socially accepted alternatives to the traditional domestic feminine role in Abergwyn. Unless and until such socially accepted alternative roles become available to these women, I predict that the menstrual cycle will continue to have the symbolic power that it currently holds for them.

7

Premenstrual Syndrome: Discipline, Work, and Anger in Late Industrial Societies

Emily Martin

There are so many roots to the tree of anger that sometimes the branches shatter before they bear. (Lorde 1982:49–50)

Recently in England and the United States there has been an enormous outpouring of magazine and newspaper articles, books, and pamphlets on the subject of the premenstrual syndrome (PMS). I propose to examine this literature for insights it can give us into current conceptions of women's role in society, women's bodies, and the kinds of human capacities that are put at a premium by late industrial societies.[1]

Perhaps the dominant model of what premenstrual syndrome is might be called the physiological/medical model. In this model PMS manifests as a variety of physical, emotional, and behavioral "symptoms" that women "suffer." The list of such symptoms varies but is uniformly negative and indeed worthy of the term "suffer." Lever's list (table 7.1) serves as an example (1981:108).[2]

The syndrome of which this list is a manifestation is a "genuine illness" (Lever 1981:1), a "real physical problem" (advertisement for a drug in *Dance Magazine*, January 1984:55), the cause of which is at base a physical one.[3] Although psychological factors may be involved as a symptom, or even as one cause, "the root cause of PMT [short for premenstrual tension, another term for PMS], no matter how it was originally triggered, is physical and can be treated" (Lever

TABLE 7.1
COMPLETE CHECKLIST OF SYMPTOMS OF PMS

Physical Changes

Weight gain	Epilepsy	Spontaneous bruising
Skin disorders	Dizziness, faintness	Headache, migraine
Painful breasts	Cold sweats	Backache
Swelling	Nausea, sickness	General aches and pains
Eye diseases	Hot flashes	
Asthma	Blurring vision	

Concentration

Sleeplessness	Lowered judgment	Lack of coordination
Forgetfulness	Difficulty concentrating	
Confusion	Accidents	

Behavior Changes

Lowered school or work performance	Avoid social activities	Drinking too much alcohol
	Decreased efficiency	
Lethargy	Food cravings	Taking too many pills

Mood Changes

Mood swings	Restlessness	Tension
Crying, depression	Irritability	Loss of sex drive
Anxiety	Aggression	

1981:47). This "root cause" is a "malfunction in the production of hormones during the menstrual cycle, in particular the female hormone, progesterone. This upsets the normal working of the menstrual cycle and produces the unpleasant symptoms of PMT" (Lever 1981:2). Although in the medical literature the percentage of women reported as experiencing PMS varies from 30 to 90 percent (Debrovner 1982:11), popular versions often stress an astonishingly high percentage, as in Lever's estimate that "more than three quarters of all women suffer from symptoms of PMT" (p. 1). In other words, according to Lever, a clear majority of all women are afflicted with a physically abnormal hormonal cycle.

Various "treatments" are described that can compensate a woman for her lack of progesterone, or her excess of estrogen or prolactin. It is claimed for such treatments that through them psychological and physical states that many women experience as extremely distressing or painful can be alleviated. The benefits of this approach are clear: a problem that had no name or known cause can be named and grasped; and some of the blaming of women for their premenstrual condition by both doctors and family members can be stopped. It seems probable that this view of PMS leads to an advance in women's well-being over their being told that "it's all in your mind," "grin and bear it," or "pull yourself together." Yet a series of assumptions about the nature of time and of society, and about the necessary roles of women and men, are also entailed in this view of PMS. These assumptions, unexamined as they are, suggest that we should scrutinize some dominant cultural conceptions in modern society and, through this, ask whether another view of PMS might give women even greater intrinsic dignity and worth.

DISCIPLINE AND WORK

Let us begin by looking at some of the negative premenstrual symptoms women report. An overriding theme in changes women notice is a loss of ability to carry on activities involving mental or physical disciplines. This is exemplified in items in Lever's list: "difficulty concentrating," "confusion," "forgetfulness," "lowered judgment," "lack of coordination," "decreased efficiency," "lowered school or work performance." Others report "an inability to string words together correctly" (Birke and Gardner 1982:ii). One book advised that if a woman finds her ability to perform some aspects of her work is impaired premenstrually, she might organize her work so that "more routine work, for example, might be carried out during this time, and work requiring more concentration and care might be kept for other times when they feel more capable of it" (Birke and Gardner 1982:24). Competitive tennis players feel their reaction times can be slower (Lever 1981:91), and professional singers report they lose voice control (Dalton 1979:102).

It is completely understandable that in a society where most people work at jobs that require and reward discipline of mind and body, these experiences would be perceived negatively. From the beginnings of industrial capitalism, factory owners (whose profit is based in part on how much value can be gotten out of laborers' work) have placed a premium on controlling the work process—the amount of time laborers work, and what they do, down to the precise movements of their hands and bodies. Indeed historically, when legislation forced a shortening of the working day, owners found it necessary to intensify labor during the hours remaining: "Machinery becomes in the hands of capital the objective means, systematically employed for squeezing more labour in a given time. This is effected in two ways: by increasing the speed of the machinery, and by giving the workman more machinery to tend" (Marx 1967:412).

Braverman and others have shown how scientific management, introduced in the late nineteenth century, has contributed to the deskilling and degradation of work: creative, innovative, planning aspects of the work process are separated from routine manual tasks, and these are then subject to extremely finely tuned managerial control (Braverman 1974). We are perhaps accustomed to the notion that assembly line factory work entails a bending of workers' bodies in time and space according to the demands of "productivity" and "efficiency." We are less likely to realize that deskilling, leading to monotony, routine, and repetition, have increasingly affected not just clerical occupations and the enormous service industry (Braverman 1974:part 4) but the professions as well. Natalie Sokolov has shown, however, that the lower edges of the medical and legal professions, edges into which women crowd, hardly have the independence, creativity, and opportunity for growth we associate with professional work. Allied health workers, legal assistants, and lawyers who work in legal clinics do tedious, boring work requiring a minimum of skill and providing little opportunity for advancement in knowledge or position (Sokolov 1984).

With respect to work, then, the vast majority of the population, and all but a very few women, are subject to physical and mental disciplines, one manifestation of what Foucault calls a "micro-physics of power," "small acts of cunning" in the total enterprise of producing "docile bodies" (Foucault 1979:139). What many women seem to be reporting is that on these days they are less willing or able premenstrually to tolerate such disciplines.[4]

An obvious next question is whether the incidence of PMS is higher among women subjected to greater work discipline. It would be interesting to know whether there is any correlation between the experience of PMS symptoms (as well as the reporting of them) and such factors as class and race. Unfortunately, the PMS literature is nearly deaf to these kinds of questions. Although the incidence of PMS in relation to age, parity, and the existence of a male living partner has been examined (and is generally found to go up with each [Debrovner 1982:11]), these are very crude indicators of the total working and living environment of particular women.

Perhaps part of the reason a more sophisticated sociological analysis is not done is that those who comment on and minister to these women do not see that the women's mental and physical state gives them trouble *only given a particular kind of industrialized society*. For these observers it is the *women* who malfunction and must have their hormonal imbalances fixed, not the organization of society and work that might be transformed so that it could demand less constant discipline and productivity.

Many PMS symptoms seem to focus on intolerance for the kind of work discipline required by late industrial societies, but what about women finding that they become clumsy? Surely this experience would be a liability in any kind of social setting. Perhaps so, and yet it is interesting that most complaints about clumsiness seem to focus on difficulty carrying out the mundane tasks of keeping house: "You may find you suddenly seem to drop things more often or bump into furniture around the house. Many women find they tend to burn themselves while cooking or cut themselves more frequently" (Lever 1981:20). "It's almost funny. I'll be washing the dishes or putting them away and suddenly a glass will just jump out of my hands. I must break a glass every month. But that's when I know I'm entering my premenstrual phase" (Witt 1984:129). Is there something about housework that would make it problematic if one's usual capacity for discipline relaxed?

First, it needs to be said that for the numbers of women who work a double day—hold down a regular job in the paid work force and come home to do most of the cooking, cleaning, and child care—such juggling of diverse responsibilities could only come at the cost of supreme and unremitting effort. For the full-time housewife, recent changes in the organization of work expected of the housewife must be taken into account. Despite the introduction of "labor-saving" machines, time required by the job has increased as a result of decline in the availability of servants, a rise in the standards of household cleanliness, and elaboration of the enterprise of child rearing (Vanek 1974; Scott 1980; Cowan 1983:208).

To this I would add the sense of how desirable it is to be "efficient" and "productive" at home, much as it is in the workplace. "Heloise's Hints" and similar columns in newspapers and magazines are full of tips on how to make every moment count and clever ways of meeting perfectionistic standards in the multitude of roles encompassed in being a housewife. Perhaps the original idea came from one of the early masters of scientific management, Frank Gilbreth, who gave his name spelled backwards (therblig) to the basic unit used in time and motion studies. Such studies, carried out with increased sophistication today, are designed to break down the human actions involved in production into their component parts so they can be controlled by management (Braverman 1974:173–175). It was a son and daughter of Gilbreth's who wrote *Cheaper by the Dozen*, a chronicle of how Gilbreth applied his notions of efficiency and productivity to his own household:

> Dad took moving pictures of us children washing dishes, so that he could figure out how we could reduce our motions and thus hurry the task. . . . Dad was always the efficiency expert. He buttoned his vest from the bottom up, instead of from the

top down, because the bottom-to-top process took him only three seconds, while the top-to-bottom took seven. (Gilbreth and Carey 1948:2)

Perhaps the need for discipline in housework comes from a combination of the desire for efficiency together with a sense of its endlessness, a sense described by Simone de Beauvoir as "like the torture of Sisyphus," "with its endless repetition: the clean becomes soiled, the soiled is made clean, over and over, day after day. The housewife wears herself out marking time: she makes nothing, simply perpetuates the present" (1952:425). Not only sociological studies (Oakley 1974:45) but also novels by women attest to this aspect of housework:

> First thing in the morning you started with the diapers. After you changed them, if enough had collected in the pail, you washed them. If they had ammonia which was causing diaper rash, you boiled them in a large kettle on top of the stove for half an hour. While the diapers were boiling, you fed the children, if you could stand preparing food on the same stove with urine-soaked diapers. After breakfast, you took the children for a walk along deserted streets, noting flowers, ladybugs, jet trails. Sometimes a motorcycle would go by, scaring the shit out of the children. Sometimes a dog followed you. After the walk, you went back to the house. There were many choices before nap time: making grocery lists; doing the wash; making the beds; crawling around on the floor with the children; weeding the garden; scraping last night's dinner off the pots and pans with steel wool; refinishing furniture; vacuuming; sewing buttons on; letting down hems; mending tears; hemming curtains. During the naps, assuming you could get the children to sleep simultaneously (which was an art in itself), you could flip through *Family Circle* to find out what creative decorating you could do in the home, or what new meals you could spring on your husband. (Ballantyne 1975:114)

Here is Katharina Dalton's example of how a premenstrual woman reacts to this routine:

> Then quite suddenly you feel as if you can't cope anymore—everything seems too much trouble, the endless household chores, the everlasting planning of meals. For no apparent reason you rebel: "Why should I do everything?" you ask

yourself defiantly. "I didn't have to do this before I was married. Why should I do it now?" . . . As on other mornings you
get up and cook breakfast while your husband is in the bathroom. You climb wearily out of bed and trudge down the
stairs, a vague feeling of resentment growing within you. The
sound of cheerful whistling from upstairs only makes you feel
a little more cross. Without any warning the toast starts to
scorch and the sausages instead of happily sizzling in the pan
start spitting and spluttering furiously. Aghast you rescue the
toast which by this time is beyond resurrection and fit only
for the trash. The sausages are charred relics of their former
selves and you throw those out too. Your unsuspecting husband opens the kitchen door expecting to find his breakfast
ready and waiting, only to see a smoky atmosphere and a
thoroughly overwrought wife. You are so dismayed at him
finding you in such chaos that you just burst helplessly into
tears. (1979:80)

Needless to say, by the terms of the medical model in which
Dalton operates, the solution for this situation is to seek
medical advice and obtain treatment (usually progesterone)
for the woman (p. 82). The content of her remarks, the substance of what she is objecting to, escape notice.

A woman who drops things, cuts or burns herself or the
food in this kind of environment has to adjust to an altogether
different level of demand on her time and energy than, say,
Beng women in Ivory Coast. There albeit menstrually instead
of premenstrually, women specifically must not enter the
forest and do the usual work of their days—farming, chop-
ping wood, and carrying water. Instead, keeping to the village, they are free to indulge in things they usually have no
time for, such as cooking a special dish made by cooking palm
nuts for a long time. This dish, highly prized for its taste,
takes hours of slow tending and cooking and is normally
eaten only by menstruating women and their close friends
and kinswomen (Gottlieb, this volume). Whatever the differ-
ing demands on Beng as opposed to Western women, Beng
social convention requires a cyclic reduction in women's usual
activities. Perhaps Beng women have fewer burned fingers.

In efforts to combat the overtly prejudicial opinions held
about women in the late nineteenth and early twentieth cen-

turies, women themselves have carried out research intended to prove that the disciplined, efficient tasks required in the workplace in industrial society could be done by women when they were menstruating as well as when they were not. In *Functional Periodicity: An Experimental Study of the Mental and Motor Abilities of Women during Menstruation*, Leta Hollingworth had twenty-four women (who ironically enough held research and academic jobs in their own lives) perform various tests of motor efficiency and controlled association both when they were and when they were not menstruating. These included tapping on a brass plate as many times as possible within a brief time; holding a 2.5 mm rod as steady as possible within a 6 mm hole and trying not to let it touch the edges; naming a series of colors as quickly as possible; and naming a series of opposites as quickly as possible. Ability to learn a new skill was also tested by teaching the subject to *type* and recording their progress while menstruating and not. The findings: that "the records of all the women here studied *agree* in supporting the negative conclusion here presented. None of them shows a characteristic inefficiency in the traits here tested at menstrual periods" (1914:93).

Similarly, in *The Question of Rest for Women during Menstruation*, Mary Putnam Jacobi shows that "women do work better, and with much greater safety to health when their work is frequently intermitted; but that those intermittences should be at short intervals and lasting a short time, not at long intervals and lasting longer. Finally that they are required at all times, and have no special reference to the period of the menstrual flow" (1877:232). Given the nature of the organization of work, men would probably also work better if they had frequent short breaks. What is being exposed in these early studies, in addition to the nature of women's capacities, is the nature of the work process to which they are subjected.

More recent research has also attempted to discover whether women's actual performance declines premenstrually. The overwhelming impression one gets from reading the popular literature on the subject is that performance in almost every respect does decline. According to Dalton's influential account, female students' grades drop, women are more likely to commit crimes and suicide, and they "cost British industry 3% of its total wage bill, which may be compared with 3% in Italy, 5% in Sweden and 8% in America" (1979: 100). Yet other accounts have been published that make powerful criticisms of the research on which these conclusions were based: they lack adequate controls, fail to report negative findings, and fail to report overall levels of performance in comparison to men (Parlee 1973:461–462). Still other studies find either increased performance or no difference in performance at all premenstrually (Golub 1976; Sommer 1973; Witt 1984:160–162).

If it is ever shown conclusively and accepted that women's actual performance is not affected by the menstrual cycle, we might still be left with women's experiential statements that they function differently during certain days, in ways that make it harder for them to tolerate the discipline required by work in our society. We could then perhaps hear these statements not as warnings of biological flaws inside women that need to be fixed but insights into flaws in society that need to be addressed.

What we see when we look at the foregoing list of negative traits is not so much a list of traits that would be unfortunate in any circumstance but ones that happen to be unfortunate in the particular social and economic system, with the kind of work it generates, that we live in. This consideration gives rise to the question of whether the losses reported by women in their ability to concentrate or discipline their attention are accompanied by gains in complementary areas. Does loss of ability to concentrate mean a greater ability to free-associate? Loss of muscle control, a gain in ability to relax? Decreased efficiency, increased attention to a smaller number of tasks?

Here and there in the literature on PMS one can find hints of these increased abilities. Women report:

No real distress except melancholy which I actually enjoy. It's a quiet reflective time for me. (Quoted in Weideger 1977:48)

My skin breaks out around both ovulation and my period. My temper is short; I am near tears, I am depressed. One fantastic thing—I have just discovered that I write poetry just before my period is due. I feel very creative at that time. (Quoted in Weideger 1977:48)

Others find they "dream more than usual, and may feel sexier than at other times of the cycle" (Birke and Gardner 1982:23).

A sculptor described her special abilities when she is premenstrual. There is a quality to my work and to my visions which just isn't there the rest of the month. I look forward to being premenstrual for its effect on my creativity, although some of the other symptoms create strains with my family. Another woman, prone to depression, described in the journal she kept, "When I am premenstrual I can write with such clarity and depth that after I get my period I don't recognize that those were my thoughts or that I could have written anything so profound" (Harrison 1984:16–17).

I don't know what it is, but I'll wake up one morning with an urge to bake bread. I can hardly wait to get home from work and start mixing the flour, kneading the dough, smelling the yeast. It's almost sensual and very satisfying. Maybe it's the earth-mother in me coming out. I don't know. But I do enjoy my premenstrual time. (Witt 1984:150)

I have heard that many women cry before their period. Well, I do too. Sometimes I'll cry at the drop of a hat, but it's a good crying. I'll be watching something tender on TV or my children will do something dear, and my eyes fill up. My heart is flooded with feelings of love for them or for my husband, for the world, for humanity, all the joy and all the suffering. Sometimes I could just cry and cry. But it strengthens me. It makes me feel a part of the earth, of the life-giving force. (Witt 1984:151)

Amid the losses that form the center of most accounts of PMS, these women seem to be describing experiences that, for them, represent increased capacities of emotional responsiveness and sensitivity, creativity, and physical sensuality. If these capacities are there, they are certainly not ones that would be given a chance to flourish or even be an advantage in the ordinary dual work day of most women. Only the exception—a sculptor or writer—would be able to put these greater emotional and associative capacities to work in her regular environment. Perhaps it is the creative writing tasks that are present in most academic jobs that lead to the result researchers find puzzling; if premenstrual women cannot concentrate as well, then why are women academics' work performance and concentration better than usual during the premenstrual phase (Birke and Gardner 1982:25)? The answer may be that there are different kinds of concentration: some requiring discipline inimical to body and soul that women reject premenstrually, some allowing expression of the depth within oneself, to which women have greater access premenstrually.

Insight into how capacities that women feel around the time of menstruation can be seen as powers and not liabilities is revealed by looking at the ethnographic case of the Yurok.[5] Buckley shows in chapter 8 how the Yurok view of menstruation (lost in ethnographic accounts until his 1982 article) held that "a menstruating woman should isolate herself because this is the time when she is at the height of her powers. Thus the time should not be wasted in mundane tasks and social distractions, nor should one's concentration be broken by concerns with the opposite sex. Rather, all of one's energies should be applied in concentrated meditation on the nature of one's life, 'to find out the purpose of your life,' and toward the accumulation of spiritual energy."

With a sense that the Yurok might appreciate of the kind of setting that would suit a premenstrual woman, Michelle Harrison, says poignantly,

> women who are premenstrual often have a need for time alone, time to themselves, and yet few women actually have that time in their lives. One woman wrote, "When I listen to music I feel better. If I can just be by myself and listen quietly, then the irritability disappears and I actually feel good. I never do it, though, or rarely so. I feel guilty for taking that time for myself, so I just go on being angry or depressed." (1984:44)

What in the right context might be released as powerful creativity or deep self-knowledge becomes, in the context of women's everyday lives in our societies, maladaptive discontent.

ANGER

A common feeling women describe premenstrually is anger. The way this anger is felt by women and described by the medical profession tells us a lot about the niche women are expected to fill in society. An advertisement in a local paper for psychotherapeutic support groups asks:

> Do you have PMS?—depression—irritability—panic attacks— food cravings—lethargy—dizziness—headache—backache— anger. How are other women coping with this syndrome? Learn new coping mechanisms; get support from others who are managing their lives. (*Baltimore City Paper,* 20 April 1984, p. 39)

Anger is listed as a symptom in a syndrome, or illness, that afflicts only women. In fuller accounts we find that the reason anger expressed by women is problematic in our society is because anger—and allied feelings such as irritability—make it hard for a woman to carry out her expected role of maintaining harmonious relationships within the family.

> Serious problems can arise—a woman might become excessively irritable with her children (for which she may feel guilty afterwards), she may be unable to cope with her work, or she may spend days crying for no apparent reason. Life, in other words, becomes intolerable for a short while, both for the sufferer and for those people with whom she lives. . . . PMT is often referred to as a potential disrupter of family life. Women suffering from premenstrual irritability often take it out on children, sometimes violently. . . . Obviously an anxious and irritable mother is not likely to promote harmony within the family. (Birke and Gardner 1982:6, 25)

This entire account is premised on the unexamined cultural assumption that it is primarily a woman's job to see to it that social relationships work smoothly in the family. Her own anger, however substantial the basis for it, must not be allowed to make life hard on those around her. If she has an anger she cannot control, she must be hormonally unbalanced and should seek medical treatment for her malfunctions. If she goes on subjecting her family to such feelings, disastrous consequences may follow that are, in the PMS literature, construed as being a woman's *fault*. For example,

> Doctor Dalton tells the story of a salesman whose commissions dropped severely once a month, putting a financial strain on the family and worrying him a great deal. Doctor Dalton charted his wife's menstrual cycle and found that she suffered from severe PMT. This affected her husband, who became anxious and distracted and so less efficient on his job. The drop in his commissions coincided with her premenstrual days. Doctor Dalton treated his wife and cured the salesman! (Lever 1981:61)

If a man's failure at work can be laid at the doorstep of a woman's PMS, so too can a man's violence. Although the PMS literature acknowledges that many battered women do nothing to provoke the violence they suffer from men, it is at times prone to suggest that women may themselves bring on battering if the man has a "short fuse": "His partner's own violent feelings and actions while suffering from PMT could supply the spark that causes him to blow up" (Lever 1981:63). Or consider this account, in which the woman is seen as the true spark to the man's blaze:

> One night she was screaming at him, pounding his chest with her fists, when in her hysteria she grabbed the collar of his shirt and ripped so hard that the buttons flew, pinging the toaster and the microwave oven. But before Susan could understand what she had done, she was knocked against the kitchen wall. Richard had smacked her across the face with the back of his hand. It was a forceful blow that cracked two teeth and dislocated her jaw. She had also bitten her tongue and blood was flowing from her mouth. . . . [Richard took her to the emergency room that night and moved out the next morning.] He was afraid he might hit her again because *she was so uncontrollable* when she was in a rage. (Lauersen and Stukane 1983:18, emphasis added)

The problems of men in these accounts are caused by outside circumstances and other people (women). The problems of women are caused by their own internal failure, seen as a biological malfunction. What is missing is any consideration of why, in Western societies, women might feel extreme rage at a time when their usual emotional controls are reduced.

That their rage is extreme cannot be doubted. Many women in fact describe themselves as being premenstrually "possessed." One's self-image as a woman—and behind this the cultural construction of what it is to be a woman—simply does not allow a woman to recognize herself in the angry, loud, sometimes violent "creature" she becomes once a month.

> I feel it is not me that is in possession of my body. My whole personality changes, making it very difficult for the people I live and work with. I've tried. Every month I say, "This month it's going to be different, I'm not going to let it get hold of me." But when it actually comes to it, something chemical happens to me. I can't control it, it just happens. (Lever 1981:25)

> Something seems to snap in my head. I go from a normal state of mind to anger, when I'm really nasty. Usually I'm very even tempered, but in these times it is as if someone else, not me, is doing all this, and it is very frightening. (Lever 1981:28)

> It is something that is wound up inside, you know, like a great spring. And as soon as anything triggers it off, I'm away. It is very frightening. Like being possessed, I suppose. (Lever 1981:6)

> I try so hard to be a good mother. But when I feel this way, it's as if there's a monster inside me that I can't control. (Angier 1983:119)

> I was verbally abusive toward my husband, but I would really thrash out at the kids. When I had these outbursts I tended to observe myself. I felt like a third party, looking at what I was doing. There was nothing I could do about it. I was not in control of my actions. It's like somebody else is taking over. (Lauersen and Stukane 1983:80)

> Once a month for the last 25 years this wonderful woman (my wife) has turned into a . (Letter in *The PMS Connection* 1982:3)

It is an anthropological commonplace that spirit possession in traditional societies can be a means for the jurally weak (often women) to express discontent and manipulate their superiors (Lewis 1971:116). But in these societies it is clear that propitiation of the possessing spirit or accusation of the living person who is behind the affliction involves the women and their social groups in setting social relationships to rights. In our own inverted version of these elements, women say they feel "possessed," but what the society sees as behind their trouble is really their own malfunctioning *bodies*. Redress for us may mean solicitous concern and attention while a remedy is sought, but it also means attention is necessarily shunted away from the social environment in which the "possession" arose. The anger was not really the women's fault, but neither was it to be taken seriously. Indeed, one of the common complaints women share is that men treat their moods casually:

> Sometimes if I am in a bad mood, my husband will not take me seriously if I am close to my period. He felt if it was "that time of the month" any complaints I had were only periodic. A few weeks ago I told him that until I am fifty-seven he will have taken me seriously only half the time. After that he will blame it on menopause. (Weideger 1977:10)

Or if moods cannot be ignored, perhaps they, instead of whatever concrete circumstances they arise from, can be treated.

> The husband of a woman who came for help described their problem as follows: "My wife is fine for two weeks out of the month. She's friendly and a good wife. The house is clean. Then she ovulates and suddenly she's not happy about her life. She wants a job. Then her period comes and she is all right again." He wanted her to be medicated so she would be a "good wife" all month. (Harrison 1984:50)

What are the sources of women's anger, so powerful it leads women to think of it as a kind of possessing spirit? A common characteristic of premenstrual anger is that women often feel it has no immediate identifiable cause: "It never occurred to me or my husband that my totally unreasonable behavior toward my husband and family over the years could have been caused by anything but basic viciousness in me" (Lever 1981:61).

> Women are often able to differentiate clearly the depression or anger of premenstrual syndrome from the depression or anger of life situations. One woman described this difference as, "Being angry when I know I'm right makes me feel good, but being angry when I know it's just me makes me feel sick inside." (Harrison 1984:36)

Anger experienced in this way—as a result solely of a woman's intrinsic badness—cannot help but lead to guilt.

I would like to suggest the possibility—though at this stage it cannot be proved—that the sources of this diffuse anger could well come from women's perception, however inarticulate, of their oppression in society: of their lowered wage scales, lesser opportunities for advancement into high ranks, tacit omission from the language, coercion into roles inside the family and out that demand constant nurturance and self-denial—to only begin the list. Adrienne Rich asks:

> What woman, in the solitary confinement[6] of a life at home enclosed with young children, or in the struggle to mother them while providing for them single-handedly, or in the conflict of weighing her own personhood against the dogma that says she is a mother, first, last, and always—what woman has not dreamed of "going over the edge," of simply letting go, relinquishing what is termed her sanity, so that she can be taken care of for once, or can simply find a way to take care of herself? The mothers: collecting their children at school; sitting in rows at the parent-teacher meeting; placating weary infants in supermarket carriages; straggling home to make dinner, do laundry, and tend children after a day at work; fighting to get decent care and livable schoolrooms for their children; waiting for child-support checks while the landlord threatens eviction . . . —the mothers, if we could look into their fantasies—their daydreams and imaginary experiences— we would see the embodiment of rage, of tragedy, of the overcharged energy of love, of inventive desperation, we would see the machinery of institutional violence wrenching at the experience of motherhood. (1976:285)

Rich acknowledges the "embodiment of rage" in women's fantasies and daydreams. Perhaps premenstrually many women's fantasies become reality, as they experience their own violence wrenching at the institution of motherhood.

Coming out of a tradition of psychoanalysis, Shuttle and Redgrove suggest that a woman's period may be "a moment of truth which will not sustain lies" (1978:58). Whereas during most of the month a woman may keep quiet about things that bother her, "maybe at the paramenstruum, the truth flares into her consciousness: this is an intolerable habit, she is discriminated against as a woman, she is forced to under-achieve if she wants love, this examination question set by male teachers is unintelligently phrased, I will not be a punch-ball to my loved ones, this child must learn that I am not the supernatural never-failing source of maternal sympathy" (p. 59). In this rare analysis some of the systematic social causes of women's second-class status (instead of the usual biological causes) are being named and identified as possible sources of suppressed anger.

If *these* kinds of causes are at the root of the unnamed anger that seems to afflict women, and if they could be named and known, maybe a cleaner, more productive anger would seem to arise from within women, tying them together as a common oppressed group, instead of sending them individually to the doctor as patients to be fixed.

In order to see anger as a blessing instead of a curse, it may be necessary for women to feel their rage is legitimate. To do so women may need to understand their structural position in society, and this in turn may entail consciousness of themselves as a group that is denied full membership in society on the basis of gender. Many have tried to describe under what conditions groups of oppressed people will become conscious of their oppressed condition. Gramsci wrote of a dual "contradictory consciousness," "one which is implicit in his activity and which in reality unites him with all his fellow-workers in the practical transformation of the world; and one, superficially explicit or verbal, which he has inherited from the past and uncritically absorbed" (1971:333).

Perhaps the rage women express premenstrually could be seen as an example of consciousness implicit in activity, which in reality unites women with their fellows: a consciousness that is combined in a contradictory way with an explicit verbal consciousness, inherited from the past and constantly reinforced in the present, which denies women's rage its truth.

It is well known that the oppression resulting from racism and colonialism entails a diffused and steady rage in the oppressed populations (Fanon 1963; Genovese 1974:647; Lerner 1972), rage that presumably makes its contribution when class war occurs. Surely it is no accident that women describing their premenstrual moods often speak of rebelling, resisting, or even feeling "at war" (Dalton 1979:80; Harrison 1984:17; Halbreich and Endicott 1982:251, 255, 256). It is important not to miss the imagery of rebellion and resistance, even when the women themselves excuse their feelings by saying the rebellion is "for no apparent reason" (Dalton 1979:80), or that the war is with their own bodies! ("Each month I wage a successful battle with my body. But I'm tired of going to war" [*PMS Connection* 1984:4].)

Elizabeth Fox-Genovese writes of the factors that lead women to accept their own oppression: "Women's unequal access to political life and economic participation provided firm foundations for the ideology of gender difference. The dominant representations of gender relations stressed the naturalness and legitimacy of male authority and minimized the role of coercion. Yet coercion, and frequently its violent manifestation, regularly encouraged women to accept their subordinate status" (1982:272–273). Looking at what has been written about PMS is certanly one way of seeing the "naturalness" of male authority in our society, its invisibility and unexamined or unquestioned nature. Coercion in this context does not consist in the violence of rape or beating: after all, it is the women who become violent. (In a best-selling novel a psychopathic killer's brutal murders are triggered by her premenstruum [Sanders 1981].) Physical coercion consists rather in focusing on women's bodies as the locus of the operation of power, and insisting that rage and rebellion, as well as physical pain, will all be cured by the administration of drugs such as progesterone, which has known tranquilizing properties (Witt 1984:205, 208; Herrmann and Beach 1978).

Credence for the medical tactic of treating women's bodies with drugs comes, of course, out of the finding that premenstrual moods and discomfort are regular, predictable, and in accord with a woman's menstrual cycle. Therefore, it is supposed, they must be caused at least partially by the changing hormonal levels known to be a part of the menstrual cycle.[7] The next step (given the logic of scientific medicine) is to try to find a drug that will alleviate the unpleasant aspects of premenstrual syndrome for the millions of women who suffer them.

Yet if this were to happen, if women's monthly cycle were to be smoothed out, so to speak, we would do well at least to notice what would have been lost. Men and women alike in our society are familiar with one cycle, dictated by a complex interaction of biological and psychological factors, that happens in accord with cycles in the natural world: we all need to sleep part of every solar revolution, and we all recognize the disastrous consequences of being unable to sleep, as well as the rejuvenating results of being able to sleep. We also all recognize and behave in accord with the socially determined cycle of the week, constructed around the demands of work-discipline in industrial capitalism (E. Thompson 1967). It has been found that men even structure their moods more strongly in accord with the week than women do (Rossi and Rossi 1977:292). And absenteeism in accord with the weekly cycle (reaching as high as 10 percent at GM on Mondays and Fridays [Braverman 1974:32]) is a cause of dismay in American industry but does not lead anyone to think that workers need medication for this problem.

Gloria Steinem wonders sardonically:

> What would happen if suddenly, magically, men could menstruate and women could not? Clearly, menstruation would become an enviable, boast-worthy, masculine event: Men would brag about how long and how much. Young boys

would talk about it as the envied beginning of manhood. Gifts, religious ceremonies, family dinners, and stag parties would mark the day. To prevent monthly work loss among the powerful, Congress would fund a National Institute of Dysmenorrhea. (1983:338)

Perhaps we might add to her list that if men menstruated, we all might be expected to alter our activities monthly as well as daily and weekly, and enter a time and space organized to maximize the special powers that seem to be felt around the time of menstruation while minimizing the discomforts.

PART IV

EXPLORATORY DIRECTIONS: MENSES, CULTURE, AND TIME

Many of the contributors to the two foregoing sections have dealt to one extent or another with biological and physiological aspects of menstruation, although such dimensions have not been central to most of their analyses and interpretations. In this section biological processes create a central context through which the three remaining contributors make sense of their ethnographic materials. Each considers the relevance of recent findings regarding "menstrual synchrony" to the anthropology of menstruation.

Martha McClintock's scientific substantiation of menstrual synchrony and suppression was first published in 1971, and replication and further testing of her findings have extended into the present decade (see chapters 8–10). It is work that has not yet entered the mainstream of either reproductive biology or anthropology. We offer the three essays of this section, then, all based on McClintock's findings, as heuristic contributions and as challenges to further investigation.

The first of these essays, Thomas Buckley's chapter 8, is composed of two distinct parts: the first ethnographic and analytic, the second biocultural and speculative. In the first part, in keeping with previous chapters, Buckley critiques interpretations of the menstrual practices of the precontact Yurok Indians of northwestern California. He views these interpretations in light both of the testimony of a contemporary Yurok woman and of older Yurok testimony and texts. Buckley argues that both sources suggest a gender-specific, traditional understanding of menstruation among aristocratic Yurok women, not solely as the negative, polluting phenomenon described by earlier ethnographers but as an ambiguous and potentially positive experience with deep implications for the spiritual and economic lives and power of women. These women, he argues, once practiced menstrual rituals that culturally paralleled the far better-known ritual training of Yurok men. In the second part of the essay Buckley relates female accumulation of power to the possibility of lunar phase-locked menstrual synchrony in precontact Yurok villages. He suggests that esoteric power existed in dialectic with women's power to dictate the temporal structure of communal life through synchronized menstruation.

Although Buckley stresses the hypothetical nature of this second argument, he urges that the hypothesis be tested in small-scale contemporary non-Western communities. To an extent this is what Frederick Lamp has done among the Temne of Sierra Leone, reporting his findings in chapter 9. Lamp's work focuses on secret male and female initiatory societies among the Temne, and because the workings of these groups are open fully only to initiates, Lamp's findings, like Buckley's, are of necessity speculative to a degree.

The Temne identify the functioning of their bodies with a variety of cosmological principles, among them those governing lunar phases and movements. From texts and his own field research Lamp has constructed a probable system of gynecological knowledge that underlies Temne male and female initiation rituals and associated rituals of sexual license. Lamp suggests that the Temne utilize knowledge (perhaps unconscious) of menstrual and ovulatory synchrony to ensure that interludes of ritual adultery do not produce illegitimate children. Thus the regular allowance of sexual license does not subvert the Temne system of patriliny, with its insistence that the legal father of a child also be the biological father.

In his concern with women's secret societies, Lamp is also interested in questions of female solidarity in face-to-face communities. Like Buckley, he relates such solidarity to the possible historical role of female reproductive biology in establishing cyclic, temporal rhythms in social life through menstrual synchrony phase-locked with the lunar cycle. Hypotheses such as Buckley's and Lamp's have significant implications not only for the anthropology of menstruation but, as Chris Knight suggests in the final chapter, for a general theory of social evolution.

As with Buckley's work, Knight's investigation of the relevance of menstrual synchrony to culture is in large part historically reconstructive; like Lamp's, his focal concern is with the possibility of powerful solidarity among women, rooted in this synchrony. But whereas Buckley and Lamp restrict themselves to single cultures and historical moments, Knight's sweep is larger. Building on his earlier studies of aboriginal Australian mythology, Knight surveys myths, rituals, and art that present images of a primal "snake" from a variety of cultures in Australia.

Knight hypothesizes that the snake, ubiquitous among Aboriginal Australian cultures, at once symbolizes synchronous menstruation and cyclic time and serves as a master metaphor of power. He marshals a variety of evidence to show that this power was once physiologically manifested in women's synchronized menstrual periods. Australian men now seek to appropriate this originally female power, however, through subincision rites and related synchronized blood-letting rituals, subverting female solidarity. Finally, Knight touches upon serpent imagery from other regions of the world, suggesting that his hypothesis may have broader significance to a full understanding of gender relations and social power than a narrow reading of his Australian materials would indicate.

Knight's provocative work may itself prove to be a "master metaphor" of intuited menstrual meaning. In the meantime, however, both menstrual synchrony and Knight's metaphorical snake are, to invoke Lévi-Strauss, good to think.

8

Menstruation and the Power of Yurok Women

Thomas Buckley

In 1976 Lowell Bean and Thomas Blackburn encouraged the ongoing renewal of anthropological interest in native California through publication of a collection of relatively recent theoretical essays. In their introduction to the volume the editors stress the possibilities inherent in the truly vast accumulation of data on aboriginal Californian peoples to be found in the descriptive ethnographies of earlier investigators, and especially in the "undigested" original field notes of these ethnographers. Bean and Blackburn (1976a: 5–10) emphasize the necessity for approaching such materials from new theoretical perspectives so as to realize their potentials. Several recent papers on Californian cultures stress such possibilities as well, suggesting that the real value in exploring these cultures lies in opportunities for developing hypotheses of significance to general theory regarding hunter-gatherers far beyond the confines of native California. Data on the area are increasingly recognized as being uniquely fruitful in just this regard (e.g., Gould 1975; Blackburn 1976).

That significant new work on native California continues to appear belies the Kroeberian notion that the ethnographic records of California's aboriginal peoples have been completed as far as possible and, moreover, that they have been exhausted analytically. Clearly more skeptical scholars have been mistaken in the conservatism of their questioning "whether late-coming ethnologists, working with . . . apparently imperfect old data and such new data as can be elicited from younger informants . . . can actually develop a viable new analytic system . . . at this late date" (Elsasser 1976:96). Specifically, I question the dim view taken in some quarters of the value of contemporary Indian consultants' testimony regarding their traditional cultures. Surviving Californian cultures have proved unexpectedly resilient. It is indeed, as Bean and Blackburn (1976a:8–9) point out, the possibility of doing sound new fieldwork in native California that in part accounts for the extreme usefulness today of older unpublished field materials.

Following these anthropologists, I suggest that contemporary research in and analyses of Californian cultures may best be undertaken in a threefold manner. New fieldwork among knowledgeable consultants should be seen in relation to earlier accounts, especially those available in various archives. Each sheds light on the other. Contemporary testimony often reveals the importance of data that were neglected in published work, and these earlier data may provide unplumbed information that could be highly useful in interpreting the nature of both cultural change and persistence in a given surviving culture. A theoretical component is needed, however, to take full advantage of the existence of these two strata of field materials, and this third component must overcome the limitations in vision implicit in prior neglect of significant portions of the earlier data. Particularly in the Californian case, such limitations seem to indicate a certain blindness to broadly suggestive, complex orders of systematic organization, variation, and interrelation in native cultures, and it is with these that I am most concerned here.

"MOONTIME"

The Yurok Indians today live largely within or near their aboriginal homelands in coastal and riverine northwestern California, close by the Klamath River and the present California-Oregon border. Their culture, though greatly changed since the time of first massive contact with European-Americans during the gold rush, retains a certain, albeit transformed, uniqueness.

One evening in 1978 I went with an Indian friend to his house to eat. He would be doing the cooking, he explained on the way, because his Yurok wife was "on her moontime" (menstruating)[1] and they were keeping the old ways as best they could. This meant that his wife went into seclusion for ten days during and after her flow, cooking and eating her own food by herself.

According to traditional "Indian law" (here, rules for conduct), a menstruating woman is highly polluting and will contaminate the family house and food supply if she comes into contact with either. Thus in the old days, a special shelter for menstrual seclusion was built near the main house, and special food for a family's menstruating women was separately collected, stored, and prepared for consumption in this shelter. In my friend's modern house a back room had been set aside for his wife's monthly use. Separate food storage as well as cooking and eating utensils were furnished in the kitchen.

I hadn't expected to find the old, seemingly anachronistic menstrual practices being approximated in this environment. Aside from the exclusion of women from ceremonial activities during their menses, and the fact that some men refrain from deer hunting while their wives and daughters are menstruating, I had not found adherence to the old menstrual rules to be widespread among contemporary Yurok—certainly not to the extent that they were being followed in this house. Even here, however, these rules were not kept to the letter. The young woman appeared when we arrived and joined the conversation, explaining to me that she often got restless in her back room and so wandered around the house talking with her husband when he was home, although they neither ate nor slept together during her "moontime." She then went on to talk about what she was doing and why and how she felt about it.

She said that she had been instructed in the menstrual laws by her maternal aunts and grandmother, who in their times were well-known, conservative Yurok women. Her understanding of menstruation came largely from these sources. She began her account of this understanding by telling me that as a foster child in non-Indian homes she had been taught that menstruation is "bad and shameful" and that through it "women are being punished." On her return to Yurok society, however, "my aunts and my grandmother taught me different."[2] The difference was that these women stressed the positive aspects of menstruation and of Yurok menstrual rules. Briefly, here is what the young woman said.

A menstruating woman should isolate herself because this is the time when she is at the height of her powers. Thus the time should not be wasted in mundane tasks and social distractions, nor should one's concentration be broken by concerns with the opposite sex. Rather, all of one's energies should be applied in concentrated meditation "to find out the purpose of your life," and toward the "accumulation" of spiritual energy. The menstrual shelter, or room, is "like the men's sweathouse," a place where you "go into yourself and make yourself stronger." As in traditional male sweathouse practice, or "training" (*hohkep-*), there are physical as well as mental aspects of "accumulation." The blood that flows serves to "purify" the woman, preparing her for spiritual accomplishment. Again, a woman must use a scratching implement, instead of scratching absentmindedly with her fingers, as an aid in focusing her full attention on her body by making even the most natural and spontaneous of actions fully conscious and intentional: "You should feel all of your body exactly as it is, and pay attention."

The woman continued: There is, in the mountains above the old Yurok village of Meri·p, a "sacred moontime pond" where in the old days menstruating women went to bathe and to perform rituals that brought spiritual benefits. Practitioners brought special firewood back from this place for use in the menstrual shelter. Many girls performed these rites only at the time of their first menstruation, but aristocratic women went to the pond every month until menopause. Through such practice women came to "see that the earth has her own moontime," a recognition that made one both "stronger" and "proud" of one's menstrual cycle.

Finally, the young woman said that in old-time village life

all of a household's fertile women who were not pregnant menstruated at the same time, a time dictated by the moon; that these women practiced the bathing rituals together at this time; and that men associated with the household used this time to "train hard" in the household's sweathouse. If a woman got out of synchronization with the moon and with the other women of the household, she could "get back in by sitting in the moonlight and talking to the moon, asking it to balance [her]."

THE CLASSIC APPROACH

My immediate reaction to all of this was somewhat as follows. The woman and her husband, who were both deeply involved in the contemporary renascence of Indian culture and identity and were committed to living in an "Indian way," as they understood it, had revived aspects of traditional menstrual practice as a means of expressing their commitment to "Indianness." Because the old Yurok menstrual rules had reflected the male-dominant gender asymmetry that ordered the underlying symbolic code—an asymmetry specifically challenged by modern notions of women's rights—these old rules had been rationalized and reinterpreted. Through this process they had come to be newly understood from a perspective that allowed resolution of conflicting desires for both a strong link to the Indian past and for political modernity.

I reacted this way because having studied the received ethnographies of traditional Yurok and neighboring cultures carefully, I found the young woman's testimony incredible. According to a composite picture drawn from published data bearing on the topic of menstruation in Yurok, Karok, Hupa, and Tolowa ethnographies, menstruation and everything associated with it was simply negative—in Yurok, *kimoɫeni* (dirty, polluting). Menstrual blood itself was thought by Yurok to be a dire poison, and menstruating women were believed to contaminate whatever they came into contact with—houses, food, hunting gear, weapons, canoes, water, trails, and, above all, the men's wealth objects central to these acquisitive societies and emblematic of spiritual ascendancy (Bushnell and Bushnell 1977). Menstruating women, beyond contaminating concrete objects, were perhaps most danger-ous through their negative effect on men's psychic or spiritual life. These women spoiled men's "luck" (*heyomoks-*)—their ability to exercise power in, among other things, the accumu-lation of wealth. A menstruating woman who seduced an unwary man was therefore *cišah* ([worse than] a dog), the lowest form of mammalian life. Strong antipathy between menstruous women and the world of spirits seems suggested by the use of menstruating virgins to drive off the spirits (*wo·gey*) that attempted to steal the "souls" (*hewec-*) of infants.

Thus menstruating women were isolated in special shel-ters, ate carefully segregated foods, and used scratching bones, being so highly charged with negative energy that they could not touch even themselves for fear of poisoning. In Yurok society, far from being permitted to travel into the very "pure" (*mɹwɹksɹyɹh*) mountains to bathe, these women bathed daily and seemingly compulsively in the Klamath River, waters already thought to be polluted by corpses, dogs, aborted fetuses, and menstrual blood—"things" (*so·k*). Final-ly, regarding discrepancies between the modern Yurok wom-an's testimony on the positive nature of menstruation and the received ethnographies, the latter nowhere explicitly sug-gest that either the moon or synchrony was a consideration in aboriginal menstrual practices.[3]

Reports of entirely negative coding of menstruation itself (as distinct from female puberty) are, of course, staples of the ethnographic accounts of a great many cultures, to the extent that they seem collectively to suggest an ethnological truism: Menstruation is, for a great many peoples, virtually the defin-itive form of pollution. Currently this apparent truism is being widely used as the basis for a strong element in more gen-eral, politically motivated critiques of male-dominant gender asymmetry in certain cultures (e.g., Delaney, Lupton, and Toth 1976). Supported by further neglected Yurok data to which I now turn, however, I suggest that we be circumspect in evaluating received ethnographies, realizing the double male biases that are implicit in a great many of them (i.e., in the descriptions of male anthropologists based on the testimony of primarily male consultants). Moreover I suggest that we be open to far more complex kinds of symbolic, or conceptual, structuring than are accommodated in what may be simplistic and overly universalistic views of menstruation qua pollution. We should bear in mind the ambivalent nature of pollution itself in many cultural systems, where, far from being a *simply* negative concept, pollution is understood to comprise an ambiguous manifestation of a neutral (hence potentially positive) energy (Douglas 1966; compare Bean 1977). Finally, we should continue to consider seriously Edwin Ardener's (1972:1–3) proposition that the world of women in culture is not characteristically defined by the same "neat, bounded categories given by the male informant" (King 1983:109).

KROEBER'S FIELD NOTES

A few weeks after the conversation sketched earlier I went to Berkeley, where I spent several days going through the A. L. Kroeber Papers, now in the Manuscript Division of the Bancroft Library, University of California, Berkeley (call number 71/83c). I was particularly interested in Kroeber's Yurok field notes (cartons 6 and 7). I discovered, in the course of my readings, a set of notes and textual transcriptions detailing interviews with a Yurok woman at the village of Wecpus in 1902 (carton 7). Kroeber never utilized either the texts or most of the descriptions collected from this woman, identified only as "Weitchpec Susie," in his various publications (but see Kroeber 1925:45).

These notes and transcriptions concern menstruation and childbirth and, along with some expository comments by Susie on these topics, include a long formula used by women in ritual bathing during menstruation, a myth relating the origins of both menstruation and these rituals, and other esoterica—fragments of prayers and myths concerning various aspects of childbirth. To my surprise, these materials to an extent confirmed the traditional authenticity of the young woman's modern understanding of menstruation as a powerful, positive phenomenon with esoteric significance. Additionally, Kroeber's notes provide a good deal of fresh insight into the structure of menstrual symbolism when viewed from a feminine perspective.

According to the myth recited in English by Susie, menstruation originated in a capricious joke, initiated by Coyote (*segep*).[4] Coyote said, "I think be best way if woman have flowers. When she have flowers she will see blood." The hero Pulekuk^werek aided and abetted Coyote, cutting his ankle and putting the blood on a girl's thigh. Coyote said, "You got flowers now." Girl: "No!" Coyote: "Yes, I see blood on your legs." Coyote and Pulekuk^werek then instituted both the girls' puberty ritual and the regimen to be followed during subsequent menses. The duration of monthly continence and ritual observance (ten days), proper costume (a bark skirt, grass arm and leg bands), specially treated foods of a limited kind (acorns gathered and stored for the purpose, similarly secured dried fish, no red meats or fresh fish), isolation in a special shelter, a program of bathing and of firewood gathering, and use of the long prayer to bring wealth are all specified (notes for 8 June 1902, pp. 1–8).

After Coyote has outlined the basic menstrual procedures he falters, not knowing how to continue. A spirit-woman speaks to him from the sky:

> Need not be afraid of that [menstruation]. We [spirits] are around here in sky, all we women thus, flowers, and we never afraid on it, because we have medicine for it. Now you look way over other side (upriver). Now I always wash way over there myself. . . . Now you can look, look at that lake right in the middle of the sky, you can see how many trails come on that lake. . . . Those trails are dentalia's trails some of them, some woodpecker head's, some white deerskin's, everything, that's where I always wash myself, because that money that's his water, his lake. Now you can look where I stand. You can see blood all around where I stand now, because I'm that way now. I'm flowers. I can go out on that lake, and wash, and they'll make me good luck just the same. . . . You tell that girl

to do that. . . . Whenever goes to wash in water anyplace, tell her just that way. . . . Tell her I wash in sky, using that water. So he'll be good luck; if talk that way, will be just same as if wash that lake on sky. (Notes 8 June 1902, pp. 4–5)

The menstrual formula (described later) comprises these instructions given by the menstruating spirit woman to Coyote and Pulekuk^{w}erek.[5]

Pulekuk^{w}erek, it should be noted, was the most ascetic and spiritual of the "Beforetime People." His total abstinence from sexual intercourse suggests asexuality, rather than the pronounced maleness of the two Yurok tricksters Coyote and Wohpekumew (a trickster-hero). It was Pulekuk^{w}erek, however, who epitomized human virtues for Yurok men, for it was he who, along with being a formidable warrior, instituted the men's sweathouse and the wealth quest austerities to be followed by men. A comparison between his and Coyote's instructions for menstruating women and Pulekuk^{w}erek's for male wealth questing is illuminating.

Ten days was the standard period for men's "training" related to all important undertakings—most significantly, here, to wealth questing and to "luck" seeking in alpine lakes. During this period men secluded themselves in the sweathouse, maintained strict continence, avoided all contacts with fecund women, and ate only specially gathered, stored, and prepared foods (the same staples as utilized in menstrual provender). These men bathed twice daily. A primary feature of such sweathouse training was the gathering of firewood for use in the sweathouse. Grass anklets were worn by these men for protection against snakebite and as an esoteric aid in traveling into the mountains to gather wood and to practice various rituals. Men in training for wealth acquisition gashed their legs with flakes of white quartz, the flowing blood being thought to carry off psychic impurity, preparing one for spiritual attainment. The common ten-day men's training periods alternated with periods of greater relaxation and less austerity, in which the "balance" of a "complete" life was restored—the aim of well-trained Yurok men being to keep "in the middle" (*wogi*). (It is relevant to note that in the sweathouse-focal training of both male and female "doctors" [*kegey*]—held to bring wealth as well as curing powers—a skirt of shredded maple bark was worn.)

The recitation of formulas was a central feature of all Yurok training, and such recitations, correctly executed, were believed to bring wealth. It has long been thought that the wealth quest and hence use of such formulas were, with the exception of female *kegey*, strictly male prerogatives. However, the menstrual formula collected from Susie not only substantiates the comparisons between male and female training suggested by the Coyote myth but calls this ethnographic assumption into question.

The formula speaks of a small lake, "up in the middle of the sky" (*wonoye?ik*), where menstruating women may see a great many *Dentalia Indianorum* (dentalium shells were prized Yurok wealth objects). Women are instructed in the formula to dive to the lake's bottom to pick up a small stone and then to return with it to their homes. As a result of these actions (and of properly reciting the formula itself), women may expect to grow wealthy in later life, their menstrual practices attracting dentalium to their houses. Translating from the Yurok text recited for Kroeber by Susie:

> You will be rich if you wash. You go in, you will be rich. Human being, money will come into your house. You go in— you'll be rich. You better go. Go up in the sky. Look! Look! Wash in the lake—just once. Sink down completely. Don't submerge yourself twice. A pile of dentalium is here.
>
> You will go in, go in the water. Only one time. You will lie with your head downstream. Take a stone. You will take it into your house so you will be rich. (Notes 8 June 1902, items 4065–4066; my translation)

The middle of the sky in Yurok cosmography is the most pure, least polluted place in the universe, the source of the most valuable and powerful of things, including many wealth objects. It may be reached, in trance, only by those who are themselves completely pure. It seems to have been a consciously metaphorical location for, as trained people well knew, they physically ascended only into the hills and mountains rising above the coastal and riverine villages.[6] In the most powerful kinds of training, the terrain of the Blue Creek drainage, above Meri·p, was utilized. Such ascents were, however, closely restricted to those who, through ritual austerities, were free of polluting influence.

Men making such ascents while seeking the power of wealth acquisition visualized dentalia and the trails of slime left by them, reciting formulas to attract the shells into their later possession. Diving in alpine lakes is a recurrent motif in accounts of male esoteric practice, as is the retrieval of wealth-attracting stone talismans from various watery places.

There are, then, direct parallels in conception, ritualization, and goal orientation between male training and female menstrual practice. However, and most important, whereas Yurok men feared menstrual pollution as, above all, driving away wealth (that is, spiritual attainment), Yurok women who used the formula understood that it was precisely during their menses that they could most easily attract wealth (i.e., attain spiritual ascendancy).

Finally, we find that whereas men considered menstruating women who seduced men to be *cišah* ([worse than] dogs), the same term was applied by women to men who forced their attentions on them during their own ten-day menstrual training periods (according to the Kroeber papers). Clearly, then, there are two gender-specific views, of which only one—that of the male—has become known through published ethnographies.[7]

The contemporary Yurok woman's notion of "accumulation" now rings true in retrospect. The primary activity of men engaged in wealth questing (that is, in a quest for spiritual advancement), while they were actually in and around the sweathouse, was "meditating" (*kocpoks*) directed toward personal centering and empowerment. It was in such meditation, according to the most knowledgeable of elderly male consultants, that one actually "made medicine" and grew "stronger," rather than in the rituals for which such "thinking" prepared one and which accompanied the meditative "accumulation" of identity, insight, and control. Wealth was believed to accrue only to those who had "done their thinking" precisely and openly (see Buckley 1979).

We find further inferential support of the traditional nature of the young woman's positive view of the power of menstruation in "Weitchpec Susie's" 1902 accounts of childbirth. Susie's English gloss of the Yurok formula for easing labor contains the passage, "*wes?onah* . . . said, 'You call my name whenever hard to come baby, then you call me to help you,' he said to Indians. 'Is my *?e?gur?* [medicine basket].' Whenever you call that to open you will hear baby crying coming." Kroeber notes that "the woman's vagina is Sky's [*wes?onah's*] *?e?gur*" (notes for 8 June 1902, p. 16). Two pieces of information are necessary to put the childbirth formula into perspective. First, the Yurok *(?)wes?onah* is polysemous, meaning "sky"; "that which exists" (the phenomenal world); and "cosmos," the universe as noumenon, a metaphysical first principle—today, in English, "creation" and/or "the Creator." Second, both traditional elkhorn dentalium purses and the medicine baskets (*?e?gur?*) used by men in the Jump Dance, which contain various power tokens, have labialike openings.

We may interpret this material in light of both the menstrual myth and formula and general tendencies in the Yurok worldview. The medicines of *(?)wes?onah,* from the "feminine" perspective, are babies, the by-products of birth, and menstrual blood—all of which are highly polluting from the "masculine" perspective. From an (aristocratic) "feminine" point of view, however, these things, while polluting in certain contexts, are *also* pure: pure enough, that is, to be to the "cosmos" what wealth and other tokens of spiritual ascendancy are to human beings. Like wealth objects, from this perspective they are themselves *mɹwɹksɹyɹh* (pure).[8] Such multiple coding is common in Yurok philosophy, which repeatedly stresses complementary perspectives in which things held to be *kimołeni* (dirty) from one perspective are revealed to be *mɹwɹksɹyɹh* from another (Buckley 1980).

COMPARATIVE MATERIALS

We find, then, that the young contemporary woman's account is quite reliable as an expression of a far older traditional Yurok women's perspective. Its reliability is founded, no doubt, in her memory of the instruction she received through her female relatives, who, it would seem, emphasized what I have characterized as an aristocratic feminine perspective over the more negative male one recorded in received ethnographies. This being so in the general case, we are obliged to pay close attention to her testimony regarding synchrony and lunar influence. Although to this point investigation has rested on solid data and clearly relevant comparison, here we can only speculate, for there are few earlier ethnographic data on these topics. There are, however, recent biological research results that appear to be pertinent.

The work of Martha McClintock (1971, 1981) has established the phenomena of human intragroup menstrual synchrony and suppression. The menstrual cycles of frequently interacting women—in college dormitories, for instance—tend to become synchronized over time, the greatest increase in synchrony among individuals occurring within four months. Such synchronization of groups within all-female populations is related to the extent and frequency of contacts between individual women, groups of close friends comprising the most evident synchronous groups (McClintock 1971). In more recent experiments (Quadagno, Shubeita, Deck, and Francouer 1979; Graham and McGrew 1980), McClintock's results have been replicated and extended to populations including both males and females.

The aboriginal Yurok residential group was an extremely flexible unit. An ideal type may be suggested through the term "household." I use this term to refer to the narrowly extended unit of population defined through consanguinity, affinity, adoption, and—above all—common residence. Such a household comprised three or four generations of patrilineally related males and their wives and unmarried daughters, those married daughters with in-marrying husbands and their children, and, in many cases, adoptive kin, both male and female. This unit was centered at a named, patrilineally inherited "family house" (ʔoʔlel). The family house was usually the property of the senior male but was strictly the domain of the women who lived and slept there with the children. The lives of most males after puberty were centered in the household's sweathouse (ʔɹʔgɹ·c), where the men spent much of their time, both waking and sleeping.

When a descent group outgrew its family house, a second one was built close by, sharing the name of the first, and its men used the sweathouse belonging to the owner of the original family house. There was approximately one sweathouse for every two family houses in a Yurok village. The people closely associated with these three structures, then, constituted the household. The normative village comprised approximately three such households, the members of each being (putatively) related to those of the others (hence exogamy was generally practiced, intravillage marriage usually being considered incestuous). By my estimate, based on 1852 census figures, each family house sheltered an average of five women and children, of whom, we may hypothesize, at least two were fertile women. Thus a *household's* potentially menstruating women would have numbered four or more (see Kroeber 1925:16–17).

We can only presume that, aboriginally, the related women of Yurok households interacted both frequently and regularly. The findings of McClintock and others are pertinent here, and a myth from the neighboring Karok encourages such comparison. The myth, relating the origins of the Pleiades, tells of several sisters who shared a house and who menstruated at the same time. The *idea* of household menstrual synchrony was indeed present in the area (Harrington 1931:142–145). Indeed, we have a historical account of women menstruating simultaneously at the coastal Yurok village of ʔespew in the later nineteenth century. According to Robert Spott, when his "aunt," the doctor Fanny Flounder, was dancing for her power in that village's sweathouse, she was secretly cursed by a menstruating woman. Trying to discover the culprit, "they summoned the menstruating women . . . only one of them would not come" (Spott and Kroeber 1942:62). At the approximate time, there were four family houses at ʔ*espew* (Waterman 1920:261).

What of the claim that synchronously menstruating women practiced the requisite rituals together? If this was indeed the case, why, we must ask, were small, individual menstrual shelters built? Why not communal shelters, like the men's sweathouses that the menstrual shelters seem functionally to parallel? It is possible that communal shelters were used. There is very little information on the subject in either ethnographic descriptions or in native texts and none on the actual size of the shelters. Although several early ethnographers mention menstrual "huts" in northwestern California, none of them ever actually saw one, for these shelters had fallen from use before the earliest trained observers arrived. Goddard (1903:17–18), working among the Hupa in 1900, noted that not even traces of the Hupa "huts" remained at the time of his fieldwork. The detailed Yurok village maps drawn by Waterman (1920) in the early part of this century, which show all structures and structural remains in each village, show neither these "menstrual huts" (*mekʷaʔr*) nor their remains. All accounts of these shelters found in ethnographic notes and publications are thus both vague and incomplete, as the minimal accounts themselves suggest.

Kroeber (1925:80), for example, tells us only that "a hut was used by Yurok women in their periodic illnesses. This was a small and rude lean-to of a few planks, near the house or against its side." Yet in northwestern California surely such flimsy shelter for valuable, necessary, and beloved women (Gould 1966; Spott and Kroeber 1942) would have been perceptibly maladaptive, even among the apparently male-dominant Yurok and especially so during the months between October and May when a great deal of cold rain customarily falls. I suggest that the paucity of ethnographic detail regarding menstrual shelters and much else reflects an understandable and pervasive bias (note Kroeber's use of the word "illnesses") and reticence in delving into and publishing material on the entire topic of menstruation, as further suggested by Kroeber's neglect of most of the Susie material in his published work.

In fact, it is quite possible that the aboriginal Yurok used large, dome-shaped communal brush menstrual shelters. Brush menstrual shelters have been reported for the Hupa of 1890 (A. R. Pilling, personal communication, 1981). In 1984 an elderly Yurok woman reported that she knew, at second hand, of three Yurok women who had undergone their first menstrual seclusion simultaneously in a single brush shelter (see later discussion). Finally, an 1850 sketch of the Yurok village of Curey by J. Goldsborough Bruff shows at least one, and possibly two, dome-shaped structures in association with plank houses (Kroeber, Elsasser, and Heizer 1977:257). If the Bruff drawing does depict one or more menstrual shelters, it indeed supports the synchrony hypothesis, for the structures shown are large ones—the clearer of the two being approximately the size of the sweathouse by which it stands. Comparative material from the Northwest Coast and the Plateau supports both the elderly woman's testimony and the drawing as evidence.

The Yurok have long been recognized as being importantly influenced by more "climactic" Northwest Coast cultures (e.g., Drucker 1963[1955]). We may legitimately turn to the farther Northwest Coast seeking comparative suggestions. We find among the Tlingit, for example, substantial brush and plank "birth houses," used for monthly menstrual seclusion as well as for labor and childbirth. These houses were heated by fires, used for sweating, and were large enough to hold four adult women (de Laguna 1972:501–502, 519, 527). The influence of Plateau cultures on those of northwestern California, though not yet systematically established, seems probable. It is of interest, then, that communal birth and menstrual seclusion houses were once common among the Chilcotin, Okanogen, Tenino, and others in the Plateau culture area (Ray 1939).

Regarding the posited use of the moon in restoring

menstrual synchrony on the occasions when it had been disrupted, we note recent biological research and findings. The timing of ovulation in certain nonhuman mammalian females and in female humans can be manipulated by exposure to light relatively stronger than that to which subjects are accustomed at a given time of day or night (Hoffman, Hester, and Towns 1965; Reinberg, Halberg, Ghata, and Siffre 1966; Matsumoto, Igarashi, and Nagaoka 1968; Dewan 1967, 1969; Presser 1974). There is evidence that light of the intensity of the full moon can affect the timing of ovulation and hence of menstruation in human females (Menaker and Menaker 1959; Hauenschild 1960; Cloudsley 1961:85–93).

More recently Dewan, Menkin, and Rock (1978) have demonstrated that the onset of menstruation itself may be directly affected by the exposure of ovulating women to light during sleep. The menstruation of ovulating women exposed to the light of a 100-watt bulb during the fourteenth through sixteenth or seventeenth nights of their cycles (counting the onset of menstruation as day 1) became regularized, with a significant number of the forty-one experimental subjects' cycles being regularized at twenty-nine days, the normative menstrual cycle (Dewan et al. 1978:582–583). The three to four nights of exposure was predicated on the natural duration of full moonlight during the lunar month (the mean synodic lunar month is 29.53 days). However, the researchers held it "probable" that one night's exposure would suffice to regularize the onset of menstruation (1978:582).

Light thus affects the onset of menstruation directly and, through affecting the onset of ovulation, indirectly as well. My young Yurok consultant did not specify in what phase of the moon women "talked" to it, "asking it to balance them." It is probable, however, that only the full moon provides enough photic stimulation (probably to the pineal gland) to affect either ovulation or, directly, the onset of menstruation twelve to fourteen days later. Such onset is at the time of the new moon, which, according to the biological model (Cloudsley 1961:85–93; Dewan et al. 1978:581), comprises the naturally occurring lunar phase for the onset of menstruation.

Elderly Yurok men have told me that intensive male training was always undertaken "during the dark of the moon." It seems probable, then, that women indeed "talked" to the full moon and that both synchronized menstruation and male training occurred during the period bracketed by the new moon. Yurok men's training for positive medicines ("luck") emphasizes light in its symbolism. Thus the intensification of training, much of it undertaken at night, during the new moon seems inconsistent—but, indeed, it makes good sense in the full biological context of village life.[9]

The Yurok word for "moon" is *wonesleg*, from *wonews* (overhead) and *leg(ay-)* (to pass regularly). There is evidence for precontact use of sweathouses as calendrical observatories in northwestern California (Goldschmidt 1940). In 1907 Kroeber gathered data on the construction and use of Yurok sweathouses for observation of both solar and lunar yearly cycles (in Elmendorf 1960:26). Such material evidence substantiates contemporary Yurok testimony on the accuracy of traditional timekeeping and the closeness of lunar prediction, and adds support to the young woman's assertion that Yurok women once utilized the moon's light in temporal regulation of biological cycles. I am suggesting, that is, a parallelism between male (sweathouse) and female uses of the moon consistent with cross-gender conceptual and ritual parallelisms discussed earlier.[10]

One important object of male lunar observation was that of correctly scheduling the great interareal ritual and ceremonial events that were once held in accordance with one-, two-, and three-year cycles in more than a dozen northwestern Californian centers. These events, customarily—if erroneously—lumped together as "world renewal dances," included esoteric components enacted by priests and their helpers, as well as public dances attended by very large audiences (Kroeber and Gifford 1949). Each had to be completed, in all aspects, within a single lunation and it had to end in the dark of the moon (p. 130; Kroeber, in Elmendorf 1960:28). The public dances themselves usually lasted approximately ten days, following the esoteric preparations. Menstruating women were prohibited from attending these dances. Whatever other symbolism was involved, the timing of these events makes particular sense in light of the biological model for menstruation at the new moon. According to this model, the two weeks before the new moon would have been the optimum time for the public dances: the time when the most women were free of menstrual restrictions and could attend.

The possible significance of menstrual synchrony in precontact Yurok culture, however, is far broader than this emphasis on ceremonialism suggests. *If* Yurok women once shared menstrual periods in synchrony and were able to control this synchrony to some degree, it would have meant that for ten days out of every twenty-nine all of the fertile women who were not pregnant were removed, as a group, from their households' mundane activities and plunged into collective contemplative and ritual exercises aimed at the acquisition of wealth objects and other spiritual boons. Logically, this would have been the ideal time for all of the younger men in the sweathouse to undertake their own ten-day periods of intense training, which, as did women's menstrual practices, emphasized continence and avoidance of contact with fecund members of the opposite sex.

Because they would have contaminated any food that they touched during their menses, all fecund women were removed from the subsistence quest for ten days out of every twenty-nine (pregnant women followed their own extended restrictions). Because the subsistence quest was *dominated* by women, who either provided foods themselves (e.g., acorns, shellfish) or were required actresses in male-focal subsistence activities—necessary for cleaning, butchering, and drying the fish and game that men caught—it is clear that during the ten-day menstrual period a woman's household's subsistence quest would have been somewhat hampered. This is even more clear in light of the fact that men could not hunt (or fight) while their wives were menstruating. If all of the women of a household menstruated in synchrony, these activities would have been very severely curtailed. If this was the case, it would be logical to think that the household's subsistence quest (and feuding) would have been brought virtually to a halt, men as well as women refraining from all but the most casual collecting of food. (Note that demand for fresh fish and game was reduced through the food avoidance rules for both menstruating women and men in training.) Such interruptions would not necessarily have been risky in northwestern California, where food supplies were abundant and dependable (cyclic occurrence of staple fish and acorns being of long duration) and where food (especially acorns and smoked-dried fish) was successfully stored in large quantities (Gould 1966, 1975).

A possibility, then, is that the monthly round transformed the Yurok household, for one-third of every month, into an esoteric training camp in which most (aristocratic) men and women between puberty and middle age devoted themselves to their respective practices aimed at the acquisition of wealth and self-knowledge, supported by both younger and older males and females (with the exception of pregnant women and new mothers, who followed their own equally restrictive regimes for the entire gestation period and for ninety days after giving birth).

This speculation accords well with both the oft-noted spirituality and asceticism of aboriginal Yurok culture and the expression of these tendencies in Yurok social organization. Male Yurok began to undertake wealth-bringing austerities at puberty, as did the women; and like the women, they had largely ceased such activities by late middle age, when, in the native theory, they began to enjoy the fruits of their labors. There was, then, a well-defined group in every household capable of managing ongoing affairs and supporting the monthly practices of the men and women between puberty and middle age. For example, the special foods of men in training were prepared by postmenopausal women and prepubescent girls, who also attended women secluded during their menses.

If we are anywhere near the mark in these speculations, it is clear that the menstrual power of Yurok women did not manifest itself only on a gender-specific, esoteric level of knowledge and practice—one that paralleled identical features of opposite-gender life—but that it had profound, pragmatic implications as well in dictating the temporal structuring of activities for entire households on a monthly basis.

CONCLUSION

I have shown that for some precontact Yurok women at least, menstruation was not viewed solely as a virulent form of contamination but was understood as spiritual potency potentially, if ambiguously, providing a route to knowledge and wealth. It is quite likely that in agreement with many contemporary native northwestern Californians other than my principal informant, and with a traditional male-dominated understanding, some aboriginal Yurok women did view their periods as times, simply, of negative pollution. It is also likely that still others were deeply ambivalent. However, some—most likely aristocratic—women held a seemingly gender-specific, at least partially positive view of menstruation, encoding it within a gender-specific mythic and ritual context.

I suggest, moreover, that the women of aboriginal Yurok households menstruated in synchrony, utilizing the light of the moon to regularize their menstrual cycles, and that the menstruating women of (aristocratic) households used their shared periods of menstrual seclusion for the practice of spiritual disciplines. Moreover I propose that both the subsistence quests and fighting patterns of all of the active men of these households, as well as their own programs of esoteric training, were keyed to the synchronous menstrual cycles of the household's women. To an extent these propositions have been justified by recent Yurok testimony, unavailable to me when I first published on these topics (Buckley 1982).

During 1984 Arnold R. Pilling, my senior colleague in Yurok studies, spent part of the summer working with the late Lowana Brantner, a Yurok woman of Meta, then in her mid-seventies. Pilling recorded on tape over twenty-two hours of data concerning Mrs. Brantner's life and Yurok traditional patterns. In the process of that interviewing he collected such data as Mrs. Brantner knew of other females' first menstruation rites and many comments on her own lengthy first menstrual seclusion. In regard to the latter, Mrs. Brantner reported that among the women who came to supervise and instruct her during this period was the renowned *kegey* Fanny Flounder (e.g., Spott and Kroeber 1942:158–164).

Mrs. Brantner also noted that she was the only girl from Meta undergoing menstrual seclusion during the year of her training and, in fact, for over a generation before, while Fanny had been the only female of her village secluded the year that Fanny had been trained at the undercut of a waterfall in a canyon along Gold Bluffs. Mrs. Brantner noted, however, that in the case of one woman with whom she had discussed first menstrual seclusion there had been three girls from a single village being secluded in one brush shelter at once. When Pilling expressed surprise that three girls from one village would have their first menstruation at the same time, Mrs. Brantner said that they *should:* since the whole village had their "mating season" at the same time (i.e., late summer–early fall), the "birthing season" fell at the same time for all as well (in May–June [compare Erikson 1943]). Therefore all the girls of a village had their first menstruation at once, according to Mrs. Brantner (Arnold R. Pilling, personal communications 1985, 1986).

Lowana Brantner's recollections add considerable weight to my own consultant's assertions regarding Yurok menstrual synchrony and menstrual practice as a context for spiritual training, which initiated the present inquiry. Still, empirical proof of the hypotheses that have grown out of that original testimony remains lacking. Unfortunately it is too late to test these hypotheses in the Yurok case. Yet as I have suggested, there are certain possibilities that can and should be explored in contemporary face-to-face societies in which strong menstrual restrictions and gender-specific knowledge and practices still exist.

Such research can be combined with a close examination of early information concerning cultures that are today much changed from their aboriginal precursors. Contemporary native testimony and far earlier ethnographic materials may stand in an intricate relationship. By exploring this relationship we may, in some cases, clarify both our received understandings of the past and our (possibly mistaken) interpretations of the present. In such analyses, particularly but not exclusively in the cases of native Californian cultures, it is especially important that we attend to the often entirely neglected raw field data of earlier investigators.

9

Heavenly Bodies: Menses, Moon, and Rituals of License among the Temne of Sierra Leone

Frederick Lamp

The behavior of women among the Temne people of Sierra Leone, West Africa, is regulated by the traditions set forth in the ceremonies of a formal initiation association of women, called Bondo. Although the secrets of Bondo allow no exegesis or even simple description of ritual procedure to outsiders, it is possible to observe the exhibition of systematic Bondo thought and practice in their public procedures, and thus to predict the sequence and character of any female ceremony. The constancy of these ceremonies seems to reflect a general correspondence in Temne female behavior patterns, and a reasonable coherence in cosmology, in routine social interaction, and even in gynecology.

One area of systematic practice among the Temne and others is ethnoastronomical observation. This is an area long neglected by scholars of Africa but now inciting new interest, leading to some startling revelations. In Africa it now seems unlikely that we will find the same kinds of precise and elaborate observatory stations and calculatory systems and symbols that are found in ancient America (Aveni 1982; Center for Archaeoastronomy 1978; Tedlock 1982; Tichy 1982; Williamson 1981). However, a sense of the importance of celestial movement to cosmological systems has recently been shown to be much more fundamental to African thought than most of us had presumed (Brooks 1984; Lamp 1982; LaPin 1983; Sawyerr 1970; Steffy 1982; R. Thompson 1981).

The human body has also emerged as a subject worthy of study in regard to African cosmological thought. The body is a contained space with dimensions that may be measured and evaluated, just as the space of a house, village clearing, acreage, or the realms of heavenly bodies. Our empirical observations about our bodies are interpreted in terms of what we understand about space generally and about movement and functions within space. I have shown elsewhere (Lamp 1982:92–98) that in Africa the human body may be seen as a microcosm representing principles of universal balance, centering, self-possession, being and not being, and the spiritual and physical planes of consciousness. Data found among several African groups parallel medieval Muslim philosophy, as expressed by the Ikwān al-Safā' (as interpreted in Nasr 1978:44, 68, 75):

> "The whole world is one . . . as man is one." Its parts are held together like the organs of a living body . . . "man can be considered as a small world. . . ." The heavenly bodies . . . are also the seats of the various faculties of the Universal Soul, which is the cause of all change in the world of generation and corruption.

There is some evidence that the body may function physically in a similarly paradigmatic manner. Unfortunately, there has been little human physiological research on Africa. Even fertility studies fail to touch on such basic issues as the menstrual cycle or impotency. We need to understand that just as culture is not universally invariable, neither is biology. We cannot assume, for example, that because in the West menses last four to six days, or because sperm can survive in the vagina for three to five days, that these are also true for Africans, for example, or with specific groups of Africans. I would predict that physiological studies on such subjects will gain more prominence in the near future, with fascinating results.

As an art historian, however, I am primarily involved in a consideration of symbols and the ritual context of art. In the art-historical method of morphology we are concerned with the use of space, its qualities, and the interrelationships of its parts. The approach may be used with painting, sculpture, architecture, theater, music, oral narrative, and dance (as in "effort-shape" analysis). In the analysis of dance ritual we seek, in cosmological thought, fundamentals in the use of the body.

One often hears Europeans in Africa sighing smugly, "The Africans have no sense of time." I found in fieldwork that art and the ritual in which it figures reveal almost an obsession with time seen qualitatively, and that spatial constructs and ritual movement in space may be graphed to show a great structural harmony with nonvisual forms of art, such as oral narrative and music, or with common and esoteric notions about the sun and the moon and other natural phenomena (Lamp 1982). That is, the body may be used to re-create the structure and the movement of the cosmos and thereby, in ritual, become one with its universe, including that universe's temporal dimension. This is a principal function of much ritual in Africa.

TEMNE SOCIETY

The Temne are the largest ethnic group in Sierra Leone, occupying an area that runs from the coast to about two hundred kilometers inland. Although they have migration legends, it is not clear when the Temne arrived in Sierra Leone. It is clear, though, that they have been in their current location since at least the fourteenth century, and that they now represent an amalgam with many other immigrant ethnic groups, such as the Susu, Kuranko, Loko, and perhaps Vai. The Temne are not now, and apparently have not been in historical times, a culturally cohesive group, but cohesion has been strong within smaller divisions, such as the Kunike, Mabanta, or Sanda Temne. In the nineteenth century these groups were at war as much with each other as with linguistic foreigners such as the Mende or Susu. Today, however, there is a very strong nationalistic sense of Temne pride.

Although since the coming of repatriated slaves the capital city of Freetown has been primarily a Temne city, the Temne are largely rural, living in small towns or villages of about ten households. Even in the larger towns the basic spatial and cultural unit is the clan-based circular enclosure, *ka-bəŋka*, consisting of extended family compounds, *kurukuru*, comprising a unit much like a small village. Ritual events usually emanate from these clan units even if they are attended by the entire town.

This "village" is a community in every sense, without the fragmentation to which we Westerners are so accustomed. The birth of a child brings all the women to the mother's house to clap their hands for her labor. "Outdooring" the child on the seventh day, the mother presents it to each household. Initiation in the ceremonial associations—Pɔrɔ or Rəbai (in different areas) for boys and Bondo for girls—in the past was universal and usually took place in early adolescence (not necessarily at puberty but as early as six and as late as the mid-twenties).

In initiation, which involves not so much practical as cultural and religious instruction through participation in ritual arts, the young learn to act cooperatively, to synchronize their behavior patterns, and to work toward a harmonious relationship with the cosmos as well as with society. To live in a community and fail to attend the public events sponsored by these associations would be the height of impropriety. When one moves to a new community it is necessary to greet the chief and all the townspeople formally and to be received by the people unanimously through a series of prescribed gestures. Upon the death of one of its members the entire community joins the bereaved family in public mourning and in the festivities of the wake.

People who do not join their neighbors in community events are suspected of harboring an antisocial, malevolent quality called *ra-ser*. These people, *aŋ-ser,* operate independently, in secret, and do not heed the commandment given to female initiates at their coming out (in Bondo): "Step as your companions are stepping." Their odd behavior leads the neighbors to categorize them as suprahuman and to ostracize them further.

In general, however, people tend to welcome outsiders

and to make a special effort to include them in daily routine. The Temne dissenter is a rarity, and people usually agree on basic philosophical issues. In discussions of religion or custom informants usually begin, "We the Temne believe . . . "

Quite a few ritual organizations exist, many specialized, that contribute to the feeling of ethnic cohesion. But in most areas in the past, ritual and cultural life was sponsored primarily by a single principal association responsible for initiating men and women into adulthood: Bondo for women, Rəbai or Pɔrɔ for men. Rəbai is now virtually defunct, although I studied a few remaining initiation groups in 1976 in western Temneland (Lamp 1978). This study focuses on the Temne of the east, for whom the men's association, since the early eighteenth century, has been Pɔrɔ, derived from the Pɔrɔ of the Bullom people to the south.

Lunar Time

Before considering the particular timing of initiation coming-out, I would like to emphasize that the lunar calendar among the Temne is ancient, predating Muslim contact and the introduction of the Islamic calendar. The earliest document is from 1506 (Fernandes 1951:100). It implies that some system of intercalation with the solar cycle was in effect: "They count their years from new year to new year, as from November to November thus they measure their new years. And they count their months by new moons." In 1623 Ruiters wrote (Hair 1975:64) that "the people do not distinguish days, but only go by the new moon and the full moon."

The Temne lunar calendar consists of twelve named non-movable months based upon the synodic lunar cycle of approximately 29.5 days, or the interval from one new moon to the next. This calendar governs all indigenous ritual, farming schedules, and much of ordinary routine. The Julian or Christian calendar is used in most business and government contexts, and the Arabic system of movable months is used in regard to Muslim ceremonies, including the installation of chiefs (most Temne are nominally Muslim).

The importance of the lunar cycle to Temne life cannot be overstated, in contrast to this phenomenon's relative unimportance elsewhere in Africa—for example, among the Kongo of Zaire as analyzed by R. Thompson (1981). Temne ritual is most concerned with the phases of the moon, whereas little attention is paid to the solar cycle in the counting of time, in notions of augury, or even in the regulation of agricultural schedules. New Year's celebrations, although apparently indigenous to groups further north (Brooks 1984), seem to have been imported by Temne entirely from Islam. The new moon, however, is observed first with anxious anticipation and then with exhilaration at its first sighting—with hand-clapping, as at the birth of a child. An eclipse of the sun is barely noted, but an eclipse of the moon occasions a furious clatter of pan-banging to chase away the cat that has caught it (Thomas 1916:179). In the Temne story of creation there is no mention of the sun, but only of the moon (Schlenker 1861:12–35).

There is, in fact, no Temne term for the sun as a heavenly body, only terms for its sensorial effects: its warmth (*a-ne*) and its brilliance (*a-ret*). The moon, on the other hand, has two ostensive names, one for the nighttime moon (*a-ŋof*) and one for the daytime moon (*kə-ləkəth*), and a number of metaphorical names as well. These metaphors have particular resonance in the rituals of the Bondo and Pɔrɔ associations. There are also eight terms for the moon's phases.

WOMEN'S AND MEN'S RITUAL
ASSOCIATIONS: THE BONDO AND PɔRɔ

The women's Bondo association is universal throughout Temneland, although the eastern Bondo seems more purely Temne while the western seems somewhat related to a similar association (Sande) found to the south and extending into northern Liberia. To become a woman, marry, and have children without Bondo initiation is unthinkable. Bondo is controlled by a hierarchy of female officials, apparently completely free of male political influence and perhaps even in defiance of it.[1] Bondo initiation lasts for one year in the east (usually less in other areas). The girls are first taken to a grove in the forest for a genital operation (allegedly ranging from labial scarification to clitoridectomy) and two weeks of healing. Then they move to a special house at the eastern end of the village where they are enclosed for the remainder of the year, hidden from the eyes of men except for brief trips to get water or for other necessary duties. Bondo ritual is secret, although the beginning and final ceremonies are quasi-public (i.e., they are ostensibly public, but certain episodes are not, and the appearance of a total stranger at any time can cause some uneasiness). Not only must the initiates refrain from talking to men and outsiders, but the Bondo officials may not refer to the proceedings to a nonmember, and it is considered a serious crime for a nonmember even to ask questions about these proceedings. Thus research on Bondo can be quite trying.

The Pɔrɔ is the strongest men's association today, prevalent (although not universal) in southeastern Temneland and among the neighboring Bullom of Sierra Leone's southern coast. It is related in structure to associations of the same name among the Mende and northern Liberian groups (although Temne Pɔrɔ privileges are completely mutual only with those of the Bullom). Like Bondo, Pɔrɔ initiation procedure is secret to nonmembers, although some research has been carried out on its public events (Dorjahn 1959, 1982; Lamp 1982). In the past initiation into Pɔrɔ lasted from three to seven years, but today an abbreviated version takes only four days. Despite this seemingly superficial initiation, a Pɔrɔ member enjoys high status and the organization holds a strong grip on the Temne.

In studying initiation into these institutions I kept charts correlating ritual timing with natural and astronomical phenomena, such as the nesting patterns of certain birds, agricultural schedules, and moon phases. The correlation with moon phases produced some definite patterns for each step in the ritual procedure, most notably for the female Bondo. I had developed a relatively comfortable rapport with some Bondo officials, so I felt free to question them on the subject of ritual scheduling. I tried every tack in my repertoire but could not elicit even the vaguest reference to the moon. Finally I simply confronted them with my charts. Undaunted, they replied that the correlations in all seven sets of initiations were thoroughly coincidental, and that the choice of timing was totally arbitrary, most definitely not lunar.

The Lunar Timing of Ritual

My charting indicated that, among many other events, the timing of coming-out ceremonies was somewhat consistent, and it is on these that I would like to focus this discussion.[2] Briefly, at the end of initiation a series of quasi-public ceremonies are held. The purpose is to present the successful initiates to the village and to reinstate them in normal society as newly reborn adults. For Pɔrɔ the event is called *aŋ-kori,* "the greeting"; for Bondo it is *aŋ-kus,* "the pouring out" (see Lamp 1988 for a full account). For three days after Pɔrɔ *aŋ-kori,* the boys are secluded in the courthouse in the center of the village and then released to their families. After the second and final day of Bondo *aŋ-kus,* the girls are kept in the courthouse for four days.[3] If the girls are betrothed (which may be the case even for infants) and are past puberty, they are now officially under the care of their new husbands, who have borne the expenses of their initiation (although pre-pubescent girls return to live with their own families, as do those girls who are not betrothed).

The timing of coming-out fell as depicted in figure 9.1:

Bondo—lasting two days, beginning either
   (1)   at the first quarter moon, or within two and a half days before; or
   (2)   at the third quarter moon, or within three and a half days after.
Pɔrɔ—either at new or full moon, with one exception (at third quarter).

Why would the moon be so important to the Temne, and specifically to Bondo women? Later I discuss the possibility

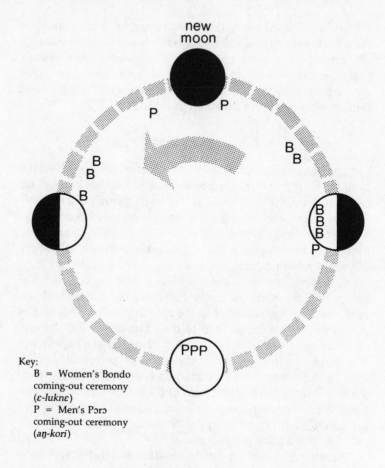

Fig. 9.1. Lunar timing of initiation coming-out ceremonies.

of a quasi-physiological relationship between women and the moon; but before turning to this, I consider first some metaphorical relationships that may be equally significant bases for the lunar timing of ritual.

First, the moon is considered female, the wife of the sun, according to some informants. Its waxing and waning are associated, by the Temne as by many peoples throughout the world, with the female condition in pregnancy and birth as well as the process of life from birth to maturity to death (see Sawyerr 1970:75 on the Mende). The names given to the various phases of the moon ascribe to it human attributes. It is first *a-ŋof a-fu,* "the new moon," just as people renewed through initiation are "new savants," *aŋ-Sema fu.* At its first sighting the people say *a-ŋof a kəl təma,* "The moon has stood up again," and they clap their hands to rejoice for its return just as they clap at the birth of a child to thank the mother for her labors. The second phase is *a-ŋof a-bərnɛ,* "the turning moon," referring metaphorically to the turning (tilling) of the soil and of women, who will be "planted" by their husbands. It also refers to the "twistin' 'n turnin'" of a seductive woman (Lamp 1982:271, 340). Of the full moon the Temne say *a-ŋof a po' lasər a yirə,* "The moon is filled up and is sitting down." Sitting is a metaphor for having arrived, or of belonging (*yi rə*), of having become a full member of society, and it is a distinctly female metaphor used, for example, when Bondo girls are presented to the village at their coming-out (they are seated, whereas male initiates stand), or in the carving of caryatid stools (never atlantid) for the seating of honored religious officials (Lamp 1982:21, 95). The third quarter of the lunar cycle is *a-ŋof a-rɔkər,* "the reaping moon," again a reference to agricultural activity. The final phase is *a-ŋof a-fi,* "the dying moon."

Without the benefit of indigenous testimony, we might draw some obvious visual conclusions. The moon at first or third quarter is only half-filled, as the Bondo girls are only at midpoint in their birth-to-death semicycle (death-to-birth being the completion, through spiritual reincarnation). The waxing of the moon beyond a hemisphere suggests pregnancy, which is, of course, out of the question for girls at this stage.

A second association of the moon may be with the butterfly, especially the *Danas chrysippus,* the most common one in Sierra Leone. Its life cycle duration is equivalent to that of the moon. This would not be notable except for the fact that the butterfly is also referred to as female, and that it is paramount in female initiation symbolism (Lamp 1985). Its metamorphosis, in four stages, parallels both the lunar cycle and the four-stage initiation of Bondo girls (entering ceremonies, seclusion in the forest, seclusion in town, exiting ceremonies). Moreover, the most important mask of the Bondo officials is a wooden helmet mask painted shiny black with rings around its base, resembling, and called specifically, "The Butterfly Chrysallis," *a-Nɔwo*. Her dance suggests the fluttering of butterflies struggling to free themselves, and it is surely a metaphor for the transformation of immature and sexless human beings into beautiful, powerful women (Lamp 1988).

A third association of the moon may be with the serpent. Certain similarities come to mind. The serpent lives in darkness or obscurity. Its form is like an elongated crescent. It regenerates itself by shedding its dead skin. In the final ceremonies of the Bondo coming-out, a white bundle is carried on an official's head in a dance explicitly symbolizing the serpent's motion, and among the neighboring Mende this is said to contain a python. Harry Sawyerr (1970:75), who studied Mende religious belief, associated the serpent with "the rhythm of life attributed to the moon" (compare Knight, this volume). "In this regard, snakes and serpents manifest the fact of 'becoming' as definitely as the life-death-life cycle noticeable in agriculture and demonstrated supremely by the phases of the moon." The serpent is associated with pregnancy in many ways and is held responsible for conception and for ease in childbirth (Lamp 1985).

SEXUAL LICENSE

I return now to the coming-out ceremonies of initiation. At the time of my field research I was told some details relating to initiation scheduling that interested me but which I simply noted down without a clue to their significance. These data I now examine here.

1. For three days after Pɔrɔ coming-out the boys are kept secluded in the house of conversation (*am-bare*) in the village square. The next day they are released and for several days

thereafter they are permitted extraordinary license, including unrestricted sexual access to consenting married women. No husband may take them to court for "woman damage" as is usually the case in adultery.

2. On the first day of girls' Bondo coming-out, one of the most important ceremonies is *ɛ-luknɛ,* meaning "transferring," but also alluding to "transplanting," and involving transvestitism in an atmosphere of wild abandon. The dance begins in the east. The entire village takes part, including the men and children. Each person selects some article that has been destroyed or violated in some way: a rotted basket, torn rags, a bottomless bucket, a broken pestle, or dried foliage. These articles are brandished in a frenzied dance in which the crowd rushes in a counterclockwise circle around the town from east to west and back east. Honorable old women dress like lorry-boys. Young men seductively shake their padded breasts in the faces of the elders. Young girls stuff gourds into the front of the men's shorts they are wearing and play the role of the village stud. And everyone, from the decrepit old grandmother to the young teenage boy, engages in the most defamatory and pornographic language. *ɛ-luknɛ* is a popular event. The Temne often say *ɛ-luknɛ ma-bɔthi ma-ti ma thasər,* "*ɛ-luknɛ*—Its sweetness is superlative." Partying is always fun, of course, but in *ɛ-luknɛ* there is a bonus.

There is a song heard at some of these occasions with the words *aŋ-Sema komande,* translated roughly as "the ritual sanction of the initiated person." The signification is that all married Bondo women are now free to have sexual intercourse with any man present without fear of reprisal from their husbands against either them or their partners.[4] The dance goes on but one senses a thinning of the crowd in the village plaza, and quick-witted young unmarried men later recall this phase of the ceremony with special relish.

MENSES AND THE MOON

How can such flagrant disregard for morality take place among a people who otherwise maintain rigid sexual prohibitions, and in a society in which the clarity of the lines of descent is critical to the ritual of ancestral supplication?[5] An explanation might be sought in the concept of ritual reversal (see Beidelman 1966; Gluckman 1963; Norbeck 1967; Babcock 1978). The focus of this discussion, however, is not on the sociosymbolic function of such behavior but on the logistics. The question here is, to what extent is ritual timing based upon either symbolic or "real" (that is, scientifically observable) concerns?

To answer this I must digress to three obscure and enigmatic references in the literature on the Temne that seem to suggest the presence of menstrual synchrony. In other societies there is some scientific evidence that women living together in close communion, as in a college dormitory or in a small isolated society, exhibit concurrent menstrual cycles (see the chapters by Buckley and Knight, this volume, and McClintock 1971). Thus in addition to the metaphorical associations with the moon mentioned earlier, there might be factors related to notions about the menstrual cycle that can explain the lunar timing of Temne initiation coming-out. The testimony of some Sierra Leoneans over a period of two centuries points, seemingly unequivocally, in this direction.

In the mid-nineteenth century the missionary Christian Schlenker compiled a book of Temne oral narratives, including an account of the creation of humanity and of the origins of the world, Temne clans, death and sexuality, and so on. The myth does not seem to survive today in Temne memory, but Schlenker apparently confirmed it with three informants, whose versions differed only slightly. In the myth the primordial couple became interested in procreation, so God gave them medicine to introduce fertility and the knowledge of coitus. Of the eight doses of medicine, the woman ate five; the man, three (Schlenker 1861:18–19): "This is the reason the woman has a stronger sexual desire; this is the reason that all women are sick in the belly, when the moon is full, again when the moon is dying."[6]

Schlenker interpreted this to refer to menses, occurring in some women at full moon and in others at new moon. But there is no way of knowing whether he just assumed this meaning or confirmed it. His alternate text for this portion reads that "all women are routinely not well at the dead moon *and* [not 'or'] at the full moon." This seems to imply that all women have two periods of "illness" per month: the Temne informants may have been referring to menses and, fifteen days after menses, the discomfort of postovulation (temperature rise caused by increased progesterone production).[7]

Even more striking is an assertion made in 1965 by a renowned physician, the late Dr. Milton Margai, first president of Sierra Leone, whose major work as a physician was with Bondo women in an attempt to upgrade their paragynecological practices. In a brief medical handbook written in Temne (1965:7–8) he included a section subtitled *Ratu ra Bomŋaŋ (kayak aŋof):* "The sickness of women (to wash the moon)":

> Every month the woman emits blood, this emission of blood is what is called "to wash the moon." [From the time] *the moon begins to appear on the last day blood stops,* until the first day of the moon when it "stands up again," so it is twenty-eight days.
>
> When the moon [i.e., the menstrual cycle?] lasts fourteen days, starting from the first day, one egg begins to come out of the house of eggs to enter the tube that leads to the uterus, in order to pass to the uterus.
>
> . . . Then the egg breaks up, blood comes out and this is what they call the coming out of the moon. Some women "wash" for three days, some four, some six.[8]

A third source, by Jean Barbot written originally in 1678, describes in general the various peoples of the coast of present-day Sierra Leone. Barbot's information is mostly secondhand, although I have not located the origin of his passage on lunar custom (1746:125) in any other source:

> At every new moon, both in the villages and open country, they abstain from all manner of work, and do not allow any strangers to stay amongst them at that time; alledging [*sic*] for their reason, that if they should do otherwise, their maiz [*sic*] and rice would grow red, the day of the *new moon being a day of blood,* as they express it; and therefore they commonly go hunting that day.[9]

Today a stranger does not stay in a house with a menstruating woman in more traditional areas, or at least the woman is kept in some kind of isolation. Women abstain from work during menses, particularly avoiding cooking and working in the fields. Coitus would be unthinkable. Perhaps the foregoing reference to hunting means that the men abandoned the village women during menses.

The names by which menstruation is known give further support to the hypothesis of new moon menses. "To wash the moon" suggests ritual washing of other kinds, such as the washing of an infant at his outdooring ceremonies; the washing of initiates when they enter the sacred grove for the first time, when they are about to begin their final ceremonies, and when they are about to "come out," or return to society; or the washing of stones representing the dead in the ancestral shrine in order to bring about the reincarnation of their spirits (see Lamp 1983:236). "Washing the moon" does not refer explicitly to a renewal of the moon as the new moon or to its disappearance as the dead moon, but disappearance is equated with washing in the case of the sun: it is said to be washed in sea water after sunset, after which it sleeps alone in the bush (Winterbottom 1969:22). Water is related to darkness in many ways—rain should fall at night, not in the day, lest it spoil the crops (Sawyerr 1970:71, 73); the rainy season is a dim season and may be associated with the inactivity and obscurity of the spiritual world and is also related to night (Lamp 1982:327–329); initiates, who are considered invisible to the villagers, are thought to exist in a land of water before they are "poured out" onto dry land at their coming-out ceremonies (Lamp 1982:chap. IV). All this suggests that washing refers to a dark, invisible state of being, a state of transition, and to a beginning, just as new moon is the beginning of the month.

Another term for "to menstruate" is *kə yi ro-kɔm,* literally "to be in the East" (Dalby 1982:145). East is significant in all Temne oral narrative as the place of beginnings. Elsewhere (Lamp 1982) I have analyzed thoroughly the cycles of time, such as days, months, seasons, and creation time, arguing that each cycle may be seen as a paradigm of the others, that time progression is based upon concepts of space and movement in space, and that time cycles organized in four segments are related to spheres of space divided into four cardinal directions. East, as the place of beginnings (the beginning of creation, the source of the ancestors, the place of birth, the site of initiation, etc.), relates to the beginnings of temporal cycles such as the day (obviously), the new moon, the sequence of months, the life cycle, and the cycle of cosmic time. The word for "east" is simply "up" (*ro-kɔm*), and "west" is "down" (*ro-pil*). The new moon and full moon, too, are associated with vertical positions as in their common descriptions: for the new moon—*a-ŋof a kəl təma,* "the moon has stood up again" (Margai 1965:7), and for the full moon—*a-ŋof a po' lasər a yirə,* "The moon has been filled and is sitting down." Therefore the period of menstruation is associated with the moon's "standing-up" phase, the new moon.

What must be on the reader's mind now is a very simple question: Why not just ask the Temne women when they menstruate? Or why not observe their behavior—for example, the isolation of menstruating women? Gynecological research on the hypothesis, of course, must be the next step, though I did not undertake it myself while among the Temne. It seems odd that the question has not been asked; but then, if the hypothesis is correct, the answer seems incredible. In fact elsewhere in West Africa researchers have been told that menses commence at the new moon, but precise data have not yet been gathered.[10]

It should be noted, however, that the observation of menstrual cycles among the Temne, as with other African groups, would not be as simple as it may seem. Harrell (1981) has shown that in such nonindustrial societies there are many mitigating factors that contribute to amenorrhea: not only pregnancy (probably about 15 percent of all Temne women) and menopause (about 15 percent), but also nursing (about 30 percent—see note 4), infertility resulting from disease (approximately 5 percent), sustained vigorous exercise (most Temne women), and malnourishment (less than 5 percent).

McClintock (1971) has shown also that women without regular contact (sexual or not) with men (probably the case for a small percentage of Temne women, who are co-wives in large polygynous families) tend to menstruate less frequently. Harrell (1981) suggests that in such a society continuous menstrual cycling may not be considered a natural female attribute, and that the "normal monthly period" is more of a Western conception. It would be difficult to calculate the percentage of Temne women in amenorrhea at any given time, but it is safe to say that most do not menstruate; therefore if Temne women are in menstrual synchrony, it is not a mass menstruation that would be easily observable.

Whether the notions of synchrony expressed in the three foregoing sources would be borne out in gynecological research, either historical or contemporary, is hard to predict. But for the purposes of the argument at hand it does not matter. We are concerned here not with biological facts but with cultural perceptions. What is important in this case is what people believe to be true. If the Temne indeed believe that menstruation should occur at the new moon, then the implications for ritual are striking.

RITUAL TIMING AND GYNECOLOGY

For the sake of argument, let us assume that Schlenker was correct—that there are, in fact, two menstrual cycles among Temne women. These two cycles, together with several other features, are charted in figure 9.2. The first cycle is identified in this figure as the primary cycle, group 1, because it is confirmed by Margai and Barbot. This cycle begins with menstruation just before and lasting through the new moon, with the probability of ovulation highest just before the full moon. (Schlenker placed the "sickness" at the "dead moon," which is the period when the moon is dark, distinct from the "new moon," when it first reappears; Margai placed the end of menstruation at the new moon; Barbot did not record the indigenous term, so his placement is ambiguous.) Group 2,

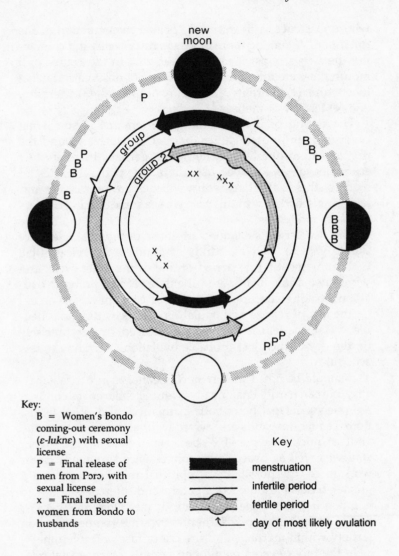

Key:

B = Women's Bondo coming-out ceremony (*ɛ-luknɛ*) with sexual license

P = Final release of men from Pɔrɔ, with sexual license

x = Final release of women from Bondo to husbands

Key

▬▬▬ menstruation

─── infertile period

◖▬◗ fertile period

↰___ day of most likely ovulation

Fig. 9.2. Hypothetical menstrual cycles and the lunar timing of sexual freedom.

whose existence is in question, begins menstruating at the full moon. Assuming more or less regular cycles and combining the two groups, it may be seen that in the course of a month there are four alternating phases of positive and negative nature: (1) infertility, (2) fertility or menses, (3) infertility, and (4) fertility or menses.[11]

The timing of Bondo coming-out (*aŋ-kus*) is somewhat consistent, as I noted earlier, enough to cluster around the first and third quarters of the moon. Perhaps there are two schedules of *aŋ-kus* because there are two schedules of menses; that is, perhaps entire villages are on distinct and opposing schedules. In this case we see some striking clusters of correspondences.

The clearest constellations are those of the final release of Bondo girls to their husbands or families. All releases fall within the most fertile period of one or the other cycle, and within two and a half days of the date of most probable ovulation, making conception possible if consummation occurs on the day of release and ovulation goes according to schedule.[12] Half the female initiates are released, in fact, precisely on the day of the most probable ovulation, according to this schedule.

It should be noted that in Sierra Leone, as in Africa generally, one can hardly imagine not wanting children, as children are one's principal heirs both in financial and ritual terms. Both Temne husbands and wives want as many as possible, and as quickly as possible, because a child brings higher status as well as prospective convenience through a larger work force, the possibility of spiritual reincarnation, and a greater base of tribute both before and after death, not to mention immeasurable pride and joy (see Dorjahn 1958:839, 842). The timing of *aŋ-kus*, then, serves the Temne accent on fertility within marriage and the critical use of fertile time.

In the other events mentioned here in which sexual freedom is an element, the object, we surmise, is to *avoid* pregnancy. Bondo *ɛ-luknɛ* (in which the period of sexual license occurs) clusters around the first and third lunar quarters to within three and a half days. The first-quarter *ε-luknε* quite safely corresponds to the infertile period of group 1 after menses. The third-quarter *ε-luknε,* however, overlaps with group 2's fertile period, although the three instances occurring precisely at the third quarter fall at the beginning of the "unsafe" period by only a day and a half, hardly much of a risk. Conversely, if there is no such group 2, then these girls are fully within the safe period just preceding menses (although their final release would correspond not with ovulation but with menses—seemingly bad timing).

If these latter three exceptions are to be considered, there are three possibilities. First, they are simply not playing according to the rules and may not be traditional enough still to have synchronic menstruation anyway. Second, they are menstruating synchronically but are several days late. Third, the song, *aŋ-Sema komande,* which signals the relaxing of the sexual prohibition, was not sung. In fact, I have personally witnessed the singing of the song on only one occasion, and that was at the first quarter moon.

What about the timing of sexual freedom for the boys finally released from the male initiation ceremony? For Pɔrɔ, this falls on "safe" (infertile), nonmenstrual days throughout the cycle of group 1; and if both groups 1 and 2 are valid, ony one of the six calculated days of Pɔrɔ release falls on a fertile period (group 2) of the last fertile day for the women, whereas none falls during a menstrual period of any women in either group. Again, a concentration of release dates at opposite poles of the lunar cycle suggests that there may be two menstrual cycles and that Pɔrɔ release is timed according to the cycle, of either group 1 or 2, in the particular village. If the Pɔrɔ boys released around the new moon and at the third quarter belong to a group 1 village, their period of sexual freedom clusters around the first few days before and after menstruation. If those released at full moon belong to a group 2 village, their freedom follows immediately the end of menstruation. In both cases sexual license would be perceived as harmless (not resulting in pregnancy).

CONCLUSION

God and ritual (to paraphrase the Christian holy book) "work in mysterious ways"; nevertheless ritual may perform not only symbolic functions but some psycho/biodemographic ones as well. In traditional polygynous Temne society, in which young women are usually given in marriage to older men who can afford them (Dorjahn 1958:843–849), ritual such as described earlier, though hardly meeting fully the sexual needs of single young men, at least provides an avenue for sexual education for the very young (in Pɔrɔ), as well as outlets several times a year for unmarried men (young men would not miss a Bondo *aŋ-kus,* which may happen in ten or more surrounding villages per year in the dry season). For women of polygynous households (for whom infertility is highest [Dorjahn 1958] and who are the most likely not to be pregnant or nursing, and thus are the most available at *aŋ-Sema komande*), the relaxing of prohibitions is probably equally welcome. This is not to say that Temne ritual is designed exclusively or explicitly around psychobiological (sexual) needs but that ritual must "work"—must perform a variety of functions—and that purely sexual as well as reproductive concerns, which are important ones, do figure in Temne ritual design.

The hypothesis on ritual scheduling given here suggests that some Africans have a great deal more knowledge about human anatomy than we have credited them with. Observers have argued that traditional Sierra Leone women are ignorant of the uterus and of the processes of conception and parturition.[13] I suspect, however, that ritual practitioners possess a considerable science of the body, perhaps obscured to us through the abundance of linguistic metaphor and through ritual secrecy. As a Bondo leader confided to me, "Schoolgirls are now reluctant to go into Bondo because they now have books that tell them everything that we in Bondo know—for example, biology books." Somehow it seems, though (as a reading of Margai's 1965 textbook suggests), that the traditional and Western sources are not quite compatible; that

Bondo knowledge of the body inculcates something of fuller meaning, an ecology of the body in a cosmological context.

The awareness of the body as demonstrated by Temne women, and the compatible association of their functions with those of other natural phenomena effected through ritual, seem to allow them to control their bodies' functions in an extraordinary way. Because of the greater social cohesion and, apparently, the uniformity of physiological function, Temne women are open to greater behavioral options and less vulnerable to the notion of physiological destiny from which Western women are struggling to free themselves. Much of the credit for this must go to Bondo; for while it is clear that Temne women are bound by custom to the priorities and prerogatives of their husbands, who are often quite demanding, a woman's allegiance to Bondo—that is, to her fellow women—is equally if not more binding in that, unlike marriage ritual (which is minimal), Bondo ritual involves a most sacred vow on the very life of the member. It is through Bondo ritual that the woman is bound to other women and that she receives her validity as woman in a universal sense. Bondo ritual may not be contravened by any man in Temne society—not even the chief—during the time that it is in control of village life, and any man who attempted to do so would be severely punished in a show of authority by the organization of women.

Just as Bondo is the patron of ritual and the arts, it is also the institution that regulates the female body. Bondo practice indicates that the body is more than a machine that functions independently according to invariable scientific principles. The body, because it functions paradigmatically with the principles of the universe as the Temne understand them, may be manipulated through ritual devices, just as the Temne universe may, according to cultural needs. In ritual dance the body is the medium of the spiritual universe and a tool of the artistic conception. Just as the body is used as a microcosm of the universe, and a tool of the arts that reflect it, so it is also a cultural artifact, a functional effect of cosmological thought.

10

Menstrual Synchrony and the Australian Ranbow Snake

Chris Knight

Over much of Aboriginal Australia men exercise ritual power through ceremonies (stated in myths once to have been the prerogative of women) in which they symbolically "menstruate" and "give birth." The resultant power is conceptualized as a rainbowlike snake, which is said to be the source of life and which "swallows" humans and then "regurgitates" them, now "reborn." This chapter discusses examples of such rituals and beliefs. It suggests that Australian Aboriginal culture in certain regions exhibits a phenomenon known in Western medical science as "menstrual synchrony," and that such synchrony has been conceptualized traditionally as "like a rainbow" and "like a snake." It is shown that Australian menstrual synchrony is also conceptualized as "like a Mother" and "like a womb." The chapter culminates in a hypothesis that links the origin of the Rainbow Snake ritual complex with menstrual synchrony. In a coda to the chapter I present some comparative evidence from ancient Greece, the ancient Near East, Western Europe, and East Asia which suggests speculatively a possible parallel to the model of linked menstrual synchrony and snake/dragon symbolism as offered in the chapter.

The discussion in this chapter forms part of a wider argument (see Knight 1983, 1984, 1985, 1986) that menstrual synchrony was once a basic experience of many of the world's women and a source of female power in society. When for various reasons menstrual synchrony in traditional cultures broke down, its formal structures may have been preserved ritually by men, with secret initiation rites (which included men ritually "menstruating" together) and male-controlled versions of the Rainbow Snake being among the results.

MENSTRUAL SYNCHRONY IN ABORIGINAL AUSTRALIA

Direct evidence of menstrual synchrony in Aboriginal Australia is scattered and sparse. We have no report comparable with, for example, Shostak's (1983:68) note on the !Kung, who "believe . . . that if a woman sees traces of menstrual blood on another woman's leg or even is told that another woman has started her period, *she* will begin menstruating as well." Nor is there an Australian counterpart to the recent reconstruction of menstrual norms among the California Yurok, among whom it has been hypothesized that in some descent groups "all of a household's fertile women who were not pregnant menstruated at the same time" (Buckley, this volume; also see Lamp, this volume). The !Kung and Yurok reports, however, are recent; in both cases the ethnographers were aware of the recent medical literature documenting menstrual synchrony among closely associated women (Burley 1979; Graham and McGrew 1980; Kiltie 1982; McClintock 1971; Quadagno et al. 1981; Russell, Switz and Thompson 1980). What indirect evidence we do have for Australian menstrual synchrony, from both early and relatively recent reports (see later discussion), was gathered at a time when menstrual synchrony was not acknowledged as a concept by social anthropologists in the field.

Yet enough exists even in the published record to indicate that Aboriginal culture acknowledged menstrual synchrony long before McClintock (1971) first documented it for Western science. Direct evidence appears in four domains:

(a) cat's cradle string figures and an associated myth of two sisters, called the Wawilak [= Wauwalak, Wauwelak, etc.] Sisters;

(b) certain other versions of the Wawilak Sisters myth;

(c) images of apparently menstruating dancing women from the Pilbara region of Western Australia;

(d) mythological images of collective menstruation from the Central Australian Aranda.

Scattered items of additional mythological evidence exist (see, for example, later descriptions in this chapter). Indirect evidence is more abundant but requires the reader's acceptance of a theoretical interpretation of male ritual and its associated mythology.

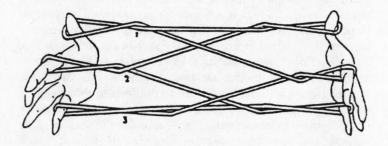

Fig. 10.1. String figure from Yirrkalla, northeast Arnhem Land.
"Menstrual blood of three women."
(From McCarthy 1960:466, Fig. 63.)

Among the Yolngu of northeast Arnhem Land (formerly known as the Murngin), menstrual synchrony is an acknowledged, ritually potent possibility. For example, at Yirrkalla, women traditionally made cats' cradles that were said to represent, among other things, "menstrual blood of three women" (McCarthy 1960:466; see figure 10.1). "The women," writes McCarthy (1960:424), "make their figures amongst themselves, and not in front of the men, particularly the old men, as a rule. The men walk past and do not look because the game belongs to the women's sphere of life." A woman may not make such figures with her husband. "Menstrual blood of three women" is not reported as a subject more frequent than topics such as "three vulvas," "birth of a baby" and many others (McCarthy 1960:419). However, the theoretically possible male counterparts of these ("three men urinating," "three penises," etc.) are not listed as subjects; moreover menstrual synchrony is stressed in the string figure origin myth: "String was first made by the two Wawilak sisters at Mudawa, near Buckingham Bay. They saw a lot of honey, about which they made a string loop." Later the elder sister made a figure of the yams in her sister's hands: "She then looked inside the latter's vagina and made another string figure." Later still, "The sisters sat down, looking at each other, with their feet out and legs apart, and both menstruated. Each one made a loop of the other one's menstrual blood, after which they put the string loops around their necks." They were subsequently swallowed by "a Snake" (McCarthy 1960:426).

Some of the remaining direct evidence for Aboriginal menstrual synchrony will now be surveyed. R. Berndt's (1951:22) version of the Wawilak myth states that ritual dancing was used by two "incestuous" women to synchronize their blood flows. With one sister already shedding quantitites of afterbirth blood, the other began to dance: "She moved her body gracefully, shuffling her feet, swaying her body from side to side, and holding in her hands feathered string from which she made cats-cradles as she danced." This, then, was a cat's cradle ritual of the "secret" kind noted by McCarthy (1960) among living Yolngu women. It was also a puberty celebration—in the words of the mythical younger sister, "a very happy time, for this is my first menstruation" (R. Berndt 1951:27). The younger sister danced on, "and as she swayed from side to side the intensive activity caused her menstruation to begin" (Berndt 1951:22–23). Blood from both women was now flowing simultaneously, and it was precisely at this moment that "the Snake" also flowed from its own womblike "waterhole" and coiled around the Two Sisters and their child. "There is the suggestion," comments Berndt (1951: 22 n.), "that the snake found the blood attractive." Certainly it is a noticeable feature of the myth in all its versions that blood must be flowing if "the Snake" is to appear; *where there is no blood, there is no Snake.*

Rock engravings from the Pilbara region of Australia include images of dancing pairs of women "suggesting the sisters in some Aboriginal mythologies" (B. Wright 1968: figures 99–115). Various of Wright's (1968) figures may show menstruating women (e.g., figs. 85, 88), two of them dancing together (fig. 112). One drawing (fig. 383) depicts dancers beneath an arc (rainbow?) and beside what may be a snake. Wright's figure 100 more clearly shows two figures with a snake, and figure 845 is reminiscent of the scene in which the two Wawilak Sisters "sat down . . . and both menstruated" (McCarthy 1960:426). If the parallel is valid, this image depicts two women conjoined by the same menstrual flow. Figure 105 again seems to show women linked by streams of their own blood, and figure 648 seems to connote cyclicity in the form of a snake. (We regret that the Wright figures were not available for publication in the present volume.—Eds.)

In western Arnhem Land women knew how to bring on their menstrual flows, if late in arriving, by "steaming, massage or violent exercise" (Berndt and Berndt 1951:45). We may speculate that dancing might have been the mythologically sanctioned form of "violent exercise" used to bring on the flow. Although there is little direct evidence for this, other regions of Australia repeat the notion as a mythological theme. Among the Aranda, for example, deposits of red ochre "blood" were formed by the mythical Unthippa women: their sexual organs dropped out from exhaustion, caused by their uninterrupted dancing over the spots where the ochre now lies (Spencer and Gillen 1927, 1:345).

Synchronous feminine bleeding appears in other Aranda myths. At a point along the Finke River is a traditionally used red ochre pit. At this spot two kangaroo women "caused blood to flow from the vulva in large quantities, and so formed the deposit of red ochre." Traveling away westward, "they did the same thing in other places" (Spencer and Gillen 1899:463–464). In Aboriginal Australia (Flood 1983:46, 238) red ochre was a much-used symbol of ritual power.[1]

In many Aranda myths women who are referred to as *alknarintja* are recognized by the fact that they are constantly decorating themselves with red ochre, are associated with water, and are "frequently represented as menstruating copiously" (Róheim 1974:150). The *alknarintja* women of Aranda songs

> . . . cut their breasts.
> On their breasts they make scars.
> They slap their thighs . . .
> They are menstruating.
> Their flanks are wet with blood.
> They talk to each other.
> They make a bull-roarer . . .
> They are menstruating.
> The blood is perpetually flowing. (Róheim 1974:138–139)

Such women possess bull-roarers and other symbols of power, and have solidarity—evoked in one song through the image of a clump of bushes "so thick and so pressed against each other that they cannot move separately" (Róheim 1974:144).

Indirect evidence such as this lends strong support to widespread menstrual synchrony among Aboriginal women of Australia. In the next section I consider the phenomenon of mythological snake women and rainbow snakes and explore their relationships to menstruous women.

AUSTRALIAN SNAKE WOMEN AND RAINBOW SNAKES

The Alawa Aborigines of western-central Arnhem Land say that certain mythic females, called "Mungamunga girls," when they go into the water, become merged in the corporate identity of their "mother," the "Kadjari." ("Kadjari" and "Kunapipi" are alternative names for this mother figure.) This awe-inspiring woman emerges from the water: she "comes out as one person, but as she stands on the dry land she is manifested as a Kadjari with a group of Mungamunga girls" (R. Berndt 1951:189–190).

The Mungamunga girls, when diving into the water, may be called Kilji:ringkiljiring. When the Wawilak Sisters have been swallowed by a Snake in a waterhole (see earlier) they change their names to Ka'lerika'lering—a name derived from the Ma:ra term (the Ma:ra are neighbors of the Alawa). "This would suggest," as R. Berndt (1951:173) comments, "that the Mungamunga and Wauwalak are identical." Ka'lerika'lering means "having been swallowed" (R. Berndt 1951:35). The sisters now "belong to the Kunapipi side—the side of the great ancestral "Mother." Becoming "at one" with "the Mother" in the water, whose all-swallowing uterus is the "inside" of "the Snake" (R. Berndt 1951:32, 43, 54), and becoming "at one" with "the Snake" in its waterhole therefore appear to be different ways of saying the same thing. This is confirmed by the fact that synchronous menstruation is practiced by the Mungamunga girls, too. In one song from the Ma:ra, a man called Bananggala "comes over and wants to copulate with the Mungamunga, but they are menstruating. They each say to him, 'I've got blood: you wait for a while'" (R. Berndt 1951:164). Another song from the same area concerns two men who encounter a group of Mungamunga girls by a lagoon: "No sooner do they seize a Mungamunga and put her on the ground, ready for coitus, than she slides away, jumps up and runs down to the lagoon, and dives into its water; then she emerges and joins the rest" (R. Berndt 1951:174). These women, then, have two ways of avoiding sex with a man: diving into the water, and menstruating. It seems that whether they are menstruating, diving into water, becoming submerged in the identity of a mother figure, or being "swallowed" by a snake, women are repudiating heterosexual intercourse and returning into a symbolic womb instead.

The mythology of western and northern Australia focuses centrally upon "swallowing" episodes of this kind. A Yolngu myth ends by describing how two sisters "decided to go into the waterhole and become a rainbow." It is explained: "They wanted to be a snake, like the rainbow, when she is standing up in the waterhole and makes lightning" (Groger-Wurm 1973:120). These sisters, then, change their form into that of a rainbow snake, just as the Wawilak Sisters change their names to Having Been Swallowed and the Mungamunga girls submerge their separate identities into the corporate one of "the Mother/Snake." The positive attitude of the women who "wanted to be a snake" is significant. The women *desired* to lose their separateness in the formation of a larger whole. There is no evidence to suggest that they would have welcomed the arrival of a monster slayer to "rescue" them from this fate (see the Coda).

Robinson (1966:61–66) provides a dramatic Murinbata story that is worth dwelling on at some length. It is reminiscent of myths from other parts of the world concerning a conflict between a winged snake or "dragon" and a male hero for the hand of a woman—except that the dragon (in the form of the rainbow snake) wins.[2] The rainbow snake Kunmanggur was in the water with a number of water-women or "Murinbungo." A man called Ngalmin approached and tried to catch one; at first they had been lying along the riverbank in the sunlight, but they saw him coming and "ran and jumped into the water." Ngalmin went away, disguised himself in mud, approached again and succeeded in seizing a young woman. He went off with her, camping at various places but always carefully avoiding "any big water." The woman kept asking for water, but Ngalmin insisted on keeping to dry places. Eventually she went off, looking for water on her own, and found a billabong (pool), where she drank:

> And when she drank, all the Murinbungo, the water-lubras, rose up out of the billabong. They had long streaming hair and they called out to her: "O, sister, sister, where have you been? We cried for you. Come back to us, sister." The water-lubras reached out their arms to her. They pulled her down to them into the water.

When Ngalmin discovered his loss he cried, cut his head, and lost all interest in life. He returned to the billabong and tried to recover his wife, but she resisted and the rainbow snake frightened him away. Again he attempted life without her but could not stop pining and crying. He returned to the water for a final time, saw his woman lying in the water and cut his head with a stone. He called out to the rainbow snake:

"You have to give me your child. I cut myself. You see this blood belonging to me? You have to be sorry for me." The rainbow snake just lay still, watching Ngalmin; the girl did not move despite the man's pleas. At last Ngalmin jumped into the water to catch a fleeing woman. Kunmanggur the rainbow snake lashed out from the water, grabbed Ngalmin, crushed and drowned him.

This, then, is a dragon-slaying myth in reverse. The heroine wants to stay with her dragon protector; it is her would-be suitor who is killed. Another myth—from the Kimberleys—makes clear that to try to detach a woman from "the Snake" is to attempt to sever bonds symbolized not only by water but above all by the presence of *blood*:

> A man called Purra was looking for a wife. One day he was crossing a creek when he noticed that its water was red. "Look," he said, "a girl must be around here. She is at the time of the passing of blood and went into the water. That is why the creek is red." He followed the water right up to its source. There he found a girl. Her lower half was in the water, but the rest of her was lying on the bank. "She is Tira's [the rainbow snake's] daughter," Purra said to himself. He took the girl, "but he knew that her father, the serpent, would be after him." He tried to run away but the Serpent followed. Purra kept lighting fires to keep the Serpent away, but one day "the big rain came"; it extinguished Purra's fire-stick and caused a flood into which Purra's wife disappeared. (Adapted from Bozic and Marshall 1972:121–123)

This myth eloquently links the notion of being wet or in the rains with a woman's menstrual state and consequent non-availability as a wife. At the same time, it emphasizes that to be "wet" and menstruating is to be under the guardianship of the serpent.

These are consistent mythological equations and themes. The great snake of the Wawilak myth "swallows" the incestuous sisters as they shed blood into a pool (R. Berndt 1951:23; Warner 1957:254). The Yolngu say that not so long ago a man took his two wives in a canoe for a trip from one island to another. One of them was menstruating. When they had gone for a short time, Yurlunggur the rainbow snake "smelt the unclean odour, came out of the subterranean depths, and swallowed them all" (Warner 1957:76). In western Arnhem Land among the Gunwinggu a menstruating woman should avoid associating with other women around waterholes or streams; she should stay in seclusion with a fire burning "to keep the Rainbow away" (C. Berndt and R. Berndt 1970:180). In Western Australia the Wagamansnake, Djagwut,

> lives in deep springs, rivers and billabongs. His spit is the "secondary" or "high" rainbow. He is the source of spirit-children and the protector of human life. He is especially dangerous to menstruating women, being able to smell them from afar (Stanner 1966:87).

Von Brandenstein (1982:58) suggests that "Muit" and similar names for the rainbow snake in western and northern parts of the continent derive from a Kariera root meaning "blood & red & multi-coloured & irridescent." When Yolngu neophytes are shown "the Snake" for the first time, it is in the form of two immense white "Muit emblems" consisting of padded poles "with the rock pythons" painted in blood on the white surfaces gleaming in the light of the many fires" (Warner 1957:304). "The Snake," then, may appear as a line of blood. The Wikmungkan of Cape York confirm this: the snake "is believed to be responsible for women menstruating" (McKnight 1975:95); seeing the red band in a rainbow, people say, "'Taipan the-rainbow-snake-has-a-'sore inside' i.e. has her menstrual pains" (McConnel 1936, 2:103). The rainbow's red band, the "snake," and the menstrual flow are, then, explicitly one and the same.

THE "SNAKE" IN AUSTRALIA

Marshack (1977:286), referring to prehistorians' difficulties in interpreting Upper Paleolithic "serpentine"/"meander" designs, notes that "what we 'see' or recognise conceptually are usually 'units' and 'patterns' in terms of our culture, units and patterns which are relevant to us in terms of equations derived from our West European training." It is central to the project of social and symbolic anthropology to escape from ethnocentrism of this kind, yet it is not certain how far we have succeeded.

Radcliffe-Brown (1930:342) argued that the rainbow snake "represents the element of water." On the basis of native statements that "the Snake" is embodied in seasonal wet/dry alternations, Warner (1957:378) concluded that it is "a weather-symbol." On the basis of other native statements that "the Snake" is identified with the production of babies, R. Berndt (1951:12–13, 31) argued that it symbolizes "the Penis," being the counterpart of the "All-Mother," who symbolizes "the uterus." For Elkin (1951:9), "no deep analysis is needed to show that the mythical Snake is a sexual symbol." For Schmidt (1953:909, quoted by Maddock 1978a:2), the creature represents "the male element (membrum virile)," or "the male idea of the penis." For Triebels (1958:129–130, cited by Maddock 1978a:2), in its snake aspect it symbolizes the spirally formed cosmic power that lay in the world's virgin waters, while as rainbow it is an emanation of the snake.

Marshack's (1977:286) note of caution is appropriate here. Snake symbolism in Australia, as elsewhere, is associated with the innermost mysteries of secret rites and cults. Because the "meaning" of the symbols is that given by these religious systems themselves, it is hardly likely to consist of a mental or physical reality—"water," "weather," "penis," or "male idea of penis"—immediately recognizable or familiar to those whose belief system is rooted in the scientific rationalism of Western culture. Maddock (1974:121) suggests "that what is called the Rainbow Serpent is but a visually striking image of force or vitality, a conception that cannot adequately be given figurative expression." As evidence he cites the Dalabon term *bolung*, which signifies not only "rainbow," "snake," and "the mother of us all" but also "ambiguity in form, creativity, power and time long past" (1974:122–123). The reality in mind "cannot be more than partially and misleadingly conveyed in visual and psychological images like rainbow or snake or mother." In fact, Maddock concludes, no Western concept or expression can hope to convey the notion of what is meant.

The rainbow snake is paradoxical to the core. As Yurlunggur of the Yolngu, he "is both in the heavens . . . and in the subterranean depths" (Warner 1957:386). "He is the highest in the sky and the deepest in the well" (1957:255 n.). Although "he" may be male, he is both "man and woman" (p. 383). Likewise the rainbow snake of the Murinbata, Kunmanggur, is bisexual: "Even those who asserted the maleness of Kunmanggur said that he had large breasts, like a woman's" (Stanner 1966:96). "It is as though paradox and antinomy were the marrow in the story's bones," comments Stanner (1966:100) on the basic Kunmanggur myth. Eliade (1973:115) writes that the rainbow snake is able to relate "to women's mysteries, to sex and blood and after-death existence" because "his structure has permitted the Rainbow Serpent to unite the opposites."

What "the Snake" is cannot be simply stated. I propose that an understanding of it may presuppose an understanding of the rhythmic core and structural basis of human culture as such. The meaning of the snake refers us to the logic of Aboriginal Australian culture—and perhaps of all human culture, if we are to trace it to its source; consequently to understand the one may be to fathom the genesis of the other (see Knight 1986). In any event, we need an explanation of the fact that the rainbow serpent "is not confined in Australia to any particular ethnological province, but is very widespread and may very possibly be practically universal," forming "a characteristic of Australian culture as a whole" (Radcliffe-Brown 1926:24). Indeed, on archaeological grounds, Flood (1983:134) speculates that the snake complex in northern Australia may represent "the longest continuing religious belief documented in the world," stretching back seven or nine thousand years.

For Maddock (1978a:1), rainbows, snakes, sisters, and related images are "a host of fleeting forms in and through which a fundamental conception of the world is expressed." As a first approach to an understanding of the Dalabon term for rainbow snake, *bolung*, he suggests that we should "lay stress on the cyclicity embedded in the concept and . . . draw attention to the role of cyclical thinking in Aboriginal thought generally" (1978b:115). Why should snakes and rainbows be used to conceptualize the force behind the changing of the seasons, the movements of the celestial bodies, the breeding times of animals and plants, and the cycles of life, death, and afterlife? "The curvilinear imagery of snakes and rainbows," Maddock (1978b:115) answers, "might be considered apt to express the abstract notion of cyclicity."

In accordance with Marshack's (1985:141–142) interpretations of serpentine symbolism cross-culturally, let us take it, then, that "the Snake" in one of its aspects connotes *cyclical time*. It would then be an Australian version of "the serpent of time, of process and continuity, the serpent of self-birth and origins, the serpent of death, birth, and rebirth, the cosmic serpent, the serpent of such processes as water, rain, and lightning, the *ouroboros* that bites its own tail in perpetuity, the guilloche serpent of endless continuity and turns" (Marshack 1985:142). "The Snake," like seasonal or any other form of cyclicity, would in this aspect express the logic of alternation, metamorphosis, and change, perpetually incorporating within itself its own opposite: it would be wet season *and* dry, the highest *and* the lowest, male *and* female, and so on.

THE HYPOTHESIS: MENSTRUAL
SYNCHRONY AS "SNAKE"

Why were the two Wawilak Sisters "swallowed" by "a Snake"? Were they swallowed by "cyclical time"? I suggest that in a sense they were. It will be remembered that in Mc-Carthy's (1960:426) version of the Wawilak myth, the sisters sat down face to face "and both menstruated." They then (*a*) *encircled* each other's necks with "loops" of "menstrual blood" and (*b*) were *swallowed* by "a Snake." Cyclical time seized ("encircled") the Wawilak Sisters in the form of their own menstrual flows. Being "encircled" by blood and being "swallowed" by a snake were not two separate experiences but are alternative metaphors for expressing the same experience.

What, then, is the Snake? On the basis of the evidence so far, the following hypothesis suggests itself.

The Snake is in the first instance a ritual phenomenon. In one of its aspects it is an *all-female* ritual presence (the opposite aspect is male and is discussed later). As female, I suggest, it is the ritual synchronization of women's reproductive cycles and menstrual and/or afterbirth flows. It is a way of describing women in such close intimacy that they feel as if they are "one flesh," "one blood"—or "one Mother." As the Aranda song put it, they resemble a clump of bushes "so thick and so pressed against each other that they cannot move separately." With their blood flows conjoining, they form a single flow or stream—its elements as harmoniously conjoined and as inseparable as those of a snake. The Two Sisters who in the myths "turn into a rainbow" or are "swallowed by a Snake" are in reality entering the "wet" phase of the menstrual cycle and becoming engulfed in their own blood-derived unity with each other. Like water-women diving into a river, they are being "swallowed up" in a collective medium that transcends the boundaries of each. Whenever an out-of-phase woman is brought back into synchrony, it is as if her "water-sisters" were claiming her back into their realm (see earlier discussion). These women are indeed "like a snake," for no creature on earth more closely resembles a river or flow, or can coil itself up into so many repeated cycles. And women are indeed "like a rainbow"—because, given the ubiquity of menstrual seclusion rules in Australia, the blood flow carries them as if from world to world. They move from dryness to wet, and also from marital life to the world of seclusion, just as the rainbow moves cyclically between sunshine and rain, dry season and wet, earth and sky.

TESTING THE HYPOTHESIS

To be of value a hypothesis should make specific predictions and be testable. It should be possible to conceive of types of evidence that, if verified in the ethnographic record, would disprove the hypothesis. The model should also prove fruitful as a research guide, enabling us to seek out evidence that the hypothesis would predict but that had not been "seen" before.

If the hypothesis is correct, we could expect that everything that can be said of menstrual synchrony would be equally true of the (rainbow) snake. We may expect synchronized women to be termed "snake women," with half of their being in a "wet" phase or element and half in the "dry." Meanwhile, so-called snakes would turn out to be human mothers. They should menstruate, give birth to human offspring, and copulate with human partners. Assuming that menstrual blood is thought of as "wet" rather than "dry," menstrual seclusion should be depictable as a snake's drawing of women into a watery world. In terms of detailed mythological imagery, the "swallowing" episodes would be associated with pools, streams, marshes, rains, storms, wet season, and so on, while the "regurgitations" would be linked with dryness (fire, dry earth, sun, dry season, etc.). A "dry" swallowing and a "wet" regurgitation would disprove the hypothesis. Menstrual seclusion in the real world is a withdrawal from exogamous sex into "one's own blood," so no union with a snake should have the characteristics of legitimate exogamous marriage. Snake marriage should be a union of blood with blood—that is, an intimacy comparable with the incestuous relationships of the Wawilak Sisters. A "correct" marriage with a snake would invalidate the hypothesis. Given that menstrual blood is taboo and is also reminiscent of the blood in meat (Warner 1957:278, McKnight 1975:85; compare Knight 1983:41–42), the snake should connote the sanctity of both women and animal flesh during the "raw" or menstrual state.

The exhaustive testing of these aspects of the hypothesis is beyond the scope of the present chapter (for further testing see Knight 1983, 1985). However, other predictions based upon the hypothesis seem already to have been validated in previous sections of this essay. Notably, if our hypothesis is correct, the Snake should be an immense blood-red cyclical phenomenon, analogous to the changing of the seasons, responsible for women's periodic "death" to marital life, embodying all opposite phases in itself and associated in the first instance with women, pregnancy, fertility, and "wet" things such as rain, storms, floods, and menstrual or other blood. It should prove hostile to marital or exogamous sex, "swallowing" women and their offspring into "incestuous" blood unity whenever and wherever blood was flowing. It should be "sacred," representing the "tabooed" state of game animals and women alike (compare Knight 1983:41–42). It should be incompatible with fire and cooking (as these destroy visible blood—Knight 1983:41–42; 1986). Although a great deal of this is substantiated by the available myths, there is a further probability not yet raised: the Snake should be a ritual entity beyond the power of men to usurp or control—except in the event that men were able to simulate menstruation and childbirth themselves.

THE SNAKE AS "PENIS" AND MALE POWER

Despite its being a "fantastically painful" operation (Gould 1969:112), subincision is practiced over an immense area of traditional Australia (fig. 10.2). The penis is cut along the underside, the incision reaching to the urethral canal; the organ then opens out wide. During rituals the wound is reopened to produce a flow of blood. The more sacred the ritual (as a general rule), the more bloody—and the more taboo it is to women.

In 1937 Ashley Montagu (1937:320–325) first put forward the theory that "subincision in the male was originally instituted in order to cause the male to resemble the female with respect to the occasional effusion of blood which is naturally characteristic of the female." He admitted that the idea "must appear fantastic" but provided ample supporting evidence. According to Róheim (1945:171), subincision ritual restrictions look "like a simple inversion of the menstruating taboo, the men saying: 'We are not allowed to see your bleeding so we shall not allow you to see ours.'" The Pitjandjara call the subincision hole a "penis womb" (Róheim 1945:164). Róheim (1945:171) notes further that subincision in general produces

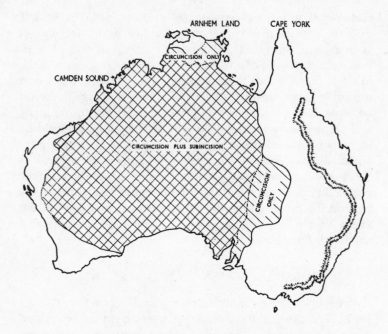

Fig. 10.2. Map showing distribution of subincision and circumcision
in Australia. (From Abbie 1969:Fig. 15.)

"a penis that is also a vagina," adding, in agreement with
earlier writers, that the bleeding men "are playing the role
of menstruating women." More recently, Berndt and Berndt
(1964:145) confirmed Montagu's original interpretation to this
effect.

If the operation is so painful, why do men do it? In keeping
with the view of cultural origins that informs this analysis
(Knight 1986), I suggest that culture begins with a tendency
toward menstrual synchrony; that this determines the symbolic language on the basis of which ritual power is expressed;
and that when—in certain regions or at certain epochs—the
synchrony breaks down, its formal structures are ritually preserved by men, whose tendencies toward dominance cannot
now so effectively be checked.

C. Berndt (1965:274) writes of menstruation as "a rite performed more or less automatically by women (although imitated artificially, in various regions, by men)." This chapter has suggested that it is the factor of synchrony that transforms the private experience of menstruation into the collective realm of "rite." In Aboriginal Australia men's "menstrual periods" are elaborately synchronized with each other, and there is evidence that the phasing was connected with the periodicity of the moon (Berndt and Berndt 1970:131, 133, 141; Maddock 1974:159; Warner 1957:296; compare Knight 1985, 1986). For example, Berndt and Berndt (1945:309–310) watched a male initiation rite in the Ooldea region of western south Australia, during which ten men simultaneously began puncturing their penis incisures:

> The blood was sprinkled on the thighs of the men, either by holding the penis at each side and letting it drip, or by moving so that the bleeding penis flopped from side to side, or upwards and downwards, the blood touching the lower buttocks and loins.

The Berndts (1945:308 n.) note that "the actual initiation was held during the period of the new moon."

Yolngu men, while not subincising, cut themselves to produce blood. The Wawilak myth tells of how men gained the necessary blood and dancing instructions from the Two Sisters, and this is how Warner (1957:278) presents an interpretation of the blood-letting phase of the corresponding Djungguan reenactment of the myth:

> *Native interpretation.*—The blood that runs from an incision and with which the dancers paint themselves and their emblems is something more than a man's blood—it is the menses of the old Wawilak women. I was told during a ceremony: "That blood we put all over those men is all the same as the blood that came from that old woman's vagina. It isn't the blood of those men any more because it has been sung over and made strong. The hole in the man's arm isn't that hole any more. It is all the same as the vagina of that old woman that had blood coming out of it."

Rituals of a similar kind are a condition of male ritual potency throughout Aboriginal Australia. To acquire ritual power a youth or man has always to "die" and "be reborn," and the symbolic language is that of pools and waterholes, wombs, blood, rainbows, and all-swallowing Mothers who are Snakes. Men not only "menstruate"; they are also the agents of their own kind's "rebirth," and they "give birth" by taking youths or boys into their collective "womb"—which may be a deep pit—and subsequently expelling ("regurgitating") them. The original womb is depicted to the uninitiated as having been a monstrous, cannibalistic Mother or Snake, always thirsty for blood. This "bad dragon"—usually associated with the evils of womankind—is said, however, to have been killed and replaced with a more benevolent male-controlled symbolic substitute that does not permanently kill those it "swallows" (Hiatt 1975).

In terms of the model presented in this chapter, it seems clear that the "bad dragon" is the menstrual synchrony and power of women; the "good" one, the male substitute. Male myths justify the usurpation of women's menstrual power by describing the female version in lurid terms as a cannibalistic monster from which humanity had to be rescued (Hiatt 1975).

Interestingly, however, these male myths are rich with ambivalence and a sense of tragedy at the loss of the original Mother/Snake. The Murinbata snake-woman Mutjingga, for example, had to be killed when she swallowed ten children alive; men cut open her belly and rescued the still-living victims, thus providing the model for contemporary male ritual rebirth (Stanner 1966:40–43). Men regard this tale as "a sorrowful story"; the Old Woman, they say, was once "truly human" and had "primal authority." With her death a disaster of almost incomprehensible dimensions had occurred. "The loss to man," say the Murinbata, "was irreparable." The symbolic substitutes for her are felt to be inadequate. "Because she died," they say, "men now have only the bull-roarer, which was made in order to take her place . . . stand for her and . . . be her emblem, symbol and sign" (Stanner 1966:43, 54, 56). The sound of the bull-roarers—heard across Australia at moments when ancestral blood is flowing—is, among the Ma:ra, explicitly thought to be the sound of the dying ogress's blood (R. Berndt 1951:150–151).

When Mutjingga swallowed the ten children, she took them down into the waters of a river (Stanner 1966:40–43). When the Wuradjeri medicine man wishes to acquire power from the water-dwelling rainbow snake (called, in this case, Wawi) he has to paint himself in red ochre, follow a rainbow to where it enters a pool, and dive down under the surface (Elkin 1977:87).

Countless other examples could be cited. In this chapter I have suggested that all such processes of immersion in water, all such intimate encounters with a Snake or Rainbow or Mother, are male replications of the female potentiality to conjoin, through menstrual synchrony, in a blood-union transcending the boundaries of the self. The Snake, as Aboriginal paintings from the Oenpelli region of Arnhem Land make clear (fig. 10.3), is a rhythmic line, a flow inseparably associated with the body of womankind. It is a symbol of periodicity—or of "the abstract notion of cyclicity" itself (Maddock 1978b:115). An implication is that the entire structure and language of ritual potency is derived by men from the opposite sex. As Yolngu men say in reenacting the myth of the two Wawilak Sisters,

> But really we have been stealing what belongs to them (the women), for it is mostly all women's business; and since it concerns them it belongs to them. Men have nothing to do really, except copulate, it belongs to the women. All that belonging to those Wuwalak, the baby, the blood, the yelling, their dancing, all that concerns the women; but every time we have to trick them. Women can't see what men are doing, although it really is their own business, but we can see their side. This is because all the Dreaming business came out of women—everything; only men take "picture" for that Julunggul [i.e., men make an artificial reproduction of the Snake]. In the beginning we had nothing, because men had been doing nothing; we took these things from women. (R. Berndt 1951:55)

To this Aboriginal analysis I add only that I am not suggesting that universal, or near-universal, patriarchy is caused by men's menstrual envy, resentment, or desire to appropriate

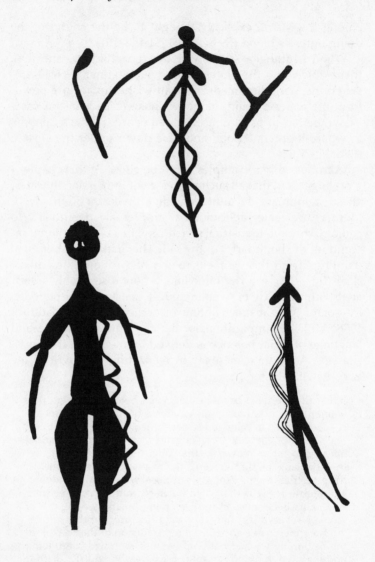

Fig. 10.3. Serpentine forms with women. Cave paintings from Oenpelli region, Arnhem Land. (From Mountford 1956:167, Fig. 49.)

women's menstrual synchrony or its associated power. What I have been trying to show is that the formal structures of men's rule in the Australian Aboriginal societies considered bear the stamp of feminine menstrual ritual.

CODA: SNAKE MOTHERS AND THE ORIGINS OF RITUAL POWER

"I will put enmity between thee and the woman," said God to the Serpent (Genesis 3:15), "and between thy seed and her seed; it shall bruise thy head and thou shalt bruise his heel."

Blacker (1978:113) has explored "the manner in which, in many parts of the world and particularly in the Far East, this commandment of God has been ignored. We find on the contrary a close and mysterious identification between serpents and women." Blacker is referring to the snake women of Asian folklore—creatures whose appearance is human until they are spied upon while in seclusion and discovered to be a snake. A Japanese version tells of a woman whose husband spied on her while she was giving birth. Within her parturition hut on the seashore, she had turned into a sea snake or dragon. Angry at having been discovered, she returned to the sea, leaving her baby behind. Her human sister then adopted the boy, married her "son" when he had come of age, and produced from this incestuous union the first imperial ruler of Japan (Daniels 1975:12).

Because structurally similar myths are to be found worldwide, and because they are particularly prominent in Aboriginal Australia, it is worth dwelling on their common features. The myths link (*a*) women in seclusion with (*b*) water, (*c*) incest, (*d*) snakes, and (*e*) the origins of ritual power or divine kingship. In Greek mythology Echidna, Delphyne, and Keto "are different names for the same monstrous snake woman or sea monster" (Fontenrose 1959:95–97). Echidna was half young woman, with bright eyes and fair cheeks, "and half snake, dwelling in the depths of the earth, eating raw meat." She was the "sister-wife" of the monstrous multicolored winged or feathered hundred-headed snake known as Typhon, who still rumbles beneath Mount Etna (Fontenrose 1959:73–74, 95–96). Under another name she was Skylla, a woman from the waist up and a fish from the waist down, described in the *Odyssey* as living in a cave opposite Etna and seizing and eating sailors as they passed through the straits of Messina (Fontenrose 1959:97). The Sumerian counterpart was the snake woman Tiamat, out of whose defeated body were created earth, sky, and the world we know (Fontenrose 1959:150).

Like the Sumerian Marduk, mythological divine kings and gods the world over are said to have acquired their power through a cosmic battle with the forces of evil or helpless femininity in association with a monstrous snake. The legend of St. George and the Dragon is, of course, a variation on the theme. Womankind, according to patriarchal ideology, stands in dire need of rescue from her original connection with sin in dragonlike or snakelike form (Frazer 1911, 2:155; Fontenrose 1959:469; Ingersoll 1928:194–195). Only once the evil has been slain is the world made safe for marriage as a sacred bond. Only then is the stable world order known today secured (compare Knight 1983).

A recurrent theme, however, is that the male hero, having slain the Dragon, usurps its extraordinary potencies for himself. A Japanese version illustrates this clearly:

> A man came to a house where all were weeping, to learn that the last of seven daughters was to be given to a seven-headed dragon, which yearly came to the seashore to claim a victim. The man assumed the girl's form, and induced the dragon to drink *sake* from seven pots. He then slew the drunken monster. From the end of its tail he took out a sword which is today the Mikado's state sword, and married the maiden himself. (Adapted from Ingersoll 1928:105)

Ingersoll (1928:148, 149) notes the dragon reputedly worn on the crest of King Arthur's helmet, and the dragons used as ensigns by Roman soldiers in their wars with the Britons; he also notes the red dragon as the current emblem of the Prince of Wales. The gold mask of Tutankhamen features a snake with two heads—one birdlike, the other that of a cobra—on the ruler's forehead (Daniel 1981: facing page 13).

It is beyond the scope of this chapter to detail the world's royal lineages whose power is symbolized by winged snakes or "dragons." It is worth noting, however, that the early emperors of China were born from a human woman's copulation with a dragon. "Such a stupendous affair," writes Schafer (1973:23), "occurred in the dawn of time when Shun's mother conceived after a visitation by a rainbow dragon." In China and Japan the emperor was termed "dragon-faced"; in view of the fatal consequences of seeing such a face, visitors granted an audience were suitably protected, hearing only a voice emanating from behind a bamboo screen (Ingersoll 1928:100).

"In China," writes Schafer (1973:28), "dragon essence is woman essence." But it should be appreciated that "the dragon" was not safe, sexually available femininity, but womankind in her ritually potent "wet" and "dangerous" phase when she was anything but "feminine." The dragon is always ferocious and therefore in a certain sense "male." "Masculine femininity" and "feminine masculinity" express the core of this creature's being. It was Frazer (1900, 3:204), following hints from Durkheim (1897), who first drew attention to a seemingly incongruous parallel that illustrates this point and with which this discussion may conclude. The divine kings of much of the ancient world were subjected to taboos that included two in particular: they were not to see the sun and not to touch the ground. "Now it is remarkable," writes Frazer (1900, 3:204), "that these two rules—not to touch the ground and not to see the sun—are observed either separately or conjointly by girls at puberty in many parts of the world." The dragon-empowered kings were treated as if they were "menstruating men" (compare Hogbin 1970), being subjected to seclusion rules uncannily like those imposed upon menstruating women throughout most of the traditional world.

Notes

1. INTRODUCTION

Acknowledgments. In writing this essay we have received valuable suggestions from many people. The following gave generous assistance in locating sources: Linda Coates (Medical Science Library), Paul Treichler (College of Medicine), Clark E. Cunningham and Lynne Mackin (Department of Anthropology), all at the University of Illinois at Urbana-Champaign; Catherine K. Levinson, Reference Librarian at the University of North Carolina at Greensboro; Mona Etienne (Yale University); and Judith Van Herik (Pennsylvania State University). In addition, Denise Lawrence and Vieda Skultans made important contributions to our review of menstruation literature. Professors Cunningham and Linda Klepinger, also of the Department of Anthropology at the University of Illinois, both offered very helpful critiques of this essay while it was in draft.

Portions of this introductory chapter were presented at a colloquium in the Department of Anthropology, University of North Carolina at Chapel Hill, and also to Professor Cunningham's Medical Anthropology seminar at the University of Illinois; we thank the faculty and students present at both of these presentations for their helpful responses.

1. This kind of danger is apparent, for example, both to Bagisu women in Uganda (La Fontaine 1972:164) and to American Blacks in Michigan (Snow and Johnson 1977:2739). In both cases if a woman's menstrual discharge, contained in a discarded tampon or pad, falls into the wrong hands, it may be used against the woman herself through sorcery that can render her sterile, according to informants. Here taboos regarding the disposal of menstrual blood seems to reflect a notion of women's vulnerability to social threats, rather than of women's threat to society.

2. There is a possibility that the reputed austerity of menstrual seclusion is, in some cases at least, a product of cultural nostalgia and guilt. In the old days, people seem to say, our grandmothers *really* followed the taboos, but we've gone downhill since the outsiders came. Like cannibalism (Arens 1979), rigid menstrual seclusion

often seems to be something practiced long ago, or by the folks over the next hill.

3. However, the vast majority of contemporary health and sex manuals that we consulted either make no mention of menstrual sex (e.g., Hongladarom, McCorkle, and Woods 1982) or, like Derbyshire's (1980:33), deem it "medically harmless." One contemporary physician does advise the use of condoms during menstrual sex, but this is to protect the woman's opened uterus from male-borne infection, rather than vice versa (Lauersen and Whitney 1983:92). Still other authors (e.g., Lanson 1984:190) suggest that sex during menstruation is of medical *benefit* to women suffering cramping and associated lower back or pelvic discomfort.

4. Though still observed in conservative Eastern orthodox churches, this taboo was abolished in the Roman Catholic Church by Pope Gregory the Great in a Papal bull of 597 (Wood 1981:713–714).

5. Kitahara (1982) and many other of the comparativists discussed here have based their research in the Human Relations Area Files (HRAF) and the *World Ethnographic Atlas*.

6. The Christian tradition is not entirely negative in its view of menstruation. Jesus, for example, is said to have cured a woman of the "plague" of "an issue of blood" that had lasted twelve years, making her "whole" (Mark 5:25–29). According to Mark, the incident occurred between Jesus's casting out of "unclean spirits" and "the devil" from the possessed (Mark 5:1–19), and his raising of the daughter of Jairus from death (Mark 5:23–24, 35–43). It is emphasized, however, that Jairus's daughter "was of the age of twelve years" (Mark 5:42), and the structural sense of the juxtaposition of the twelve years of dysmenorrhea, in the sick woman, and the girl's age—when coupled with other Judeo-Christian references to the age of women at menarche—is that Jesus restored the daughter of Jairus to life in the sense of full, fecund womanhood; that is, that "life" in this instance is equated positively with menarche (Jorunn Jacobsen Buckley, personal communication, 1984).

Ambivalence may well be embedded in the very way Westerners talk about menstruation. In an early study of menstrual euphemisms in several European languages, Joffe found that such expressions fall into five general categories of metaphor: time, color, visitors, other persons, and disabilities (1948:184). Terence Hays (n.d.) is currently researching this subject, and when combined with Joffe's work, Hays's preliminary findings make it clear that in English and other European languages women express diverse perceptions of their own menstrual periods though euphemisms.

7. The notion of shared substances is not only pertinent to the analysis of some menstrual customs, such as joint husband/wife restrictions and rituals, but also to other types of beliefs regarding

menstruation. The ideology that menstrual blood is inherited from the mother is widespread, especially in matrilineal societies. Mary Douglas (1969) and Wyatt MacGaffey (1969), however, have both pointed out that it is not just menstrual blood that is thought to be so inherited but veinous blood as well, and that such beliefs are not restricted to matrilineal societies. Here the topic of shared substance—an underinvestigated one, we think—connects with a wide variety of ideas regarding the composition of fetuses, examined below.

8. Ford (1945:44–46) gives nine examples of societies that hold the fetus to be composed wholly or in part from menstrual blood. Richards (1950:222–223) and M. Wilson (1957:299) both propose that such a view is found in societies in which descent is reckoned matrilineally. But in accord with Douglas and MacGaffey (see note 7), we do find evidence of this notion being associated with patrilineal descent as well, as it is among the Azande of the Sudan, the Kwoma of New Guinea, and the Lepcha of Tibet and Mongolia (Ford 1945:44).

9. Conversely, doctors of the medieval Christian Church, following Aristotle, specified the week following cessation of the menstrual flow as women's most fertile time (Wood 1981:716–717).

10. For example, before contact with Euro-Americans, Yurok women had an extremely restricted sexual life and an intentionally low rate of pregnancy (Erikson 1943). Therefore menstruation among these women could not have been as strongly suppressed by pregnancy and lactation as among Harrell's rural Taiwanese or Winslow's Sri Lankan women (1980).

2. MENSTRUAL COSMOLOGY AMONG THE BENG OF IVORY COAST

Acknowledgments. The field research upon which this chapter is based was conducted from September 1979 to December 1980 and from June to August 1985. The first trip was supported by the U.S. Social Science Research Council; the second trip was supported by the United States Information Agency and by the University of Illinois (Center for African Studies; Research Board; and International Programs and Studies). My thanks for the generous support of all these bodies are hereby gratefully acknowledged. I am appreciative to my Beng friend and main informant, A, who fearlessly provided the majority of the data presented in this paper. I would also like to thank the following readers, who all gave interesting and helpful comments, only some of which could be incorporated into the chapter: Thomas Buckley, J. Christopher Crocker, Frederick H. Damon, Robbie Davis-Floyd, Mona Etienne, Irving Goldman, Philip Graham, J. David Sapir, Roy Wagner, and James Wilkerson.

The first version of this article under the title "Pregnant Sex, Menstrual Sex and the Cuisine of Menstruation: The Beng Case," was presented at the twenty-second Annual Meeting of the Northeastern Anthropological Association in Princeton, New Jersey (March 1982), where it was the winner of the Graduate Student Paper Competition. Another version appeared in *Africa*, vol. 52 (1982). The current chapter represents a revision of the latter, based on field research in summer 1985.

1. At least two Beng villages have two or three named Earths associated with their territory, and one of these Earths is considered to be spiritually "stronger" than the other(s). It is not clear to me whether all Beng villages have such a distinction. Without such a "strong" Earth, the third taboo—against men eating food cooked by menstruating women—might be irrelevant.

2. The Beng word *zozoa* may be translated as "polluted" in some circumstances. It has a wide spectrum of meanings, ranging from "broken" (as in a typewriter) to "all messed up" (as the situation in a serious dispute) to, finally, "polluted" (in the religious sense, as when the Earth is transgressed against by human sins).

In contrast, there is no Beng word for "polluting," and the transitive verb "to pollute" (*zozo*) does not permit intransitive constructions; one can say "she pollutes the Earth" (*o ba zozo*) but not "she is polluting" or "she pollutes" (* *o zozo*). I believe that this linguistic fact may reflect a wider theme in Beng culture (compare Gottlieb forthcoming) that substances are not polluting in themselves but only when they come into contact with certain other substances. Certainly this is the case for menstrual blood, as I shall be suggesting in this chapter (see Gottlieb forthcoming). As originally used by Douglas (e.g., 1966), the English word "polluting" implied a wide range of moral states, but it has since taken on a popular meaning (possibly influenced by the environmental movement) with only pejorative connotations. On one level this essay is a plea for a return to the potentially multivocal meaning of "pollution": things out of place (see part I of this volume).

3. If the funeral or wedding were in another village, however, a menstruating woman at the heaviest part of her period would attend only if she had a hostess in that village in whose bathhouse she could wash out her menstrual cloth at noontime.

4. If the wife whose "turn" it is to sleep with the shared husband happens to be menstruating and her husband does not mind not making love that night because of the blood, he will sleep with her. If he wants to make love that night he will sleep with his co-wife out of turn or, more rarely, he might make love with the menstruating wife.

5. I believe that the model of menstruation presented in this article, to the extent that it is a consciously realized one, is shared

by Beng men and women. Individual men did not view menstrual blood as disgusting. Indeed, I frequently discussed the topic of menstruation with several male friends of all ages, none of whom evinced disgust or even embarrassment. Whether or not the ideology of fertility that lies behind this behavior is widely known—and it may well be fairly esoteric, articulable only by Masters of the Earth and other intellectuals—the daily attitudes that accompany it certainly seem to be held virtually universally.

6. The wife's maternal half brother died suddenly after developing a headache and fainting. Two or three days after his death, one of this man's daughters died of chicken pox. About a month later the wife's matrilateral parallel-cousin, who was nine months pregnant, developed heart pains and died the same day without having gone into labor; the couple's own daughter died of a snakebite in the forest. The husband's sister's daughter lost a great deal of weight and died, and the house of the husband's patrilateral cross-cousin caught fire and all the possessions inside, including his wives' food stores and kitchen implements as well as the house itself, were ruined.

7. The cost of a cow is $150 to $300. It is bought by the guilty man or, if he is young and unmarried, by his father; in either case his own matriclan members contribute. The average yearly income of a Beng nuclear family nowadays ranges from $500 to $1,000.

My informant didn't know what the king would do with the couple's polluted clothes, but in any case the intent is clear: separate the guilty man and woman from the pollution to cleanse them as well as the Earth. The fact that it is the king who is given the clothes serves to affirm his ultimate "ownership" of the Earth. The ritual itself can suggest various interpretations. One, which fits with a theme that is common in Beng symbolism, is the principle that "two negatives equal a positive": in this case the sin of sex in the forest is expiated by a repetition of that act.

8. Two examples can be offered of the parallelism between the fertility of fields and of humans. The first concerns hot/cold symbolism. Cold is seen as an attribute of both forms of fertility and a beneficial quality. In contrast, heat is seen as inimical to fertility in both women and crops. Regarding field fertility, it is said that cool dew is good for the crops, as are cool weather in general and the occasional hail (which is seen as cool) that falls at the beginning of the growing season. Parallel examples regarding women's fertility are given below. On another level, it may be noted that the cutting-progeny of rootstock crops—for example, the yams that grow from the planted tuber—are called "children" (*lɛŋ*).

9. It is said that the Earth came before the Sky and for this reason, as in other areas of Beng life in which seniority rules, the Earth in some contexts has priority over the Sky. (The word *eci* refers to the

Sky, but Beng who speak French often translate it as *Dieu*, or "God." Because the Earth in some senses "rules" the Sky, I am not convinced that "God" is an accurate translation of *eci*.) My informants pointed out, however, that the boundaries of the Earth and the Sky are uncertain; the two are "friends" (*gwe*) and thus look out for each other's interests. In keeping with this, when the Earth is polluted, the Sky withholds rain to punish humans and protect its "friend."

10. It is useful to compare briefly the Beng treatment of menstruation with that of the Baule, the Bengs' immediate neighbors to the west and south. Although they belong to different language groups (Beng to the Mande family, Baule to the Akan family), Beng nevertheless claim that many of their social forms are similar or identical to those of the Baule. In this instance, however, there are profound differences. The cult of the Earth is not nearly as developed among the Baule as it is among the Beng, and many Baule groups, especially the southern Baule, have no Master of the Earth positions. Correspondingly, menstruating Baule women, at least in recent times, are not prohibited from working in the forest (Mona Etienne, personal communication). They are forbidden all sexual contact with any men, but this is because of spirits and cults with which men are associated and not because of any violation (direct or indirect) of the Earth (Etienne 1981:29, n. 7). This accords with the observation that in general Baule cosmology human actions and misfortunes are tied or attributed to spirits far more than they are to the Earth (Susan Vogel, personal communication; Mona Etienne, personal communication). All this, of course, is in direct contrast with the Beng situation as I have outlined it and thus serves as further confirmation that the elements I have grouped together—the Beng taboo on menstruating women entering the forest, and the worship of the Earth—form a complex or a unit of meaning, neither of whose two main elements the Baule have developed to any large extent.

11. This is unlike other systems of hot/cold symbolism, such as those found throughout Southeast Asia, in which the aim is to achieve a *balance* between the two extremes of hot and cold (compare, e.g., Laderman 1981).

12. It is perhaps pertinent to observe here that the model of menstruation presented in this article is almost certainly a traditional one. That is, there is no hint that in the past menstruation was viewed more negatively and surrounded by more taboos but that such a belief is now fading in the face of modern influences. Other acts that were highly polluting in the past, such as copulating in the forest, are still so today, and I have no reason to suspect that menstrual blood, on the contrary, once would have been equally polluting but is now seen as harmless. Rather, I believe that the Beng notions of fertility argue for a traditional lack of extensive

menstrual taboos and against a negative view of menstruation generally. The two—ideas concerning fertility and paucity of menstrual taboos—form a complex, each element giving meaning to the other.

13. Women form exchange relationships with other women of their own choosing—normally friends or matrilaterally related kin. Though my data are incomplete on this, it is my impression that only women (and their daughters and very young sons) eat the food that they exchange. It is conceivable, however, that some men (see note 1 and below) might consume food cooked by menstruating women who are acting as their hostesses when they are visiting in other villages, or if they are eating with friends or kin in their own village.

14. That there is a symbolic connection between palm nuts and menstrual blood is confirmed by data concerning a certain medical remedy. If a woman has severe menstrual cramps, a treatment consists of her cooking palm nuts, extracting the threads (*saŋ*) that separate from the nuts while cooking, and, late at night when there is no one awake to observe her in an embarrassing position, squatting over a fire and steaming the palm-nut threads' vapors up her vagina. This remedy shows clearly that cooked palm nuts are associated on yet another level with menstruation.

3. MORTAL FLOW; MENSTRUATION IN TURKISH VILLAGE SOCIETY

1. It must also be noted that there is little, if any, mention of menstruation in the Turkish literature on health and family planning. Although there is no government policy on sex education, the passing of the Population Planning Law in 1965 made available information about and devices for contraception. The focus of these planners is on contraception, but very little attention has been given to education about the physiology of reproduction.

2. Although the other world (*öbür dünya*) is divided into *Cehennem* (Hell) and *Cennet* (Paradise/Garden), villagers normally mean *Cennet* when they speak of the other world. As the original and eventual home of Muslims, among many life is felt to be a kind of temporary exile. At the same time it must be made clear that Islam, to Muslims, is not a separate religion but the one true faith given in the beginning and thus the one to which all must submit (be *muslim*). Paradise is therefore not reserved for one religious group; it is not exclusive but inclusive. One need only return to the true faith.

3. Because of the lack of awareness of the discrepancy in understanding of procreation between the educated urban elite and the rural population, the education these midwives (young unmarried girls) are given is not made culturally sensitive. The scientific medical

knowledge they receive is little more than a veneer discarded quickly under the impact of more pervasive cultural notions. A midwife's primary duty is to deliver babies and to provide some pre- and postnatal care. She may give information about contraception to married women, but she must refer them to a town medical center for insertion of IUDs (the most prevalent method of contraception, after coitus interruptus).

4. With regard to Turkey, the ethnographic literature on this topic or anything relating to the body is all but silent. Engelbrektsson (1978) and Magnarella (1974) speak of menstruation as polluting, but they assume rather than explore the meanings of this. More general confirmation of attitudes toward and practices relating to menstruation in other Islamic societies can be gleaned from Dwyer (1978), Good (1980), Mernissi (1975), Minai (1981), and Saadawi (1980). The latter gives the most comprehensive account of the way the female body is perceived and of practices relating to it. An excellent recent article by Julie Marcus (1984) came to my attention too late to be referred to in the text. It confirms some of the observations made in this text.

5. The seed-field theory of procreation has been mentioned in a number of ethnographies of Turkey—Engelbrektsson (1978), Erdentuğ (1959), Magnarella (1974), and Meeker (1970)—but the full meaning and implications have nowhere been explored or elaborated. For a full account see Delaney (1984).

6. That the child is considered to belong to the man because he produced it and that this is a central concern is indicated by the following: (1) A father is often referred to as *çoçuk sahıbı*, lit. "child owner." (2) There is a widespread belief that no *man* can care for another *man's* child. (3) In the case of divorce or widowhood, the children do not normally accompany the mother if she remarries, remaining instead with their paternal grandparents. (4) There is no legal adoption until after the husband is age forty and proves that he has not been able to produce a child of his own. (5) In the past a man could take a second wife if the first was unable to bear a child; although this practice is now illegal, it still occurs in villages. Expressed in all of these practices is the belief that it is important for a man not just to have a child but to have one from his own seed.

7. The relationship between the "honor and shame complex" and this specific theory of procreation is taken up in Delaney (1987b).

8. Sometimes women inexplicably stopped menstruating but they were clearly not pregnant, nor were they menopausal. Conversely, a woman who was quite obviously pregnant was having blood taken from her finger by the village midwife as a check for anemia. The midwife had a difficult time obtaining even a drop of blood. A friend said to the pregnant woman, "You must be

menstruating," implying that menstruation draws blood away from other parts of the body. When a few of the other women laughed, she realized her mistake.

9. Most disease is felt to be airborne, which is why people protect themselves from drafts and certain odors and keep babies tightly swaddled.

10. Denise Lawrence (this volume) describes a similar kind of fear in relation to sausage making which, in Portuguese society, is metaphorically related to the process of procreation. For a very interesting discussion of the relation between the theories of procreation and food processing, see Ott (1979). Ott makes, however, no mention of menstruation or menstrual blood.

11. Because bearing children is what women were created for and is their primary function and role in life, the cessation of menses can be a traumatic time for women in Turkish society. The transition can be made more smoothly if the woman has fulfilled her proper role—namely, by producing at least one son. This son will marry and be expected to bring his wife to live in his parents' home, where she will help with the burden of domestic work and produce children to continue the line. With the disruption of rural society, however, particularly the outmigration of many young men for work, the trauma of menopause is intensified, leaving many older women embittered.

4. Menstruation among the Rungus of Borneo: An Unmarked Category

Acknowledgments. From 1959 to 1960 and 1961 to 1963 I carried out research among the Rungus on religion and women's activities. My husband, George N. Appell, was conducting research among the Rungus during this period under the auspices of the Department of Anthropology, Research School of Pacific Studies, the Australian National University. The brief description of Rungus social organization that follows is derived from the works of G. N. Appell (1965, 1966, 1967, 1968, 1976a, 1976b, 1978).

I am indebted to my husband for his patience in reading all previous drafts of this chapter and offering innumerable valuable comments, but mostly for giving me the opportunity to accompany him in the extended fieldwork that resulted in our making many lasting friendships.

I owe a tremendous debt of gratitude to my faithful informant and dear friend the late Itulina binte Magoi, who had the courage to tell me about matters religious and sexual not often imparted to outsiders.

Finally, I want to thank my daughter, Laura Appell-Warren, who at the age of five months accompanied her parents to the field and, as a beguiling baby, elicited much information on child rearing.

1. I use the term "bride-price" here, rather than "bride wealth," which some prefer, as the Rungus themselves use the word *harga*— "price"—in explaining its purpose.

2. In the days of warfare men did have spirit familiars that guarded them in fighting. Head-hunting played no part in Rungus culture, according to our informants. However, the sacrifice of human captives purchased from coastal Muslim groups, for purposes of increasing fertility, was a significant aspect of their religion. Warfare in the past was for the purpose of obtaining property such as gongs and jars. Such warfare was on the wane by the time the British assumed control in the late 1800s.

3. A frequent statement by young girls about a bride-to-be is that they feel sorry for her.

4. Anna Tsing (personal communication) notes that the management of menstruation among the Meratus of South Kalimantan may have certain similarities with Rungus practice. Very little has been published on the handling of menstruation among the indigenous peoples of Borneo, and it is an area in which interesting comparative research could be done.

5. MENSTRUAL POLITICS: WOMEN AND PIGS IN RURAL PORTUGAL

Acknowledgments. The present chapter represents a revised version of a paper entitled "Reconsidering the Menstrual Taboo: A Portuguese Case" published in *Anthropological Quarterly*, vol. 55, no. 2 (1982). A preliminary version was presented to the Faculty Seminar on Feminist Theory organized by the Center for the Humanities at the University of Southern California, 1979, sponsored by an NEH Challenge Grant. I wish to thank the members of that seminar for comments offered during the early stage of writing. In addition, the following individuals provided further critical insights: Alma Gottlieb, Anne Geyer, Carol Mukhopadhyay, and Andrei Simic.

1. The issue of male-public/female-domestic spheres is a complex and important one because it has been used widely to discuss asymmetry in female status. An initial definition by Rosaldo focused on the distinction in institutional and activity foci of men and women (1974:23). Woman's identification with domestic activities derives from her primary role as a childbearer/carer but assumes in the definition a geographical limitation on her activity. Later Rosaldo shifted emphasis away from these distinctions to the further understanding of "relationships of women and men as aspects of a wider social context" (1980:414). Still, the fact that societies differ in the manner and degree to which male and female activities are separated

seems an important observation. European peasant cultures appear to be especially appropriate for general descriptions of these kinds (Friedl 1967; Riegelhaupt 1967). Reiter (1975), however, approaches the differences in male/female-dominated spheres of activities in various cultures by drawing attention to the distinction between prestate and state societies. In prestate societies kinship systems operate as the template by which most major social, economic, and political institutions are organized. With the rise of the state, however, kinship is relegated to a narrower sphere of activity, the domestic arena, as the state takes over the other societal functions based primarily in nonkinship relations. Women, as primary childbearer/ carers in all societies, are often subsumed within the kinship structures dominated by men in prestate societies, whereas in states reproduction is relegated to an almost separate sphere from that of other societal functions (Reiter 1975).

2. This pattern is observed throughout southern Europe (see Banfield 1958; Cronin 1977; J. Davis 1977; Pitt-Rivers 1961).

3. Fieldwork was conducted from August 1976 to July 1977.

4. For example, most women say that bathing, and especially hair washing, can be dangerous to a menstruating woman's health. Eating ice cream or consuming cold beverages during the menstrual period can "shock" the system. Women may also avoid whitewashing the exterior of their houses because they say that exposure to too much sun is dangerous to one's health during the menstrual period. Cutileiro (1971) interprets this behavior symbolically. He argues that menstruating women, because they are in a polluted state, do not whitewash their houses to avoid contaminating the sacred purity of the home (1971:99). This argument is typical of the view that women are seen primarily as agents of pollution, the standard anthropological interpretation of menstruation. It is not argued here, however, that women are *not* seen and do not see themselves as polluters. Rather, the emphasis is placed on the extent to which they use this view to further their own ends.

5. Symbolic connections between menstruation and the moon in Western European folk culture are widespread and well documented (Chadwick 1932; Eliade 1963). These essential links between menstruation and the moon emphasize the monthly cycles of each.

6. Details of this study can be found in Lawrence (1979).

7. All but one were postmenopausal women: mothers or aunts.

8. Only one other couple claimed not to believe in the effects of menstrual pollution, although the husband believed in the potentially dangerous effects of the moon.

9. For example, infants and young children are protected with amulets tied together in a cloth pouch and secured under their clothing. Families of the bride and groom may paint protective crosses on critical corners of their houses and garden walls before the wed-

ding to protect against the envious feelings of others. Certain older women confidentially explain that they or someone they know has the power to cure afflictions caused by the evil eye. Although residents do not openly discuss it, its influence remains, not necessarily by name but expressed in action.

10. Cutileiro (1971) notes these distinctions in a comprehensive discussion of the evil eye in rural southern Portugal.

11. The symbolic relations between pregnancy and food-processing activities are potentially rich and complex. Pliny (1963) and Ploss, Bartels, and Bartels (1935), among others, mention repeatedly the taboo that Western European peasant cultures place on menstruating women in activities related to cheese and wine production, bread baking, and curing pork. Although the connections are highly suggestive, there exist other kinds of taboo elements (for example, causing flowers or plants to wilt, causing milk to spoil, etc.) which do not involve any kind of "preservation" process but are thought to be caused immediately and directly by the menstruating woman's touch. Thus the relation between the menstrual taboo and food processing is not an exclusive one. Rather, it is part of a complex of taboo behavior related to a variety of items and situations.

12. Ott (1979) describes a similar food-reproduction analogy among the Basques, who liken the formation of the fetus to the hardening of cheese. She documents through historical references the presence of the same cheese analogy throughout Europe from early times. It seems likely that additional food-reproduction analogies might also exist, forming a European complex of beliefs with varied expressions and societal contexts, and that these may give clues to the origins of these notions.

13. Lois Paul also mentions the pride Guatemalan women take in being competent at their domestic tasks, with such competence being a common indicator in female prestige rankings (1974:285).

6. MENSTRUAL SYMBOLISM IN SOUTH WALES

Acknowledgments. I would like to thank the Tudor-Harte family for their encouragement and hospitality, and my informants for their willing cooperation in a difficult area. I also thank Dr. Joe Loudon, my supervisor, for his meticulous questioning; Dr. Alma Gottlieb and Dr. Thomas Buckley for their scrupulous editing; and Vicki Kelly for her inexhaustible patience and typing skills. This chapter represents a major revision of an article that appeared in *Man*, vol. 5 (1970).

1. Though it might be a plausible explanation, the perceived dangers of menstruation and menopause (see later discussion) do not seem to be related to attitudes about family size or premarital

intercourse. There appear to be neither well-organized attempts to limit family size nor excessively censorious attitudes toward premarital or extramarital sex. Indeed, 80 percent of women are married after they become pregnant. Once they are married extramarital activity, according to privileged village gossip, is abundant, especially among those women approaching middle age. The situation seems to confirm the local saying, "A cut cake goes twice as fast."

Likewise, there seems to be no correlation between family size and attitudes toward menstruation. For example, women whom I characterize later as "unhappy" (who do not conform to gender-role expectations) and those whom I characterize as "happy" (who do conform to such expectations) do not differ appreciably in the number of children they bear.

2. Although connections between attitudes toward menstruation and sociological and medical factors were not immediate, there were certain socioeconomic and medical patterns apparent at less immediate levels. These patterns emerge when women are considered not in terms of their attitudes toward menstruation per se but in relation to the categories of "happy" and "unhappy" (to be described later).

The three women I interviewed who had had a grammar school education all fell into the "unhappy" category. Similarly, three of the four working women in my sample were "unhappy." Finally, "unhappy" women were more likely to suffer from gynecological complaints, and their visits to the doctor were likely to be slightly more frequent than those of "happy" women.

It may be that the notion that women cannot be either educated or working and have a contented married life contributes to the formation of a subcategory of "unhappy" women who are either educated or working outside the home.

3. The main elements of menstrual "ritual" in Abergwyn involved belief in unknown dangers, in inner badness or excess, and in taboos on washing, especially washing the head. The symbolic equation of the head and the womb, apparent in washing prohibitions, is also present in the etiology of "hot flushes." Menopause is seen not merely as the cessation of menstrual bleeding, but as a suppression of menstrual blood that is then directed to the head, causing hot flushes. Implicit in this account is the idea that the female system needs regular purging and that when the usual channel is blocked the system seeks alternative outlets.

The substitution of head for womb is a move from the private to the public part of the body. As such, the symbolism is particularly well suited to conveying the link between biological function and social role (see also Delaney, this volume).

Finally, this symbolism seems to depend upon the same conceptual structures as the nineteenth-century argument against higher education for women: intensive study was thought to direct menstrual blood away from the reproductive organs to the brain, weakening the reproductive potential of young women (e.g., Ehrenreich and English 1974).

4. Becker illustrates this analysis of menopausal depression by a reexamination of Freud's case study of a fifty-three-year-old female patient. The woman came to see Freud because she had suddenly been "flooded" by an insane jealousy of a young career woman with whom she imagined her husband to be having an affair. Freud's interpretation of the situation was that through the use of this jealousy language, the woman was trying to conceal her own libidinal urges toward her young son-in-law.

Becker's view of the situation is very different. For him the significant elements are, first, that "this woman senses the decline of her only value to men—her physical charm" (Becker 1963:360) and, second, the differences between her own status and that of the younger woman.

According to Becker the jealous wife had played the social game according to all of the conventional rules, but something had gone wrong. She now found herself alone, without usable skills, without children, and without her accustomed beauty. The situation was rendered doubly poignant by the fact that the woman was "without words in which to frame her protest," and thus the protest against "helplessness and potential meaninglessness takes the form of jealousy accusations" (1963:361). For Becker this jealousy language makes indirect reference to the woman's exclusion from the male world—indirect of necessity because the exclusion was so complete as to deprive the woman of the language in which a direct protest could be voiced.

On the nature of menopausal depression and its connection with social role, see also Kirk's (1964) study of childless marriage and adoption.

7. PREMENSTRUAL SYNDROME: DISCIPLINE, WORK, AND ANGER IN LATE INDUSTRIAL SOCIETIES

Acknowledgments. I thank Sarah Begus, Thomas Buckley, Alma Gottlieb, Judith Leavitt, Leith Mullings, Lorna AmaraSingham Rhodes, and Jane Sewell for their helpful comments on this essay. An expanded version of this chapter appears in *The Woman in the Body* (Beacon Press, 1987).

1. I am in the process of doing a large-scale study, based on extensive interviews, of women's body image through the life cycle in the United States. Because I have not sought out women with PMS for that study, and because my focus here is on what can be

made of public representations of PMS, I have not included interview material. However, the extremely negative imagery with which
women of all ages talk about menstruation is certainly in the back
of my mind as I write. It is also relevant to note that I do not
experience severe manifestations of PMS, and there is a possibility
for that reason that I do not give sufficient credit to the medical
model of PMS. I have, however, experienced many similar manifestations during the first three months of each of my three pregnancies, so I have some sense that I know what women with PMS are
talking about.

2. Other examples of uniformly negative symptomatology are
Halbreich and Endicott (1982) and Dalton (1979).

3. Few authors reject the description of PMS as a disease. One
who does is Witt, who prefers the more neutral term "condition"
(1984:11–12).

4. I have not done historical research to determine when in relation to the development of industrial society premenstrual syndrome
was first experienced or described. The first scientific publication
describing it was Frank (1931). This is clearly an important topic for
future research.

5. Like Buckley, M. Powers (1980) suggests that the association
generally made between menstruation and negative conditions such
as defilement may be a result of a priori Western notions held by
the investigator. She argues that the Oglala Plains Indians have no
such association. This does not mean that menstruation is *never*
regarded negatively, of course (see Price 1984:21–22).

6. On isolation of housewives see Gilman (1903:92).

7. The issue of how emotional states are related to hormonal
levels is too complex for me to take on here. On the difficulty of
showing invariant relationships between hormonal states and particular behavioral and emotional states, see Lowe (1983:53–54).

8. MENSTRUATION AND THE POWER OF YUROK WOMEN

Acknowledgments. I especially thank Tela Lake, Yurok, without whose
testimony this work could not have been done, and Martha McClintock, Committee on Human Development, University of Chicago,
who also contributed in important ways. I am grateful, too, to the
late Dewey George, Yurok, and the late Harry K. Roberts for information on male esoteric training used in this chapter, and to Arnold
R. Pilling and Richard Keeling for a variety of ethnographic details.
Of course I take full responsibility for the uses I have made of
everyone's respective contribution. Research undertaken in California and incorporated here was supported by the Jacobs Research
Fund of the Whatcom Museum Foundation in 1976 and 1978 and by

the Danforth Foundation in 1978. I also thank the Bancroft Library, University of California at Berkeley, and Professor Karl Kroeber for their kind permission to quote from the A. L. Kroeber Papers at the Bancroft.

An earlier version of this chapter appeared in *American Ethnologist*, vol. 9, no. 1 (1982):47–60. The present version, in which I have corrected certain errors and have made several additions, should be regarded as the more definitive of the two.

1. The English language euphemism "moontime," used by some Yurok today in reference to menstrual periods, reflects a central symbolic relationship between the moon and menses in contemporary Yurok culture. It is not clear, however, just when "moontime" came into use among English-speaking Yurok, nor are there sufficient data to establish a likely time. In 1902 one of Kroeber's consultants used the English "flowers" in reference to menstruation, and "moontime" does not appear in any of the other early published or archival material on the Yurok. We cannot, then, use the term "moontime" as evidence of a moon/menses relationship in aboriginal Yurok culture. (Both flowers and moon-related menstrual imagery are very widespread, far beyond the confines of both native California and the modern era [Delaney, Lupton, and Toth 1976; Gottlieb, this volume].)

The explicit Yurok verb meaning "to menstruate" is *kɪkɪcp-*, the prefix *kɪkɪ-* indicating both cyclic and erratic oscillation. This verb is not used, however, in any of the Yurok texts collected by Kroeber. Here the common Yurok term for a menstruating woman, *wespurawok*, is euphemistic, alluding to a woman who bathes in the (Klamath) river. Such euphemisms are frequently used in Yurok in avoidance of more explicit terms, use of which under many circumstances is considered to be offensive and even polluting.

2. The woman was perhaps dramatizing her relationship to her far older female relatives. It is quite possible that she did not herself receive the information from them but at second hand, from her mother, for the youngest of the women of whom she spoke died while she herself was a young girl in a foster home. (Such dramatization is frequently encountered among Yurok today, many of whom stress their links with the past by telescoping time and people in accounts of their own nurture.)

Later I argue that the value of the young woman's testimony is established by its resonance with a far older account, that given in 1902 by Weitchpec Susie, and with the contemporary testimony of another, elderly Yurok woman. Again, the evaluation of contemporary testimony in dialectic with other evidence is a central methodological concern in the present chapter.

3. The classic ethnographic accounts in which the earliest published data on menstrual practices in northwestern California are to

be found are S. Powers ([1877] 1976); Goddard (1903); Kroeber (1925); Harrington (1932); and Drucker (1937). Information on male training for wealth acquisition among these peoples, referred to later, is found in the same sources. Additional material on Yurok training appears in Spott and Kroeber (1942); Elmendorf (1960); Kroeber (1976); and Pilling (1978).

4. No reason is given in the Kroeber notes for Coyote's action. A parallel Chilula Indian account, however, states that a girl had rejected the trickster's sexual advances and that he acted out of spite. The Chilula once neighbored the Yurok.

5. Note that in this text the perpetual purity of the spirits—the *wo·gey*—is cast in quite a different light than in the received ethnography (e.g., Erikson 1943): the female *wo·gey* themselves menstruate, even in the "spirit world." The fact is but one of many that needs attention in a careful reconsideration of traditional Yurok world view, male and female.

6. A Yurok woman fully trained as a *kegey* (doctor) told Kroeber about using the angelica roots she gathered in the mountains. The full account was recorded in English in 1907 and is among the Kroeber Papers, carton 7. I include a partial version here.

> I . . . always throw *woʔlp'eʔy* [angelica] in the fire. I talk this way: "Now this *woʔlp'eʔy*, I got it *wesʔonah hiwoʔnik*, right up in the middle of the sky. . . . "
>
> It didn't come from there in fact, but one just talked that way and threw it in the fire, so that all kinds of money would just come right to this house.

Clearly the "lake in the middle of the sky" comprises such metaphorical usage, this lake being symbolized by any water used to bathe in during menstruation, most commonly the Klamath River and, far less certainly, the "moontime pond" above Meri·p.

7. In all likelihood the actual situation was far more complex. Some women undoubtedly shared what I have characterized here as a "male" perspective, viewing menstruation as a dire pollutant. Again, one old Yurok-trained "aristocratic" male voiced the kind of perspective I here characterize as female in conversations with me in 1970, long before I had begun the present inquiry. Finally, it is probable that some—perhaps many—women were highly ambivalent and shared *both* "male" and "female" perspectives on menstruation. Susie herself, for instance, told Kroeber that menstruous women polluted trails.

Such diversity was probably resolved to an extent by Yurok quasi-class structure. Esoteric knowledge among Yurok tended to be concentrated in the upper echelons of aboriginal society among what, for lack of a better term, may be called "aristocratic" descent groups (see Buckley 1980). Weitchpec Susie was a member of such a group, as was the old man mentioned earlier, and as is—although less significantly today—the young woman whose testimony initiated the present study.

It is likely, and in keeping with what may be known of the sociology of aboriginal Yurok knowledge, that the positive view of menstruation developed here was class- as well as gender-specific, but also that its occurrence to some extent crossed both class and gender lines. In any case the present analysis must be viewed as pertaining particularly to aboriginal Yurok women of aristocratic descent groups. As Pilling (1978) points out, these groups over-whelmingly have provided ethnographers, informants, and we know far more about them than about the lower strata of traditional Yurok society.

8. Erikson (1943:295) writes that the Yurok "believe [that] babies come from the sky." The Kroeber notes discussed here, however, suggest that the meaning of this "belief" was far more complex, at least for "educated" (*teno·wok*) aristocratic women. Babies come from *(ʔ)wesʔonah* (the cosmos) by way of its "medicine basket" (the uterus).

9. Menstruation at the new moon is in accord both with Cloudsley's and Dewan's biological model and with the folk-physiological models of many nonindustrial peoples. However, these models contrast with Cutler's (1980) findings that statistically correlate menstruation among a sample of contemporary women in Philadelphia and the "light" lunar period (between the first and third lunar quarters). If Cutler's findings are significant (and the variables here are extraordinarily complex), more comprehensive cross-cultural models should perhaps be pursued. Lamp's hypothesis (this volume) that menstruation occurs among Temne women in two groups—a "light" lunar phase group and a "dark" one, in Cutler's terms—may be relevant to this still unresolved matter.

10. Harry K. Roberts, who spent much of his youth in the Spott household at Requa, told me that "old-time" women kept careful track of their monthly cycles using stick calendars in order to plan for travel and ritual. Pregnancy, according to Roberts, was also carefully charted, a stick being set aside each month rather than each day (as is the case with menstrual stick calendars).

9. HEAVENLY BODIES: MENSES, MOON, AND RITUALS OF LICENSE AMONG THE TEMNE OF SIERRA LEONE

Acknowledgments. This chapter is a revision of a paper of the same title presented at the Twenty-fifth Annual Meeting of the African Studies Association, November 1982, Washington, D.C., in a symposium on "African Cosmology, Astronomy and World View." I would like to thank several people who read that paper and offered suggestions: Deirdre LaPin (University of Arkansas at Little Rock), Allen Roberts (University of Michigan), and Alma Gottlieb. Susan Vogel, director of the Center for African Art, New York, first suggested this investigation to me. Editorial suggestions have been made by Audrey Frantz and Dawn Schnably (The Baltimore Museum of Art). My research among the Temne (the first art-historical field research conducted there) was sponsored in 1976 by the National Endowment for the Arts, Fellowships for Museum Professionals, and in 1979–1980 by the Social Science Research Council, International Doctoral Research Fellowship. I gratefully acknowledge their support. From 1967 to 1969 I served among the Temne as a Peace Corps volunteer.

1. When Bondo begins its session it wrests control of the village from the men through a series of rituals, and it cedes control in the same manner at the end of its term (see Lamp 1982:259). D'Azevedo (1983:18–22) has suggested that among the Gola the men somewhat resent what they see as total female political freedom and dominance; therefore the suggestion of some observers that the women simply enforce what is substantially male control is debatable.

2. My sample consists of the seven Bondo ceremonies and three Pɔrɔ ceremonies that I observed. In addition, I have added to the sample one Bondo ceremony (three days after third quarter) observed by Dorjahn (personal communication), one Pɔrɔ ceremony (a half-day before full moon) observed by Dorjahn (1961:38), and two Pɔrɔ ceremonies of the Bullom (both full moon, or thereabouts) recorded by Banbury (1888:187–189) and Gervis (1952:204). Bullom and Temne Pɔrɔ are identical in most structural respects (although I cannot say whether the Bullom dates are relevant to the following discussion). Lunar dates on the chart are approximated to the nearest half-day. Bondo coming-out begins in the late afternoon; Pɔrɔ begins just before midnight. The Temne sample is from eastern Temneland. I have not included Bondo dates recorded in Maforki Chiefdom in western Temneland because Bondo structure there is heavily influenced by Mende Sande, the dates are less consistent, and I have not been able to document any knowledge of the song, *aŋ-Sema komande* (discussed later), in use there. Neither have I included dates of the boys' Rəbai initiation because it is not found in the East, because I had too few data, and because in its deterioration its traditions are perhaps "diluted."

3. Three and four are, respectively, male and female ritual numbers, totaling seven, the number of completion. For example, deceased men are said to take three days and women four days to reach the world of the dead. In initiation ritual boys circle the town three times, put on their clothes three times, repeat certain phrases

three times, and so on, while girls do the same things four times.

4. It should be noted, however, that even with the lifting of sexual prohibitions in either male or female ritual, only a small percentage of women would actually be available. Most would be off-limits: (1) unmarried women, who must preserve their virginity; (2) pregnant women from about their sixth month of pregnancy on (Dorjahn 1958:849); and (3) nursing mothers up to two years after parturition (Dorjahn 1958:849). Infertile young women would be available, but we can also eliminate (4) those past menopause, as these women frequently take unmarried male lovers, having little to risk, and are of little interest to the men at the special time of *ε-luknε*.

Exact demographic data to measure these four categories of women are not available, but I have informally estimated that they would add up to approximately 80 percent of all women. This would leave approximately only 20 percent of all women as eligible participants in the *ε-luknε* ritual of sexual license. Further research is needed to provide more precise figures on this point.

5. Although the Temne tend to absorb illegitimate children into extended families fairly easily, such children are apparently still regarded as the legitimate heirs of their physiological fathers, unless the true facts of conception are hidden by the mother (although this is unusual—Dorjahn 1958:839, 842). Female virgins are inviolable, and violators are liable for very steep compensation to the parents. (Only virgin brides remain their husbands' wives after death [Dorjahn 1958:855] and a husband's payment to the parents of a nonvirgin bride is minimal.) Female (but not male) adultery is a crime for which the wife is often beaten and her lover charged with a heavy fine (generally as much as two months' salary). All sexual activity is restricted to the night, between sundown and the first crow of the cock (about 3:30 A.M.), and to the bedroom (intercourse in the forest is severely punished).

6. *Tsiəŋ ɔ-bera ɔ thas təka a-fela; tsiəŋ a-bera bε ŋa ma tsu kor, ma a-ŋof ŋa las, talɔm ma a-ŋof ŋa fi.* I have retranslated his text into English and retranscribed the Temne text according to the standard International Phonetic Alphabet.

7. *Tsiəŋ a-bera bε ŋa yeŋk hε sɔ ma-der ka a-ŋof a-fi, de ka a-ŋof a-las.* See note 6. In his primary text, *tsu kor* is used to indicate "belly sickness," and although this is most frequently used to refer to menstruation, it may refer to any internal pain in the belly. In the alternate text the term is *yeŋk hε,* meaning simply "not well." One other phrase is a critical mistranslation: where I write "when the moon is dying," Schlenker wrote "when the moon is new." In both his Temne versions, however, the text reads *a ŋof a-fi* (or *a ŋof ŋa-fi*), which is literally "the dying (or dead) moon" (as he indicates, him-

self, in a footnote). There is a distinction. "The dying/dead moon" refers to its final crescent disappearance, whereas "new moon" (*a ŋof a-fu*) refers to its crescent reappearance. The crucial implication is that menstruation begins just before, not precisely at, new moon.

8. *ŋof ɔ ŋof ɔ-wunibom ɔ wur mə-tir, kə-wur mə-tir a-ke ka ma a tela kə-yak a-ŋof. A-ŋof aŋ təp gbo kə-wur-e ka aŋ-re a ləpsɔ mə-tir mə-poŋ, haŋ kə-kɔ ka aŋ-re a-tɔtɔkɔ ŋa a-ŋof maŋ kəl təma-e, pəyimɔ mə-re kəgba-thamthrɛsas. Ka a-ŋof ka ba kati mə-re tɔfɔt-maŋlɛ, kə-təp ka aŋ-re a-tɔtɔkɔ, rə-mɛs din rə wur kə-wur ka aŋ-seth ŋa ɛ-mɛs kə-woŋ ka ka-sul a-ke kɔ ka aŋ-pɔru-e ta ka-thas ka aŋ-pɔru . . . ɔwa ra-mɛs ra gbaiɛa ɔwa ma-tir mə tə wur a-me ma a tela a-ŋof mə tə-wur. Aŋ-fəm a-bom a-lɔm aŋ tə yak tə ma-re məsas aŋ-lɔm maŋlɛ aŋ-lɔm thamthrukin.* Translation and emphasis are mine, with a retranscription of the Temne text (see note 6). Margai probably wrote the original in English. In a number of passages the translator (into Temne) appears to confuse the beginning of menstruation with the end. Apparently the translator was not clear either on the duration of menstruation or on whether it begins or ends at new moon. It is difficult to tell how much of this text is simply from straight textbook sources and how much is based on indigenous thought. It may also be noted that the menstrual cycle is thought to begin with menstruation, not with ovulation. I have interpreted the text to say that menstruation ends as the new moon appears, thus agreeing with Schlenker that it begins just before new moon (see note 7). The text refers to ovulation fourteen days after the beginning of the moon cycle, but this certainly should be fourteen days after the beginning of the menstruation, unless we are to believe that Temne menstruation lasts only a day or two. The days from the moon's reappearance to its next "first day" is given as twenty-eight days, but this is certainly again a confusion between textbook gynecology and the Temne lunar menstrual cycle as implied in the text.

9. Emphasis mine. Much of Barbot's information came from Ol- fert Dapper, but Barbot apparently visited the Sierra Leone Estuary personally and probably received information from the European traders there.

10. Alma Gottlieb (personal communication) was told by the Beng of Ivory Coast that "most women menstruate at the new moon or at the full moon." She was not told of any ritual or other reasons or associations for this, however, nor was she able to verify this statement. Susan Vogel (personal communication) was told by the Baule of Ivory Coast that women menstruate synchronically, al- though she doubted it, and believes that menstruation is unlikely to occur at the new moon (as that is a time of festivities in which they take part). Deirdre LaPin (1983) was told by the Ngas of Nigeria

that the menstrual cycle "is governed by the moon." She describes a ritual called "shooting the moon" performed annually just before harvest at the new moon. One of the opening acts of the ritual is the removal of refuse from the town, and a principal purpose of the ritual is to cleanse the villagers of their past evil. Perhaps this clearing of the way also refers to menstruation, associated with the new moon? The cleansing of evil is said to ensure reproductivity with the initiation of a new cycle, and the post-moonshot period is the favorite time for marriages.

Outside of Africa, the tendency toward new moon menstruation is suggested also in Menaker (1967) and Menaker and Menaker (1959) (compare Buckley, this volume).

11. The period of fertility here is calculated on this basis: (1) thirteenth to seventeenth days after the beginning of menstruation—ovulation is likely; (2) ninth to twelfth days—active sperm from previous coitus may survive in the uterus; (3) eighteenth day—an egg entering the uterus on the seventeenth day may live to be fertilized for one day (Kramer 1981:18–19, 54–55). The period of fertility is certainly one of great variation, and a sexually active woman relying solely on charts such as mine would be playing a risky game indeed. Some women argue, in fact, that there are no "safe days" outside of menstruation. Still, I think it is not unreasonable to use such a chart in this case. First, ritual functions not on the basis of proven fact but more on a basis of theory, which may be somewhat independent of empirical evidence. Second, if the Temne are guided by a schedule so uniform as to account for no menstruation apart from new or full moon, it may be reasonable to assume that ovulation also is thought to adhere rather strictly to schedule. Further investigation among the Temne by anthropologists and/or gynecologists is needed to clarify this and related points.

12. That is, sperm deposited in the women of group 1 (who are released only a day and a half before the date of most probable ovulation) would ordinarily survive three to five days; and the egg dropped in the women of group 2, who are released the latest (two and a half days after the date of most probable ovulation), could still be capable of fertilization.

13. Carol MacCormack (personal communication) claims that the Bullom have no knowledge of or word for the uterus, but only a concept of the belly. This seems doubtful, as their neighbors, the Temne, distinguish stomach (*kor*) from uterus (*aŋ-pɔru*), although the same word, distinguished by male or female modifiers, signifies both womb and sperm (as containers of potential life—although sperm has also another term, *ma-runi*, which means literally "that of man"). MacCormack also points out that pregnant women tie cords around their waists to discourage the fetus from moving up-

ward and departing the body in the wrong direction. I believe that this is only a metaphorical notion. The Temne, by way of comparison, seem to have a notion, expressed in visual and oral arts, that the conception of a child occurs through the head (Lamp 1982:152–153, n. 75), yet they clearly understand the function and consequence of coitus (see the famous debate on human parthenogenesis in Douglas 1969; Leach 1967, 1968; Needham 1969; Schwimmer 1969; Spiro 1968; P. Wilson 1969). Lyrics sung in initiation, for example, compare coitus with the planting of seeds. We need to be able to read through the very richly metaphoric content so often dominant in African expression, and in this an essential facility in the indigenous language is only a beginning.

10. Menstrual Synchrony and the Australian Rainbow Snake

Acknowledgments. An earlier version of this chapter was presented at the World Archaeological Congress in September 1986 (Southampton, England).

Note. Readers should be aware that much of the previously published material cited by Knight in this chapter is deemed both sacred and secret by the Aboriginal peoples of Australia. We republish these readily available ethnographic materials respectfully, for scholarly purposes only, and in hopes that our doing so may ultimately serve the interests of the native peoples of Australia. —Eds.

1. This was also the case in Upper Paleolithic Europe (Leroi-Gourhan 1968:40, Shimkin 1978:271; Klein 1969:226).

2. I deal with non-Australian "dragon," "snake," and other serpent myths in the Coda. It seems clear that use of the term "snake" in reference to the Australian rainbow serpent is a matter of cultural conditioning (and perhaps bias). The mythological creature is a flying serpent—as easily called a "dragon," in English, as a "snake." For this reason I use the English "snake" and "dragon" interchangeably in the following discussion.

References

Abbie, A. A.
    1969   *The original Australians*. London: Muller.

Ahern, Emily Martin
    1975   The power and pollution of Chinese women. In *Women and the family in rural Taiwan*, ed. M. Wolf and R. Witke, 193–214. Palo Alto: Stanford University Press.

Anderson, Peter
    1983   The reproductive role of the human breast. *Current Anthropology* 24, no. 1:24–45.

Angier, Natalie with Janet Witzleben
    1983   Dr. Jekyll and Ms. Hyde. *Reader's Digest* (February), pp. 119–121.

Appell, George N.
    1965   *The nature of social groupings among the Rungus of Sabah, Malaysia*. Ph.D. dissertation, Australian National University.

    1966   Residence and ties of kinship in a cognatic society: The Rungus Dusun of Sabah, Malaysia. *Southwestern Journal of Anthropology* 22:280–301.

    1967   Observational procedures for identifying kindreds: Social isolates among the Rungus of Borneo. *Southwestern Journal of Anthropology* 23:192–207.

    1968   The Dusun languages of Northern Borneo: Rungus Dusun and related problems. *Oceanic Linguistics* 7:1–15.

    1976a   The cognitive tactics of anthropological inquiry: Comments on King's approach to the concept of the kindred. In *The societies of Borneo*, ed. G. N. Appell, 146–151. Washington, D.C.: American Anthropological Association.

    1976b   The Rungus: social structure in a cognatic society and its symbolization. In *The societies of Borneo*, ed. G. N. Appell, 66–86. Washington, D.C.: American Anthropological Association.

    1978   The Rungus of Sabah, Malaysia. In *Essays on Borneo societies*, ed. Victor T. King, 143–171. Hull Monographs on South-East Asia 7. Oxford: Oxford University Press.

Appell, George N., ed.
    1976   *The societies of Borneo: Explorations in the theory of cognatic social structure*. Special Publication no. 6. Washington, D.C.: American Anthropological Association.

Ardener, Edwin
1972   Belief and the problem of women. In *The interpretation of ritual, Essays in honour of A. I. Richards*, ed. Jean la Fontaine, 135–158. London: Tavistock.

Arens, William
1979   *The man-eating myth*. New York: Oxford University Press.

Augé, Marc
1982   *The anthropological circle: Symbol, function, history*, trans. Martin Thom. Cambridge: Cambridge University Press. (Original: *Symbole, fonction, histoire: les interrogations de l'anthropologie*. Paris: Hachette, 1979.)

Aveni, A. F., ed.
1982   *Archaeoastronomy in the New World*. Cambridge: Cambridge University Press.

Babcock, Barbara A.
1978   *The reversible world: Symbolic inversion in art and society*. Ithaca, N.Y.: Cornell University Press.

Bailey, F. G.
1969   *Stratagems and spoils: A social anthropology of politics*. New York: Schocken.

Bakhtin, Mikhail
1984   *Rabelais and his world*, trans. Hélène Iswolksy. Bloomington: Indiana University Press. (Original: *Tvorchestvo Fransua Rable i narodnaia kul'tura srednevekov'ia i Renessansa*. Moscow: Khudozhestvennia literatura, 1965.)

Ballantyne, Sheila
1975   *Norma Jean the termite queen*. New York: Penguin.

Balzer, Marjorie Mandelstam
1981   Rituals of gender identity: Markers of Siberian Khanty ethnicity, status and belief. *American Anthropologist* 83:850–867.

1985   On the scent of gender theory and practice: Reply to Child and Child. *American Anthropologist* 87:128–130.

Banbury, George A. L.
1888   *Sierra Leone, or the white man's grave*. London: S. Sonnenschein, Lowrey & Co.

Banfield, Edward
1958   *The moral basis of a backward society*. New York: Free Press.

Barbot, Jean
1746   *A description of the coasts of North and South Guinea; and of Ethiopia inferior, vulgarly Angola; a new and accurate account of the western maritime countries of Africa*. London: Henry Lintot & Jean Osborn.

Barrett, Samuel Alfred
1976   *Pomo Indian basketry*. Glorieta, New Mexico: The Rio Grande Press. (Originally published in *University of*

California Publications in American Archeology and Ethnology 7, no. 3, 1908.)

Bean, John Lowell
1977 Power and its applications in native California. In *The anthropology of power*, ed. Raymond D. Fogelson and Richard N. Adams, 117–131. New York: Academic Press.

Bean, John Lowell and Thomas C. Blackburn
1976a Introduction. In *Native Californians: A theoretical retrospective*, ed. J. L. Bean and T. C. Blackburn, 5–10. Socorro, N.M.: Ballena Press.

Bean, John Lowell and Thomas C. Blackburn, eds.
1976b *Native Californians: A theoretical retrospective*. Socorro, N.M.: Ballena Press.

Becker, Ernest
1963 Social science and psychiatry. *Antioch Review* 23:353–365.

Beidelman, T. O.
1966 Swazi royal ritual. *Africa* 36:373–405. Reprinted in *Africa and change*, ed. Colin Turnbull, 382–421. New York: Knopf, 1973.

Berndt, C. H.
1965 Women and the "secret life." In *Aboriginal man in Australia*, ed. R. M. Berndt and C. H. Berndt, 238–282. Sydney: Angus & Robertson.

Berndt, Catherine H. and Ronald M. Berndt
1945 *A preliminary report of field work in the Ooldea Region, western South Australia*. Sydney: University of Sydney. (Originally published in *Oceania* 12–15.)
1951 *Sexual behavior in western Arnhem Land*. New York: Viking Fund Publications in Anthropology 16.
1964 *The world of the first Australians*. London: Angus and Robertson.
1970 *Man, land and myth in North Australia*. Sydney: Ure Smith.

Berndt, Ronald M.
1951 *Kunapipi: A study of an Australian Aboriginal religious cult*. Melbourne: Cheshire.

Bettelheim, Bruno
1954 *Symbolic wounds: Puberty rites and the envious male*. New York: Free Press.
1978 *The uses of enchantment*. Harmondsworth: Penguin.

Biersack, Aletta
1983 Bound blood: Paiela "conception" theory interpreted. *Mankind* 14:85–100.

Birke, Lynda and Katy Gardner
1982 *Why suffer? Periods and their problems*. London: Virago.

Blackburn, Thomas C.
1976 Ceremonial integration and social interaction in aborigi-

nal California. In *Native Californians: A theoretical retrospective,* ed. J. L. Bean and T. C. Blackburn, 225–244. Socorro, N.M.: Ballena Press.

Blacker, C.
1978   The snake woman in Japanese myth and legend. In *Animals in folklore,* ed. J. R. Porter and W. M. S. Russell, 113–125. Totowa, N.J.: Rowman Brewer, and Cambridge: Littlefield, for the Folklore Society.

Bleier, Ruth
1984   *Science and gender: A critique of biology and its theories on women.* Elmsford, N.Y.: Pergamon.

Bozic, S. and A. Marshall
1972   *Aboriginal myths.* Melbourne: Gold Star.

Brandenstein, C. G. von
1982   *Names and substance of the Australian subsection system.* Chicago: University of Chicago Press.

Braverman, Harry
1974   *Labor and monopoly capital.* New York: Monthly Review Press.

Brazelton, T. Berry
1970   Effect of prenatal drugs on the behavior of the neonate. *American Journal of Psychiatry* 126:1261–1266.

Brooks, George E.
1984   The observance of All Souls' Day in the Guinea-Bissau region: A Christian Holy Day, an African harvest festival, an African New Year's celebration, or all of the above (?). *History in Africa* 11:1–34.

Brown, Paula and Georgena Buchbinder, eds.
1976   *Man and woman in the New Guinea highlands.* Special Publications no. 8. Washington, D.C.: American Anthropological Association.

Bruner, Edward M. and Victor W. Turner, eds.
1986   *The anthropology of experience.* Urbana: University of Illinois Press.

Bryant, J. A., D. G. Heathcote, and V. R. Pickles
1977   The search for "menotoxin." *The Lancet* 2 April:753.

Buchler, Ira and K. Maddock, eds.
1978   *The rainbow serpent.* The Hague: Mouton.

Buckley, Thomas
1979   Doing your thinking: Aspects of traditional Yurok education. *Parabola* 4, no. 4:29–37.

1980   Monsters and the quest for balance in native northwest California. In *Manlike monsters on trial: Early records and modern evidence,* ed. Marjorie Halpin and Michael Ames, 152–171. Vancouver: University of British Columbia Press.

1982   Menstruation and the power of Yurok women: Methods in cultural reconstruction. *American Ethnologist* 9: 47–60.

Bukhari, (al-) Muhammed Ibn Isma'il
1903   *Les traditions islamiques,* vol. 1, trans. Octave Victor
        Houdas and William Marcais. Publications of the Ecole
        des Langues Orientales Vivantes, 4th series, Vol. 3.
        Paris: Imprimerie Nationale/Ernest Leroux.

Bulmer, Ralph
1967   Why is the cassowary not a bird: A problem in zoological
        taxonomy among the Karam of the New Guinea High-
        lands. *Man* 2:5–25.

Burley, Nancy
1979   The evolution of concealed ovulation. *The American Nat-
        uralist* 114:835–858.

Bushnell, John and Donna Bushnell
1977   Wealth, work, and world view in native northwest
        California. In *Flowers in the wind,* ed. Thomas C.
        Blackburn, 120–182. Socorro, N.M.: Ballena Press.

Bynum, Caroline Walker
1984   Womens' stories, women's symbols: A critique of Victor
        Turner's theory of liminality. In *Anthropology and the
        study of religion,* ed. Robert L. Moore and Frank E.
        Reynolds, 105–125. Chicago: Center for the Scientific
        Study of Religion.

Campbell, J. K.
1964   *Honour, family and patronage.* New York: Oxford Univer-
        sity Press.

Center for Archaeoastronomy
1978   *Archaeoastronomy 1.* College Park: University of Maryland
        Press.

Chadwick, Mary
1932   *The psychological effects of menstruation.* New York: Ner-
        vous & Mental Diseases.

Child, Alice B. and Irvin L. Child
1985   Biology, ethnocentrism and sex differences. *American
        Anthropologist* 87:125–128.

Cloudsley, T. J. L.
1961   *Rhythmic activity in animal physiology and behavior.* New
        York: Academic Press.

Collier, Jane Fishburne
1974   Women in politics. In *Woman, culture and society,* ed.
        M. Z. Rosaldo and L. Lamphere, 89–96. Stanford: Stan-
        ford University Press.

Cowan, Ruth Schwartz
1983   *More work for mother: The ironies of household technologies
        from the open hearth to the microwave.* New York: Basic
        Books.

Crawford, Marian
1970   What happens at "the change." *New Society* 16 (10 Oc-
        tober):771–773.

Crawfurd, Raymond
    1915   Notes on the superstitions of menstruation. *The Lancet*
            18 December:1331–1336.
Cronin, Constance
    1977   Illusion and reality in Sicily. In *Sexual stratification*, ed.
            A. Schlegel, 67–93. New York: Columbia University
            Press.
Cutileiro, Jose
    1971   *A Portuguese rural society.* Oxford: Clarendon Press.
Cutler, Winnifred Berg
    1980   Lunar and menstrual phase locking. *American Journal of
            Obstetrics and Gynecology* 137:834–839.
Dalby, T. David P.
    1982   *Temne-English dictionary.* Unpublished manuscript.
Dalton, Katharina
    1979   *Once a month.* Pomona, Calif.: Hunter House.
Daniel, G.
    1981   *A short history of archaeology.* London: Thames & Hudson.
Daniels, F. J.
    1975   Snakes as wives and lovers in Japanese myth, legend
            and folk-tale. *Bulletin of the Japan Society of London* 75:
            12–21.
Davis, Geoffrey
    1974   "Menstrual toxin" and human fertility. *The Lancet* 8 June:
            1172–1173.
Davis, J.
    1977   *People of the Mediterranean.* London: Routledge & Kegan
            Paul.
Davis, Natalie Zemon
    1971   The reasons of misrule: Youth groups and charivaris in
            sixteenth-century France. *Past and Present* 50:41–75.
    1984   Ritual, antistructure and the historian's order. Paper pre-
            sented at the 83rd Annual Meeting of the American
            Anthropological Association, Denver (November).
d'Azevedo, Warren L.
    1983   *The Zogbenya of Gola Sande and the meaning of friendship.*
            Unpublished manuscript.
de Beauvoir, Simone
    1952   *The second sex*, trans. and ed. H. M. Parshley. New York:
            Knopf. (Original publication: *Le deuxième sexe*, 2 vols.
            Paris: Gallimard, 1949.)
Debrovner, Charles, ed.
    1982   *Premenstrual tension: A multidisciplinary approach.* New
            York: Human Sciences Press.
de Laguna, Frederica
    1972   *Under Mount Saint Elias: The history and culture of the*

Yakutat Tlingit, 3 vols. Smithsonian Contributions to Anthropology, vol. 7. Washington, D.C.: Smithsonian Institution Press.

Delaney, Carol
1977   The legacy of Abraham. In *Beyond androcentrism: New essays on women and religion*, ed. Rita M. Gross, 217–236. Missoula, Mont.: Scholars Press, for the American Academy of Religion.
1984   *Seed and soil: Symbols of procreation and the creation of a world*. Ph.D. dissertation, Anthropology Department, University of Chicago.
1987a   The meaning of paternity and the virgin birth debate. *Man* 21, no. 3:494–513.
1987b   Seeds of honor, fields of shame. In *Honor and shame and the unity of the Mediterranean*, ed. David D. Gilmore. 35–48. Washington, D.C.: American Anthropological Association, Special Publication no. 22.

Delaney, Janice, Mary Jane Lupton, and Emily Toth
1976   *The curse: A cultural history of menstruation*. New York: Dutton.

Derbyshire, Caroline
1980   *The new woman's guide to health and medicine*. New York: Appleton-Century-Crofts.

Deutsch, Helene
1950   The psychiatric component in gynecology. *Progress in Gynecology* 2:207–217. Reprinted in *Neurosis and character types*, 305–318. New York: International University Press, 1965.

Devereux, George
1950   The psychology of feminine genital bleeding. *International Journal of Psycho-Analysis* 31:237–257.

Dewan, E. M.
1967   On the possibility of a perfect rhythm method of birth control by periodic light stimulation. *American Journal of Obstetrics and Gynecology* 99:1016–1019.
1969   Rhythms. *Science and Technology* 20:20–28.

Dewan, E. M., M. F. Menkin, and J. Rock
1978   Effect of photic stimulation on the human menstrual cycle. *Photochemistry and Photobiology* 27:581–585.

Dorjahn, Vernon R.
1958   Fertility, polygyny and their interrelations in Temne society. *American Anthropologist* 60:838–860.
1959   The organization and functions of the *Ragbenle* Society of the Temne. *Africa* 29:156–170.
1961   The initiation of Temne Poro officials. *Man* 61:35–40.
1982   The initiation and training of Temne Poro members. In

African religious groups and beliefs, ed. Simon Ottenberg, 35–62. Evanston: Northwestern University Press.

Douglas, Mary
1966   *Purity and danger: An analysis of concepts of pollution and taboo*. London: Routledge & Kegan Paul.
1968   The relevance of tribal studies. *Journal of Psychosomatic Research* 12:21–28. Reprinted as Couvade and menstruation: The relevance of tribal studies. In *Implicit meanings*, M. Douglas, 60–72. London: Routledge & Kegan Paul.
1969   Correspondence: Virgin birth. *Man* 4:133–134.
1970   *Natural symbols*. London: Barrie & Rockliff.
1972   Self-evidence. The Henry Myers Lecture. *Proceedings of the Royal Anthropological Institute* for 1972:27–43. Reprinted in *Implicit meanings*, M. Douglas, 276–318. London: Routledge & Kegan Paul.
1975   *Implicit meanings*. London: Routledge & Kegan Paul.

Doyle, James C.
1952   Unnecessary hysterectomies. *Journal of the American Medical Association* 151:360–365.

Drucker, Philip
1937   The Tolowa and their southwest Oregon kin. *University of California Publications in American Archaeology and Ethnology* 36, no. 4:221–300.
1963   *Indians of the Northwest coast*. Garden City, N.Y.: Natural History Press. (Original edition: New York: McGraw Hill for the American Museum of Natural History, Anthropological Handbook No. 10, 1955.)

Dumont, Louis
1957   For a sociology of India. *Contributions to Indian Sociology* 1:7–22.

Durkheim, Émile
1897   La prohibition de l'inceste et ses origines. *L'Année Sociologique* 1:1–70.
1915   *The elementary forms of the religious life*, trans. Joseph Ward Swain. London: George Allen & Unwin. (Original publication: *Les formes élémentaires de la vie religieuse, le système totémique en Australie*. Paris: F. Alcan, Travaux de l'Année Sociologique, 1911.)

Dwyer, Daisy Hilse
1977   Bridging the gap between the sexes in Moroccan legal practice. In *Sexual stratification*, ed. A. Schlegel, 41–66. New York: Columbia University Press.
1978   *Images and self-images: Male and female in Morocco*. New York: Columbia University Press.

Eggan, Fred
1954   Social anthropology and the method of controlled comparison. *American Anthropologist* 56:743–763.

Ehrenreich, Barbara and Deirdre English
1974   *For her own good; 150 years of the experts' advice to women.* New York: Doubleday.

Eliade, Mircea
1963   *Patterns in comparative religion.* New York: Meridian Books.
1973   *Australian religions: An introduction.* New York: Cornell University Press.

Elkin, A. P.
1951   Introduction. In *Kunapipi: A study of an Australian Aboriginal cult,* R. M. Berndt. Melbourne: Cheshire.
1977   *Aboriginal man of high degree.* St. Lucia: University of Queensland Press.

Elmendorf, William W.
1960   The structure of Twana culture with comparative notes on the structure of Yurok culture by A. L. Kroeber. *Washington State University Research Studies* 28, no. 3, Monographic Supplement 2. Pullman, Washington.

Elsasser, Albert B.
1976   Review of Native Californians. *Journal of California Anthropology* 3, no. 2:95–96.

Engelbrektsson, Ulla-Britt
1978   *The force of tradition. Turkish migrants at home and abroad.* Göteburg, Sweden: Acta Universitatis Gothoburgensis. Gothenburg Studies in Social Anthropology, no. 1.

Erdentuğ, Nermin
1959   A study on the social structure of a Turkish village. *Publications of the Faculty of Languages, History and Geography* 30. Ankara, Turkey: University of Ankara.

Erikson, Erik H.
1943   Observations on the Yurok: Childhood and world image. *University of California Publications in American Archaeology and Ethnology* 35, no. 10:257–302.

Etienne, Mona
1977   Women and men, cloth and colonization: The transformation of production-distribution relations among the Baule (Ivory Coast). *Cahiers d'Études Africaines* 17, no. 65:41–64.
1981   Gender relations and conjugality among the Baule (Ivory Coast). *Culture* 1, no. 1:21–30.

Etienne, Mona and Eleanor Leacock, eds.
1980   *Women and colonization: Anthropological perspectives.* New York: Praeger/Bergin.

Evans-Pritchard, E. E.
1932   Heredity and gestation as the Zande see them. *Sociologus* 8:400–413.
1956   *Nuer religion.* Oxford: Clarendon Press.

1965*a*   The comparative method in social anthropology. In *The position of women in primitive societies and other essays in social anthropology*, 13–36. London: Faber and Faber.
1965*b*   *Primitive religion*. Oxford: Oxford University Press.

Faithorn, Elizabeth
1975   The concept of pollution among the Kafe of the Papua New Guinea Highlands. In *Toward an anthropology of women*, ed. R. R. Reiter, 127–140. New York: Monthly Review Press.

Fanon, Frantz
1963   *The wretched of the earth*, trans. Constance Farrington. New York: Grove Press. (Original publication: *Les damnés de la terre*. Paris: Maspéro, 1961.)

Fausto-Sterling, Anne
1985   *Myths of gender: Biological theories about women and men*. New York: Basic Books.

Fernandes, Valentim
1951   *Description de la Cote Occidentale d'Afrique (Sénégal au Cap de Monte, Archipels)*, trans. T. Monod, A. Teixeira da Mata and R. Mauny. Bissau, Guinea-Bissau: Centro de Estudos da Guine Portuguesa. Mem. 11.

Fiawoo, D. K.
1974   Characteristic features of Ewe ancestor worship. In *Ancestors*, ed. William H. Newell, 263–281. The Hague: Mouton.

Firth, Raymond
1973   *Symbols: Public and private*. Ithaca, N.Y.: Cornell University Press.

Flood, J.
1983   *Archaeology of the Dreamtime*. Sydney and London: Collins.

Fontenrose, J.
1959   *Python: A study of Delphic myth and its origins*. Berkeley and Los Angeles: University of California Press.

Ford, Clellan
1941   *Smoke from their fires*. New Haven: Yale University Press.
1945   *A comparative study of human reproduction*. New Haven: Yale University Press.

Foster, George
1967   *Tzintzuntzan: Mexican peasants in a changing world*. Boston: Little, Brown.

Foucault, Michel
1979   *Discipline and punish: The birth of the prison*, trans. Alan Sheridan. New York: Pantheon. (Original publication: *Surveiller et punir: naissance de la prison*. Paris: Gallimard, 1975.)

Fox-Genovese, Elizabeth
1982   Gender, class and power: Some theoretical considera-
         tions. *The History Teacher* 15:255–276.
Frank, Robert T.
1931   The hormonal causes of premenstrual tension. *Archives
         of Neurology and Psychiatry* 26:1053–1057.
Frazer, James George
1900   *The golden bough*, 2d ed. London: Macmillan.
1911   *The golden bough*, 3d ed. London: Macmillan.
1963   *The golden bough: A study in magic and religion*, abridged
(1950)   ed. New York: Macmillan. (First ed. 1890, London: Mac-
         millan.)
Freeman, Susan
1970   *Neighbors: The social contract in a Castilian hamlet*. Chicago:
         University of Chicago Press.
Freud, Sigmund
1930   *Civilization and its discontents*, rev. ed., 1963, trans. Joan
         Riviere, ed. James Strachey. London: Hogarth Press.
         (Original publication: *Das Unbehagen in der Kultur*. Vien-
         na: Internationaler Psychoanalytischer Verlag, 1930.)
1931   Female sexuality. In *Collected papers*, vol. 5, trans. Joan
         Riviere, ed. James Strachey, 252–272. London: Hogarth
         Press. (Original publication: Uber die weibliche Sexuali-
         tät, *Int. Z. Psychoanal.* 17, 1931, 317 ff.)
1950   *Totem and taboo: Some points of agreement between the mental
         lives of savages and neurotics*, trans. James Strachey. New
         York: Norton. (Reprinted: London: Routledge & Kegan
         Paul, 1960. Original publication: Totem und Tabu. *Imago*
         1–2, 1912–1913.)
1955   *The interpretation of dreams*, trans. James Strachey. New
         York: Basic Books. (Original publication: *Die Traumdeu-
         tung*. Leipzig and Vienna: Deuticke, 1900.)
Friedl, Ernestine
1967   The position of women: Appearance and reality. *An-
         thropological Quarterly* 40, no. 3:97–108.
1975   *Women and men: An anthropologist's view*. New York: Holt,
         Rinehart & Winston.
Frisch, Rose E.
1975   Demographic implications of the biological determinants
         of female fecundity. *Social Biology* 22, no. 1:17–22.
Geertz, Clifford
1966   *Person, time and conduct in Bali: An essay in cultural analysis*.
         Southeast Asia Studies, Cultural Report Series no. 14.
         New Haven: Yale University Press. Reprinted in *The
         interpretation of cultures*, C. Geertz, 360–411. New York:
         Basic Books.

1968 *Islam observed: Religious development in Morocco and Indonesia*. Chicago: University of Chicago Press.

1973 *The interpretation of cultures*. New York: Basic Books.

1976 Art as a cultural system. *Modern Language Notes* 91: 1473–1499.

1984 Anti anti-relativism. *American Anthropologist* 86:263–278.

Genovese, Eugene D.

1974 *Roll, Jordan, roll: The world the slaves made*. New York: Random House.

Gervis, Paul

1952 *Sierra Leone story*. London: Cassell.

Gilbreth, Frank B. and Ernestine Gilbreth Carey

1948 *Cheaper by the dozen*. New York: Bantam.

Gill, W.

1969 *Petermann Journey*. London: Angus & Robertson.

Gilman, Charlotte Perkins

1903 *The home: Its work and influence*. Urbana: University of Illinois Press. (Reprinted 1972.)

Gluckman, Max

1954 *Rituals of rebellion in South-East Africa*. The Frazer Lecture for 1952. Manchester: Manchester University Press. Reprinted in *Order and rebellion in tribal Africa: Collected essays with an autobiographical introduction*, Max Gluckman, 110–366. New York: Free Press.

1956 The license in ritual. In *Custom and conflict in Africa*, 109–135. London: Basil Blackwell.

1963 *Order and rebellion in tribal Africa*. New York: Free Press.

Goddard, P. E.

1903 Life and culture of the Hupa. *University of California Publications in American Archaeology and Ethnology* 1, no. 1:1–88.

Goffman, Erving

1959 *The presentation of self in everyday life*. Garden City, N.Y.: Doubleday.

Goldschmidt, Walter R.

1940 A Hupa calendar. *American Anthropologist* 42:176–177.

Golub, Sharon

1976 The effect of premenstrual anxiety and depression on cognitive function. *Journal of Personality and Social Psychology* 34:99–104.

Golub, Sharon, ed.

1985 *Lifting the curse of menstruation: A feminist appraisal of the influence of menstruation on women's lives*. New York: Harrington Park Press.

Good, Mary-Jo DelVecchio
  1980   Of blood and babies: The relationship of popular Islamic physiology to fertility. *Social Science and Medicine* 14B, no. 3:147–156.
Gottlieb, Alma
  1982   Sex, fertility and menstruation among the Beng of the Ivory Coast: A symbolic analysis. *Africa* 52, no. 4:34–47.
  1983   *Village kapok, forest kapok: Notions of separation, identity and gender among the Beng of Ivory Coast.* Ph.D. dissertation, Department of Anthropology, University of Virginia.
  1986a   Birth order, cousin marriage and gender: Alliance models among the Beng of Ivory Coast. *Man* 21, no. 4:697–722.
  1986b   Dog: Ally or traitor? Mythology, cosmology and society among the Beng of Ivory Coast. *American Ethnologist* 13, no. 3:65–76.
  1988   Witches, kings and identity; or, the power of paradox and the paradox of power among the Beng of Ivory Coast. In *The creativity of power*, ed. Ivan Karp and William Arens. Washington, D.C.: Smithsonian Institution Press.
  forth-   Reflections on "female pollution" among the Beng of
  coming   Ivory Coast. In *Beyond the second sex: Essays in the anthropology of gender*, ed. Peggy Sanday.
Gould, Richard A.
  1966   The wealth quest among the Tolowa Indians of northwestern California. *Proceedings of the American Philosophical Society* 110:67–87.
  1969   *Yiwara: Foragers of the Australian desert.* London and Sydney: Collins.
  1975   Ecology and adaptive response among the Tolowa Indians of northwestern California. *Journal of California Anthropology* 2, no. 2:148–170.
Graham, C. A. and W. C. McGrew
  1980   Menstrual synchrony in female undergraduates living on a coeducational campus. *Psychoneuroendocrinology* 3:245–252.
Graham, Susan Brandt
  1985   Running and menstrual dysfunction: Recent medical discoveries provide new insights into the human division of labor by sex. *American Anthropologist* 87:878–882.
Gramsci, Antonio
  1971   *Selections from the prison notebooks of Antonio Gramsci,*

trans. and ed. Quintin Hoare and Geoffrey Nowell Smith. New York: International Publishers. (Original publication: *Quaderni del Carcere*. Turin: G. Einaudi, 1948–1951.)

Gregory, James R.
1984   The myth of the male ethnographer and the woman's world. *American Anthropologist* 86:316–327.

Groger-Wurm, H. M.
1973   *Australian Aboriginal bark paintings and their mythological interpretation*, vol. 1. *Eastern Arnhem Land*. Canberra: Australian Institute of Aboriginal Studies.

Hair, Paul E. H.
1975   Sources on early Sierra Leone 4: Ruiters (1623). *Africana Research Bulletin* 5, no. 3:52–70.

Halbreich, Uriel and Jean Endicott
1982   Classification of premenstrual syndromes. In *Behavior and the menstrual cycle*, ed. Richard C. Friedman, 243–266. New York: Marcel Dekker.

Hammond, Dorothy and Alta Jablow
1976   *Women in cultures of the world*. Menlo Park, Calif.: Benjamin Cummings.

Hanson, F. Allan
1970   The Rapan theory of conception. *American Anthropologist* 72:1444–1447.

1975   *Meaning in culture*. London: Routledge & Kegan Paul.

Harding, Susan
1975   Women and words in a Spanish village. In *Toward an anthropology of women*, ed. R. R. Reiter, 283–308. New York: Monthly Review Press.

Harlow, Siobán D.
1986   Function and dysfunction: A historical critique of the literature on menstruation and work. In *Culture, society and menstruation*, ed. Virginia L. Olesen and Nancy Fugate Woods, 39–50. Washington: Hemisphere Publishing Corp./Harper & Row.

Harrell, Barbara B.
1981   Lactation and menstruation in cultural perspective. *American Anthropologist* 83:796–823.

Harrington, J. P.
1931   Karuk texts. *International Journal of American Linguistics* 6:121–161, 194–226.

1932   *Tobacco among the Karuk Indians*. Bureau of American Ethnology, Bulletin 94. Washington, D.C.: Government Printing Office.

Harris, Grace
   1957   Possession "hysteria" in a Kenya tribe. *American Anthropologist* 61:1046–1066.
Harris, Marvin
   1977   *Cannibals and kings: The origins of cultures.* New York: Random House.
Harrison, Michelle
   1984   *Self-help for premenstrual syndrome.* Cambridge, Mass.: Matrix Press.
Hauenschild, C.
   1960   Lunar periodicity. *Cold Spring Harbor Symposium on Quantitative Biology* 25:491–497.
Hays, Terence E.
   n.d.   *Menstrual expressions and menstrual attitudes.* Unpublished manuscript.
Herdt, Gilbert H., ed.
   1982   *Rituals of manhood.* Berkeley, Los Angeles, London: University of California Press.
Herrmann, W. M. and R. C. Beach
   1978   Experimental and clinical data indicating the psychotropic properties of progestogens. *Postgraduate Medical Journal* 54:82–87.
Hiatt, L. R.
   1975   Swallowing and regurgitation in Australian myth and rite. In *Australian Aboriginal mythology: Essays in honour of W. E. H. Stanner,* ed. L. R. Hiatt, 143–162. Canberra: Australian Institute of Aboriginal Studies.
Hoebel, E. Adamson
   1960   *The Cheyennes: Indians of the Great Plains.* New York: Holt, Rinehart & Winston.
Hoffman, R. A., J. A. Hester, and C. Towns
   1965   Effect of light and temperature on the endocrine system of the golden hamster. *Comparative Biochemistry and Physiology* 15:525–533.
Hogbin, Ian
   1970   *The island of menstruating men: Religion in Wogeo, New Guinea.* London: Chandler.
Holden, Constance
   1986   Proposed new psychiatric diagnoses raise charges of gender bias. *Science* 231 (24 January):327–328.
Hollingworth, Leta
   1914   *Functional periodicity: An experimental study of the mental and motor abilities of women during menstruation.* New York: Teacher's College.

Hongladarom, Gail, Ruth McCorkle, and Nancy Fugate Woods
    1982   *The complete book of women's health.* Englewood Cliffs,
            N.J.: Prentice-Hall.
Honigmann, John J.
    1954   *The Kaska Indians: An ethnographic reconstruction.* Publica-
            tions in Anthropology no. 51. New Haven: Yale Univer-
            sity.
Horney, Karen
    1931   *Feminine psychology.* London: Routledge & Kegan Paul.
            (Reprinted 1967.)
Horton, Robin and Ruth Finnegan, eds.
    1973   *Modes of thought: Essays on thinking in Western and non-
            Western societies.* London: Faber & Faber.
Howell, Nancy
    1979   *Demography of the Dobe !Kung.* New York: Academic
            Press.
Hubert, Henri and Marcel Mauss
    1898   Essai sur la nature et la fonction du sacrifice. *L'Année
            Sociologique* 2:29–138. (English translation, *Sacrifice: Its
            nature and function.* London: Cohen & West, 1964.)
Hunte, Pamela A.
    1985   Indigenous methods of fertility regulation in Afghanis-
            tan. In *Women's medicine: A cross-cultural study of indige-
            nous fertility regulation,* ed. Lucile F. Newman, 43–75.
            New Brunswick, N.J.: Rutgers University Press.
Ingersoll, E.
    1928   *Dragons and dragon-lore.* New York: Payson & Clarke.
Jacobi, Mary Putnam
    1877   *The question of rest for women during menstruation.* New
            York: G. P. Putnam's Sons.
Jetté, A. Julius
    1911   On the superstitions of the Ten'a Indians (middle part
            of the Yukon Valley, Alaska). *Anthropos* 6:95–108, 241–
            259, 602–615, 699–723.
Joffe, Natalie F.
    1948   The vernacular of menstruation. *Word* 4, no. 3:181–186.
Johnson, W. O.
    1939   Emotional disturbances with pelvic symptoms. *Southern
            Surgeon* 8:373–383.
Kaberry, Phyllis M.
    1939   *Aboriginal woman: Sacred and profane.* London: George
            Routledge and Sons.
Kahn, Morton
    1931   *Djuka: Bush Negroes of Dutch Guiana.* New York: Viking
            Press.

Keesing, Roger M.
1985   Conventional metaphors and anthropological meta-
        physics: Problematic of cultural translation. *Journal of
        Anthropological Research* 41:201–218.

Kerns, Virginia
1983   *Women and the ancestors: Black Carib kinship and ritual.*
        Urbana: University of Illinois Press.

Kessler, Evelyn
1976   *Women: An anthropological view.* New York: Holt, Rinehart
        & Winston.

Kharrazi, Lily
1980   State of separation: Syrian Jewish women and menstru-
        ation. *National Women's Anthropology Newsletter* 4, no.
        2:13–14, 27.

Kiltie, R.
1982   On the significance of menstrual synchrony in closely
        associated women. *American Naturalist* 119:414–419.

King, Helen
1983   Born to bleed: Artemis and Greek women. In *Images of
        women in antiquity,* eds. Averil Cameron and Amelie
        Kuhrt, 109–127. Detroit: Wayne State University Press.

Kippley, Sheila
1975   *Breast-feeding and natural child spacing.* New York: Pen-
        guin. (First ed., Cincinnati: K. Publishers, 1969.)

Kirk, David
1964   *Shared fate.* New York: Free Press.

Kirksey, Matthew
1984   Dying. *Grassroots 1984* (Southern Illinois University at
        Carbondale), 32–35.

Kitahara, Michio
1982   Menstrual taboos and the importance of hunting. *Amer-
        ican Anthropologist* 84:901–903.

Klein, R. G.
1969   *Man and culture in the late Pleistocene.* San Francisco:
        Chandler.

Knight, Chris
1983   Lévi-Strauss and the dragon: *Mythologiques* reconsidered
        in the light of an Australian Aboriginal myth. *Man* 18:
        21–50.

1984   Correspondence: Snakes and dragons. *Man* 19:152–157.

1985   Menstruation as medicine. *Social Science and Medicine*
        21:671–683.

1986   *The hunter's "own kill" rule; a new theory of symbolic cultural
        origins.* Paper presented at the Fourth International Con-
        ference on Hunting and Gathering Societies, London.

Koeske, Randi Daimon
    1985   Lifting the curse of menstruation: Toward a feminist perspective on the menstrual cycle. In *Lifting the curse of menstruation*, ed. S. Golub, 1–16. New York: Harrington Park Press.
Kramer, Ann
    1981   *Woman's body*. New York: Simon & Schuster.
Kroeber, A. L.
    1925   *Handbook of the Indians of California*. Bureau of American Ethnology, Bulletin 78. Washington, D.C.: Government Printing Office.
    1976   *Yurok myths*. Berkeley, Los Angeles, London: University of California Press.
Kroeber, A. L. and E. W. Gifford
    1949   World renewal: A cult system of native northwest California. *Anthropological Records* 13.
Kroeber, Theodora, A. B. Elsasser, and R. F. Heizer
    1977   *Drawn from life: California Indians in pen and brush*. Socorro, N.M.: Ballena Press.
Kuper, Hilda
    1947   *An African aristocracy: Rank among the Swazi*. London: Oxford University Press for the International African Institute.
Laderman, Carol
    1981   Symbolic and empirical reality: A new approach to the analysis of food avoidances. *American Ethnologist* 8, no. 3: 468–493.
Ladurie, Emanuel Le Roy
    1979   *Montaillou: The promised land of error*. New York: Random House. (Original publication *Montaillou, village occitan de 1294 à 1324*. Paris: Gallimard, 1975.)
La Fontaine, Jean S.
    1972   Ritualization of women's life-crises in Bugisu. In *The interpretation of ritual, essays in honour of A. I. Richards*, ed. Jean S. LaFontaine, 159–186. London: Tavistock.
    1977   The power of rights. *Man* 12:421–437.
    1985   *Initiation; ritual drama and secret knowledge across the world*. Harmondsworth: Penguin.
Lamp, Frederick J.
    1978   Frogs into princes: The Temne Rabai initiation. *African Arts* 11, no. 2:38–49, 94–95.
    1979   Relief of an Aztec goddess in the Olsen collection. *Yale Art Gallery Bulletin* 37, no. 2:24–32.
    1982   *Temne rounds: The arts as spatial and temporal indicators in a West African society*. Ph.D. dissertation, Department of the History of Art, Yale University.

1983 House of stones: Memorial art of fifteenth century Sierra Leone. *The Art Bulletin* 65, no. 2:219–237.

1985 Cosmos, cosmetics, and the spirit of Bondo. *African Arts* 18, no. 3:28–43, 98–99.

1988 An opera of the West African Bondo: The act, ideas, and the word. *The Drama Review* 32, no. 1.

Lamphere, Louise

1974 Strategies, cooperation and conflict among women in domestic groups. In *Woman, culture and society*, ed. M. Z. Rosaldo and L. Lamphere, 97–112. Stanford: Stanford University Press.

Lanson, Lucienne

1984 *From woman to woman: A gynecologist answers questions about you and your body*. New York: Pinnacle Books.

LaPin, Deirdre

1983 *Astronomy and lunar ritual among the Ngas of Nigeria*. Paper presented at the First International Conference on Ethnoastronomy, Washington, D.C.

Laqueur, Thomas

1986 Orgasm, generation, and the politics of reproductive biology. *Representations* 14 (Spring):1–41. Special issue: Sexuality and the Social Body in the Nineteenth Century.

Lauersen, Niels H. and Eileen Stukane

1983 *PMS Premenstrual syndrome and you: Next month can be different*. New York: Simon and Schuster.

Lauersen, Niels and Steven Whitney

1983 *It's your body: A woman's guide to gynecology*. New York: Berkley. (Original ed. 1977.)

Lawrence, Denise

1979 *Festas: Cooperation in rural southern Portugal*. Ph.D. dissertation, Department of Anthropology, University of California, Riverside.

Leach, Edmund

1967 Virgin birth. *Proceedings of the Royal Anthropological Institute* for 1966, pp. 39–49.

1968 Correspondence: Virgin birth. *Man* 3:129, 655–656.

1976 *Culture and communication: The logic by which symbols are connected; an introduction to the use of structuralist analysis in social anthropology*. Cambridge: Cambridge University Press.

Leacock, Eleanor

1975 Class, commodity, and the status of women. In *Women cross-culturally: Change and challenge*, ed. Ruby Rohrlich-Leavitt, 601–616. The Hague: Mouton.

1978 Women's status in egalitarian society: Implications for social evolution. *Current Anthropology* 19:247–255.

Lederman, Rena
    forth-   Contested order: Gender and society in Highland New
    coming   Guinea. In *Beyond the second sex,* ed. Peggy Sanday.
Lerner, Gerda, ed.
    1972   *Black women in white America.* New York: Random House.
Leroi-Gourhan, A.
    1968   *The art of prehistoric man in Western Europe.* London:
            Thames & Hudson.
Lever, Judy with Michael G. Brush
    1981   *Pre-menstrual tension.* New York: Bantam.
Lévi-Strauss, Claude
    1963a   Language and the analysis of social laws. In *Structural
             anthropology,* 55–66. New York: Basic Books. (Essay orig-
             inally published 1951.)
    1963b   Linguistics and anthropology. In *Structural anthropology,*
             67–80. (Essay originally published 1952.)
    1963c   Structural analysis in linguistics and in anthropology. In
             Structural anthropology, 31–54. (Essay originally pub-
             lished 1945.)
    1963d   *Structural anthropology,* trans. Claire Jacobson and Brooke
             Grundfest Schoepf. New York: Basic Books. (Original:
             Anthropologie Structurale. Paris: Plon, 1960.)
    1963e   *Totemism,* trans. Rodney Needham. Boston: Beacon.
             (Original: *Le Totémisme aujourd'hui.* Paris: Plon, 1962.)
    1966   *The savage mind,* trans. anon. Chicago: University of
            Chicago Press. (Original: *La Pensée sauvage.* Paris: Plon,
            1962.)
    1969   *The elementary structures of kinship,* trans. Rodney
            Needham, et al. London: Eyre and Spottiswoode. (Orig-
            inal: *Les structures élémentaires de la parenté.* Paris: Plon,
            1949; rev. ed. 1967.)
    1970   *The raw and the cooked: Introduction to a science of mythology
            vol. 1,* trans. John and Doreen Weightman. London:
            Jonathan Cape. (Original: *Le cru et le cuit.* Paris: Plon,
            1964.)
    1973   *From honey to ashes. Introduction to a science of mythology,*
            vol. 2, trans. John and Doreen Weightman. New York:
            Harper & Row. (Original: *Du miel aux cendres.* Paris:
            Plon, 1966.)
    1976a   Jean-Jaques Rousseau, founder of the sciences of man.
             In *Structural anthropology,* vol. 2, 67–80. New York: Basic
             Books. (Essay originally published 1962.)
    1976b   *Structural anthropology,* vol. 2, trans. Monique Layton.
             New York: Basic Books. (Original: *Anthropologie struc-
             turale,* vol. 2. Paris: Plon, 1973.)

1978   *The origin of table manners. Introduction to a science of mythology*, vol. 3, trans. John and Doreen Weightman. New York: Harper & Row. (Original: *L'Origine des manières de table*. Paris: Plon, 1968.)

1981   *The naked man. Introduction to a science of mythology*, vol. 4, trans. John and Doreen Weightman. New York: Harper & Row. (Original: *L'Homme nu*. Paris: Plon, 1971.)

Lewis, I. M.

1971   *Ecstatic religion: An anthropological study of spirit possession and shamanism*. Harmondsworth: Penguin.

Lincoln, Bruce

1975   The religious significance of women's scarification among the Tiv. *Africa* 45:316–326.

Lorde, Audre

1982   *Chosen poems: Old and new*. New York: Norton.

Lowe, Marian

1983   The dialectic of biology and culture. In *Woman's nature: Rationalizations of inequality*, ed. Marian Lowe and Ruth Hubbard, 39–62. New York: Pergamon.

Lowie, Robert

1931   Women and religion. In *The making of man: An outline of anthropology*, ed. V. F. Calverton, 744–757. New York: Random House.

1963   *Indians of the plains*. Garden City, N.Y.: Natural History Press.

McCarthy, F. D.

1960   The string figures of Yirrkalla. In *Records of the American-Australian Scientific Expedition to Arnhem Land*, vol. 2, *Anthropology and nutrition*, ed. C. P. Mountford. Melbourne: Melbourne University Press.

McClintock, Martha K.

1971   Menstrual synchrony and suppression. *Nature* 229, no. 5285:244–245.

1981   Social control of the ovarian cycle and the function of estrous synchrony. *American Zoologist* 21:243–256.

McConnel, Ursula H.

1936   Totemic hero cults in Cape York Peninsula, North Queensland, part 2. *Oceania* 7:69–105.

MacCormack, Carol P. and Marilyn Strathern, eds.

1980   *Nature, culture and gender*. Cambridge: Cambridge University Press.

MacGaffey, Wyatt

1969   Correspondence: Virgin birth. *Man* 4:457.

McKnight, D.

1975   Men, women and other animals: Taboo and purification among the Wikmungkan. In *The interpretation of symbolism*, ed. Roy Willis, 77–97. London: Malaby.

Maddock, K.
1974   *The Australian Aborigines: A portrait of their society.* London: Penguin.
1978a   Introduction. In *The rainbow serpent*, ed. I. Buchler and K. Maddock, 1–12. The Hague: Mouton.
1978b   Metaphysics in a mythical view of the world. In *The rainbow serpent*, ed. I. Buchler and K. Maddock, 99–118. The Hague: Mouton.

Magnarella, Paul J.
1974   *Tradition and change in a Turkish town.* Cambridge, Mass.: Schenkman.

Maloney, Clarence, ed.
1976   *The evil eye.* New York: Columbia University Press.

March, Katherine S.
1980   Deer, bears, and blood: A note on nonhuman animal response to menstrual odor. *American Anthropologist* 82:125–127.

Marcus, Julie
1984   Islam, women and pollution in Turkey. *Journal of the Anthropological Association of Oxford* 15, no. 3:204–218.

Margai, Milton A. S.
1965   *Akafa Kɔlɔl ka kaKomsir,* trans. H. Kamara. Bo, Sierra Leone: Provincial Literature Bureau.

Marshack, Alexander
1977   The meander as a system: The analysis and recognition of iconographic units in upper palaeolithic compositions. In *Form in indigenous art*, ed. P. J. Ucko, 286–317. London: Duckworth.
1985   On the dangers of serpents in the mind. *Current Anthropology* 26:139–145.

Martin, Emily
1987   *The woman in the body: A cultural analysis of reproduction.* Boston: Beacon Press.

Marx, Karl
1967   *Capital: A critique of political economy,* vol. 1. *The process of capitalist production,* ed. Frederich Engels, trans. Samuel Moore and Edward Aveling. New York: International Publishers (Original: *Das Kapital,* 1867.)

Marx, Karl and Frederich Engels
1947   *The German ideology,* parts 1 and 3, ed. R. Pascal, trans. W. Lough and C. P. Magill. New York: International Publishers. (Original: *Die deutsche Ideologie. Kritik der neuesten deutschen Philosophie, in ihren Repräsentanten,*

Feuerbach, B. Bauer und Stirner, und des deutschen Sozialismus in seinen verschiedenen Propheten. MSS., 1845–1846.) (Reprinted, New York: International Publishers, 1967.)

Matsumoto, S., M. Igarashi, and Y. Nagaoka
1968   Environmental anovulatory cycles. *International Journal of Fertility* 13:15–23.

Mauss, Marcel
1979   Body techniques. In *Sociology and psychology, Essays by Marcel Mauss,* trans. Ben Brewster, 95–123. London: Routledge & Kegan Paul. (Original French publication 1935.)

Mead, Margaret
1928   *Coming of age in Samoa.* New York: William Morrow.
1970   *The mountain Arapesh II: Arts and supernaturalism.* Garden City, N.Y.: The Natural History Press. (Originally published 1938–1940 as *The Mountain Arapesh,* Part 1: *An importing culture;* Part 2: *Supernaturalism.* New York: American Museum of Natural History, Anthropological Papers, 36, no. 3; 37, no. 3.)

Meeker, Michael
1970   *The Black Sea Turks: A study of honor, descent and marriage.* Ph.D. dissertation, Department of Anthropology, University of Chicago.
1976   Meaning and society in the Middle East: Examples from the Black Sea Turks and the Levantine Arabs. *International Journal of Middle East Studies* 7, no. 2:243–270; 7, no. 3:383–422.

Meggitt, Mervyn J.
1964   Male-female relationships in the Highlands of Australian New Guinea. *American Anthropologist* 66, no. 4, pt. 2:204–224.

Meier, Fritz
1971   The ultimate origin and the hereafter in Islam. In *Islam and its cultural divergence,* ed. G. L. Tikku, 96–112. Urbana: University of Illinois Press.

Menaker, W.
1967   Lunar periodicity with reference to live births. *American Journal of Obstetrics and Gynaecology* 99:1016–1019.

Menaker, W. and A. Menaker
1959   Lunar periodicity in human reproduction: A likely unit of biological time. *American Journal of Obstetrics and Gynaecology* 77:905–914.

Mernissi, Fatima
1975   *Beyond the veil: Male-female dynamics in a modern Muslim society.* London: Halsted Wiley.

Miller, Norman F.
   1946   Hysterectomies: Therapeutic necessity or surgical
           racket? *American Journal of Obstetrics and Gynaecology*
           51:804–810.
Millet, Kate
   1970   *Sexual politics.* New York: Doubleday.
Minai, Naila
   1981   *Women in Islam: Tradition & transition in the Middle East.*
           London: John Murray.
Montagu, M. F. Ashley
   1937   *Coming into being among the Australian Aborigines.* London:
           Routledge.
   1940   Physiology and the origins of the menstrual prohibi-
           tions. *Quarterly Review of Biology* 15, no. 2:211–220.
   1957   *Anthropology and human nature.* NewYork: McGraw-Hill.
Montgomery, Rita E.
   1974   A cross-cultural study of menstrual taboos, and related
           social variables. *Ethos* 2:137–170.
Mountford, C. P.
   1956   *Art, myth and symbolism. Records of the American-Australian
           scientific expedition to Arnhem Land,* vol. 1. Melbourne:
           Melbourne University Press.
   1978   The rainbow-serpent myths of Australia. In *The rainbow
           serpent,* eds. I. Buchler and K. Maddock, 23–97. The
           Hague: Mouton.
Nasr, Seyyed Hossein
   1978   *An introduction to Islamic cosmological doctrines.* Boulder,
           Colo.: Shambhala.
Needham, Rodney
   1969   Correspondence: Virgin birth. *Man* 4:457–458.
   1972   *Belief, language, and experience.* Chicago: University of
           Chicago Press.
New York Times
   1986   Ideas and trends: Psychiatrists versus feminists. *New
           York Times,* 6 July, section 4, p. 7.
Niangoran-Bouah, Georges
   1964   *La Division du temps et le calendrier rituel des peuples
           lagunaires de Cote-d'Ivoire.* Paris: Institut d'Ethnologie.
Norbeck, Edward
   1967   African rituals of conflict. In *Gods and rituals,* ed. John
           Middleton, 197–226. New York: American Museum of
           Natural History.
Novak, Emil, M.D.
   1916   The superstition and folklore of menstruation. *Johns Hop-
           kins Hospital Bulletin* 27, no. 307:270–274 (26 September).

Nunley, M. Christopher
   1981   Response of deer to human blood odor. *American An-thropologist* 83, no. 3:631–634.
Oakley, Ann
   1974   *The sociology of housework*. New York: Pantheon.
O'Flaherty, Wendy Doniger
   1980   *Women, androgynes, and other mythical beasts*. Chicago: University of Chicago Press.
Ortner, Sherry B.
   1974   Is female to male as nature is to culture? In *Woman, culture and society*, ed. M. Z. Rosaldo and L. Lamphere, 67–87. Stanford: Stanford University Press.
Ortner, Sherry B. and Harriet Whitehead
   1981   Introduction: Accounting for sexual meanings. In *Sexual meanings*, ed. S. B. Ortner and H. Whitehead, 1–27. Cambridge: Cambridge University Press.
Ortner, Sherry B. and Harriet Whitehead, eds.
   1981   *Sexual meanings: The cultural construction of gender and sexuality*. Cambridge: Cambridge University Press.
Ott, Sandra
   1979   Aristotle among the Basques: The cheese analogy of conception. *Man* 14:699–711.
Paige, Karen Ericksen and Jeffery M. Paige
   1981   *The politics of reproductive ritual*. Berkeley, Los Angeles, London: University of California Press.
Parlee, Mary
   1973   The premenstrual syndrome. *Psychological Bulletin* 80:454–465.
Parsons, Anne
   1969   Is the Oedipus complex universal? The Jones-Malinowski debate revisited. In *Belief, magic, and anomie; Essays in psychological anthropology*, 3–66. New York: Free Press.
Patterson, Carolyn Bennett
   1986   In the far Pacific at the birth of nations. *National Geographic* 170, no. 4:460–499.
Paul, Lois
   1974   The mastery of work and the mystery of sex in a Guatemalan village. In *Woman, culture and society*, ed. M. Z. Rosaldo and L. Lamphere, 281–299. Stanford: Stanford University Press.
p'Bitek, Okot
   1966   *Song of Lawino*. Nairobi: East African Publishing House.
Pescatello, Ann M.
   1976   *Power and pawn: The female in Iberian families, societies, and cultures*. Westport, Conn.: Greenwood Press.

Pickles, V. R.
  1974   "Menstrual toxin" again. *The Lancet,* 22 June:1292–1293.
Pilling, Arnold R.
  1978   Yurok. In *Handbook of North American Indians,* vol. 8, ed.
           R. F. Heizer, 137–154. Washington, D.C.: Smithsonian
           Institution Press.
Pitt-Rivers, J. A.
  1961   *People of the Sierra.* Chicago: University of Chicago Press.
Pliny, The Elder
  1963   *The Natural History,* book 28, chap. 23, trans. W. H. S.
           Jones. Cambridge: Harvard University Press.
Ploss, Herman, Max Bartels, and Paul Bartels
  1935   *Woman: An historical gynaecological and anthropological com-
           pendium.* London: Heinemann.
The PMS Connection
  1982–   *PMS connection.* Madison, Wis.: PMS Action.
  1984
Poole, Fitz John Porter
  1982   The ritual forging of identity: Aspects of person and self
           in Bimin-Kuskusmin male initiation. In *Rituals of man-
           hood,* ed. G. H. Herdt, 9–154. Berkeley, Los Angeles,
           London: University of California Press.
Powers, Marla N.
  1980   Menstruation and reproduction: An Oglala case. *Signs* 6,
           no. 1:54–65.
Powers, Stephen
  1976   *Tribes of California.* Berkeley, Los Angeles, London: Uni-
           versity of California Press. (Original edition 1877.
           Washington, D.C.: Government Printing Office.)
Presser, H. B.
  1974   Temporal data relating to the human menstrual cycle. In
           Biorhythms and human reproduction, ed. M. Ferin, F. Hal-
           berg, R. M. Richart, and R. L. Van de Wiele, 145–160.
           New York: Wiley.
Price, Sally
  1984   *Co-wives and calabashes.* Ann Arbor: University of Michi-
           gan Press.
Quadagno, D. M., H. M. Shubeita, J. Deck, and D. Francouer
  1979   A study of the effects of males, exercise, and all-female
           living conditions on the menstrual cycle. (Abstract.) *Con-
           ference on Reproductive Behavior,* Tulane University, New
           Orleans.
  1981   Influence of male social contacts, exercise and all-female

living conditions on the menstrual cycle. *Psychoneuroen-docrinology* 6:239–244.

Radcliffe-Brown, A. R.
1926   The rainbow serpent myth of Australia. *Journal of the Royal Anthropological Institute of Great Britain and Ireland* 56:19–25.
1930   The rainbow-serpent myth in southeastern Australia. *Oceania* 1:342–347.

Rahman, Fazlur
1980   *Major themes of the Qur'an.* Chicago: Bibliotheca Islamica.

Rattray, R. S.
1927   *Religion and art in Ashanti.* Oxford: Clarendon Press.

Ray, Verne F.
1939   *Cultural relations in the plateau of northwestern America.* Los Angeles: F. W. Hodge Anniversary Fund, Southwest Museum, Vol. 2.

Reid, Helen E.
1974   The brass-ring sign. *The Lancet* (18 May):988.

Reinberg, A., F. Halberg, J. Ghata, and M. Siffre
1966   Spectre thermique (rhythmes de la température rectale) d'une femme adulte avant, pendant, et après son isolement souterrain de trois mois. *Comptes Rendus de l'Académie Scientifique D.* 262:782–785.

Reiter, Rayna Rapp
1975   Men and women in the south of France: Public and private domains. In *Toward an anthropology of women,* ed. R. R. Reiter, 252–282. New York: Monthly Review Press.
1977   The search for origins: Unraveling the threads of gender hierarchy. *Critique of Anthropology* 3, nos. 9–10:5–24.

Reiter, Rayna Rapp, ed.
1975   *Toward an anthropology of women.* New York: Monthly Review Press.

Rich, Adrienne
1976   *Of woman born.* New York: Norton.

Richards, Audrey
1950   Some types of family structure amongst the Central Bantu. In *African systems of kinship and marriage,* ed. A. R. Radcliffe-Brown and Daryll Forde. London: Oxford University Press.
1956   *Chisungu: A girl's initiation ceremony among the Bemba of northern Rhodesia.* London: Faber.

Riegelhaupt, Joyce
1967   Saloio women: An analysis of informal and formal poli-

tical and economic roles of Portuguese women. *Anthropological Quarterly* 40, no. 3:109–126.

Rivière, Peter G.
1974–   Couvade: A problem reborn. *Man* 9:423–435; 10:476.
1975

Robinson, R.
1966   *Aboriginal myths and legends.* Melbourne: Sun Books.

Rogers, Susan Carol
1978   Woman's place: A critical review of anthropological theory. *Comparative Studies in Society and History* 20, no. 1:123–161.

Róheim, Geza
1945   *The eternal ones of the dream.* New York: International Universities Press.
1974   *Children of the desert: The western tribes of central Australia.* New York: Basic Books.

Rohrlich-Leavitt, Ruby, Barbara Sykes, and Elizabeth Weatherford
1975   Aboriginal woman: Male and female anthropological perspectives. In *Women cross-culturally: Change and challenge,* ed. Ruby Rohrlich-Leavitt, 567–580. The Hague: Mouton.

Rome, Esther
1986   Premenstrual syndrome (PMS) examined through a feminist lens. In *Culture, society, and menstruation,* ed. Virginia L. Olesen and Nancy Fugate Woods, 145–151. Washington: Hemisphere Publishing Corp./Harper & Row.

Rosaldo, Michelle Zimbalist
1974   Woman, culture and society: A theoretical overview. In *Woman, culture and society,* ed. M. Z. Rosaldo and L. Lamphere, 17–42. Stanford: Stanford University Press.
1980   The use and abuse of anthropology: Reflections on feminism and cross-cultural understanding. *Signs* 5, no. 3:389–417.

Rosaldo, Michelle Zimbalist and Jane Monnig Atkinson
1975   Man the hunter and woman: Metaphors for the sexes in Ilongot magical spells. In *The interpretation of symbolism,* ed. Roy Willis, 43–75. London: J. M. Dent & Sons, Ltd.; New York: John Wiley & Sons.

Rosaldo, Michelle Zimbalist and Louise Lamphere, eds.
1974   *Woman, culture and society.* Stanford: Stanford University Press.

Rossi, Alice S. and Peter E. Rossi
1977   Body time and social time: Mood patterns by menstrual cycle phase and day of the week. *Social Science Research* 6:273–308.

Russell, M. J., G. M. Switz, and K. Thompson
  1980   Olfactory influences on the human menstrual cycle. *Pharmacology, Biochemistry, and Behavior* 13:737–738.

Saadawi, Nawal el
  1980   *The hidden face of Eve: Women in the Arab world.* London: Zed Press.

Sacks, Karen
  1974   Engels revisited: Women, the organization of production, and private property. In *Woman, culture and society,* ed. M. Z. Rosaldo and L. Lamphere, 207–223. Stanford: Stanford University Press.

Sahlins, Marshall
  1976   *Culture and practical reason.* Chicago: University of Chicago Press.

Sanday, Peggy
  1981   *Female power and male dominance: On the origins of sexual inequality.* Cambridge: Cambridge University Press.

Sanders, Lawrence
  1981   *The third deadly sin.* New York: Berkley Books.

Sawyerr, Harry A. E.
  1970   *God: Ancestor or creator.* London: Longmans.

Schafer, E. H.
  1973   *The divine woman: Dragon ladies and rain maidens in T'ang literature.* Berkeley, Los Angeles, London: University of California Press.

Schlegel, Alice
  1972   *Male dominance and female autonomy; Domestic authority in matrilineal societies.* New Haven: Human Relations Area Files Press.

Schlegel, Alice, ed.
  1977   *Sexual stratification; A cross-cultural view.* New York: Columbia University Press.

Schlenker, Christian F.
  1861   *A collection of Temne traditions, fables, and proverbs.* London: Christian Missionary Society.

Schmidt, W.
  1953   Sexualismus, Mythologie und Religion in Nord-Australien. *Anthropos* 48:898–924.

Schwimmer, Erik G.
  1969   Correspondence: Virgin birth. *Man* 4:132–133.

Scott, Joan Wallach
  1980   The mechanization of women's work. *Scientific American* (March):167–185.

Shapiro, Judith
  1979   Cross-cultural perspectives in sexual differentiation. In *Human sexuality; a comparative and developmental perspec-*

tive, ed. H. A. Katchadourian, 269–308. Berkeley, Los Angeles, London: University of California Press.

Shimkin, E. M.
1978   The Upper Paleolithic in north-central Eurasia: Evidence and problems. In *Views of the past: essays in Old World prehistory and paleoanthropology*, ed. L. G. Freeman, 193–315. The Hague: Mouton.

Shostak, Marjorie
1981   *Nisa: The life and words of a !Kung woman.* Cambridge: Harvard University Press.
1983   *Nisa: The life and words of a !Kung woman.* Harmondsworth: Penguin.

Shuttle, Penelope and Peter Redgrove
1978   *The wise wound: Menstruation and everywoman.* London: Victor Gollancz Ltd.

Silberbauer, George B.
1963   Marriage and the girl's puberty ceremony of the G/wi Bushmen. *Africa* 33, no. 4:12–26.

Silberman, Isidor
1950   A contribution to the psychology of menstruation. *International Journal of Psycho-Analysis* 31:258–267.

Singer, Milton
1980   Signs of self. *American Anthropologist* 82:485–507.

Skandhan, K. P., A. K. Pandya, S. Skandhan, and Y. B. Mehta
1979   Synchronization of menstruation among intimates and kindreds. *Panminerva Medica* 21:131–134.

Skultans, Vieda
1970   The symbolic significance of menstruation and the menopause. *Man* 5:639–651.

Snow, Loudell F. and Shirley M. Johnson
1977   Modern day menstrual folklore: Some clinical implications. *Journal of the American Medical Association* 237, no. 25 (20 June):2736–2739.

Snowden, Robert and Barbara Christian, eds.
1983   *Patterns and perceptions of menstruation; A World Health Organization international collaborative study in Egypt, India, Indonesia, Jamaica, Mexico, Pakistan, Philippines, Republic of Korea, United Kingdom and Yugoslavia.* New York: St. Martin's Press.

Sokolov, Natalie
1984   *Women in the professions.* Lecture in series, "Women in History, Culture and Society." Baltimore: Johns Hopkins University.

Sommer, Barbara
1973   The effect of menstruation on cognitive and perceptual-motor behavior: A review. *Psychosomatic Medicine* 35:515–534.

1984 PMS in the courts: Are all women on trial? *Psychology Today* 18, no. 8 (August):36–38.

1985 How does menstruation affect cognitive competence and psychophysiological response? In *Lifting the curse of menstruation*, ed. S. Golub, 53–90. New York: Harrington Park Press.

Spencer, B. and F. J. Gillen
1899 *The native tribes of central Australia*. London: Macmillan.
1927 *The Arunta*. 2 vols. London: Macmillan.

Spiro, Melford E.
1968 Virgin birth, parthenogenesis and physiological paternity: An essay in cultural interpretation. *Man* 3:242–261.

Spott, Robert and A. L. Kroeber
1942 Yurok narratives. *University of California Publications in American Archaeology and Ethnology* 35:143–256.

Stanner, W. E. H.
1966 *On Aboriginal religion*. Sydney: University of Sydney: University of Sydney Press. Oceania, Monograph 11.

Steffy, Philip C.
1982 The serious astronomy in the "Sirius Mystery" Part II: Spinning worlds, spiraling stars, and siguis; the solar system folklore of the Dogon. *Griffith Observer* (Los Angeles) 46, no. 2:16; no. 3:16–20; no. 4:18–20; no. 5:19–20; no. 8:19–20.

Steinem, Gloria
1983 *Outrageous acts and everyday rebellions*. New York: Holt, Rinehart & Winston.

Steiner, Franz
1956 *Taboo*. London: Penguin.

Stephens, William N.
1961 A cross-cultural study of menstrual taboos. *Genetic Psychology Monographs* 64:385–416.
1962 *The Oedipus complex: Cross-cultural evidence*. New York: Free Press.
1967 A cross-cultural study of menstrual taboos. In *Cross-cultural approaches: Readings in comparative research*, ed. Clellan Stearns Ford, 67–94. New Haven: Human Relations Area Files Press.

Strathern, Marilyn
1972 *Women in between: Female roles in a male world*. London: Seminar Press.
1980 No nature, no culture: The Hagen case. In *Nature, culture and gender*, ed. C. P. MacCormack and M. Strathern, 174–222. Cambridge: Cambridge University Press.

Suárez, Maria
1968 *Los Warao*. Caracas: Instituto Venozolano de Investigaciones Cientificas.

Tambiah, S. J.
   1969   Animals are good to think and good to prohibit. *Ethnology* 8, no. 4:423–459.

Tanner, Nancy Makepeace
   1981   *On becoming human.* Cambridge: Cambridge University Press.

Tedlock, Barbara
   1982   *Time and the highland Maya.* Albuquerque: University of New Mexico Press.

Thomas, Northcote W.
   1916   *Anthropological report on Sierra Leone,* vol. 1. London: Harrison and Sons. (Reprint, Westport, Conn.: Greenwood Press, 1970.)

Thompson, Catherine
   1985   The power to pollute and the power to preserve: Perceptions of female power in a Hindu village. *Social Science and Medicine* 21, no. 6:701–711.

Thompson, E. P.
   1967   Time, work-discipline, and industrial capitalism. *Past and Present* 38:56–97.

Thompson, Robert F., and Joseph Cornet
   1981   *The four moments of the sun: Kongo art in two worlds.* Washington, D.C.: National Gallery of Art.

Tichy, Franz, ed.
   1982   *Space and time in the cosmovision of Mesoamerica.* Munich: Wilhelm Fink.

Triebels, L. F.
   1958   *Enige aspecten van de regenboogslang: Een vergelijkende studie.* Nijmegen: Gebr. Janssen.

Turner, Victor
   1967a   Color classification in Ndembu ritual: A problem of primitive classification. In *The forest of symbols,* 59–92. Ithaca, N.Y.: Cornell University Press.
   1967b   *The forest of symbols.* Ithaca, N.Y.: Cornell University Press.
   1967c   Symbols in Ndembu ritual. In *The forest of symbols,* 19–47.
   1968   *The drums of affliction.* Oxford: Clarendon Press.
   1969   *The ritual process: Structure and anti-structure.* Chicago: Aldine.
   1977   Process, system and symbol: A new anthropological synthesis. *Daedalus* 106, no. 3:61–80.

Vanek, Joann
   1974   Time spent in housework. *Scientific American* (November):116–120.

Van Gennep, Arnold
  1909   *Les rites de passage.* Paris: A. et J. Picard. (Reprinted 1981.)
  1960   *The rites of passage,* trans. M. Vizedom and G. Caffee. Chicago: University of Chicago Press.
Van Herik, Judith
  1982   *Freud on femininity and faith.* Berkeley, Los Angeles, London: University of California Press.
Vosselmann, Fritz
  1935   *La menstruation: Légendes, coutumes et superstitions.* Lyon: Faculté de Médicine et de Pharmacie de Lyon. Année Scolaire 1935–1936, no. 23. Thèse de Docteur en Medicine.
Warner, W. Lloyd
  1957   *A black civilization,* rev. ed. New York: Harper. (Original edition 1937.)
Waterman, T. T.
  1920   Yurok geography. *University of California Publications in American Archaeology and Ethnology* 16, no. 5:177–314.
Weideger, Paula
  1977   *Menstruation and menopause: The physiology and psychology, the myth and the reality.* New York: Delta.
Weiner, Annette B.
  1976   *Women of value, men of renown; new perspectives in Trobriand exchange.* Austin: University of Texas Press.
  1980   Reproduction: A replacement for reciprocity. *American Ethnologist* 7:71–85.
Williamson, Ray A., ed.
  1981   *Archaeoastronomy in the Americas.* College Park: Center for Archaeoastronomy, University of Maryland.
Wilson, Bryan R.
  1977   *Rationality.* Oxford: Basil Blackwell.
Wilson, Monica
  1951   *Good company.* Boston: Beacon Press.
  1957   *Rituals of kinship among the Nyakyusa.* London: Oxford University Press.
Wilson, Peter J.
  1969   Correspondence: Virgin birth. *Man* 4:286–288.
Winslow, Deborah
  1980   Rituals of first menstruation in Sri Lanka. *Man* 15:603–625.
Winterbottom, Thomas
  1969   *An account of the Native Africans in the neighborhood of Sierra Leone,* vol. 1. London: Frank Cass. (First ed., J. Hatchard & J. Mawman, 1803.)

Witt, Reni L.
1984   *PMS: What every woman should know about premenstrual syndrome.* New York: Stein and Day.
Wolf, Margery
1972   *Women and the family in rural Taiwan.* Stanford: Stanford University Press.
Wolf, Margery and Roxane Witke, eds.
1975   *Women in Chinese society.* Stanford: Stanford University Press.
Wood, Charles T.
1981   The doctors' dilemma: Sin, salvation, and the menstrual cycle in medieval thought. *Speculum* 56:710–727.
Wright, B. J.
1968   *Rock art of the Pilbara region, northwest Australia.* Canberra: Australian Institute of Aboriginal Studies.
Wright, Anne
1982   Attitudes toward childbearing and menstruation among the Navajo. In *Anthropology of human birth*, ed. Margarita Artschwager Kay, 377–394. Philadelphia: F. A. Davis Co.
Yalman, Nur
1964   Sinhalese healing rituals. *Journals of Asian Studies* 23:115–150.
Young, Frank W.
1965   *Initiation ceremonies: A cross-cultural study of status dramatization.* New York: Bobbs-Merrill.
Young, Frank W. and Albert Bacdayan
1965   Menstrual taboos and social rigidity. *Ethnology* 4:225–240.

Contributors

Laura W. R. Appell is a research associate at the Social Transformation and Adaptation Research Institute, Phillips, Maine. She has done fieldwork, together with her husband, G. N. Appell, among the Dogrib Indians of the Northwest Territories, Canada, and the Bulusu' of East Kalimantan, Indonesia, as well as the Rungus Dusun of Sabah, Malaysia, the subjects of her present essay. Her research focuses on religion, spirit mediums, and the domestic family.

Thomas Buckley is assistant professor of anthropology and director of the Linguistics Program at the University of Massachusetts at Boston. He did intermittent fieldwork in northwestern California between 1976 and 1981. His work has appeared in *American Ethnologist, Language in Society, Semiotica,* and other publications. His ongoing research focuses on religion, language, and history in Native North America, and the history of anthropology.

Carol Delaney is assistant professor of anthropology at Stanford University. She did fieldwork in Turkey in 1979–1982 and returned for a shorter stay in 1986. Her work on gender and religion has appeared in *Special Publication 22* of the American Anthropological Association, and in *Man.*

Alma Gottlieb is assistant professor of anthropology at the University of Illinois at Urbana-Champaign. She conducted research in Ivory Coast in 1979–1980 and in 1985. Her articles have appeared in *Africa, American Ethnologist, Man,* and elsewhere. Her current research interests include symbolic and interpretive theory, gender issues, and social organization.

Chris Knight lectures in anthropology for the Extra-Mural Department of the University of London. His Ph.D. research at University College, London, was on the significance of menstruation to human cultural origins. He has lectured and published widely on Australian Aboriginal mythology, and his articles have appeared in *Man* and *Social Science and Medicine*, among other publications.

Frederick Lamp is curator of the Arts of Africa, the Americas, and Oceania at the Baltimore Museum of Art. He worked at the National Museum of African Art, Washington, from 1973 to 1977. He lived among the Temne of Sierra Leone for many years, and they are the subject of his doctoral dissertation (Yale, 1982). He has published articles in *African Arts*, *The Drama Review*, and elsewhere.

Denise L. Lawrence teaches in the Departments of Architecture and Landscape Architecture at California State Polytechnic University, Pomona. Her present contribution is based on fieldwork in southern Portugal in 1976–1977. With return visits between 1979 and 1985, her research has been extended to the study of changing Portuguese patterns of gender relations and territoriality as expressed in vernacular housing forms. Other current research in urban symbolic structures includes studies of parades and fiestas in Pasadena, California, and Valencia, Spain. Results of her research have appeared in *Anthropological Quarterly* and in *Urban Anthropology*.

Emily Martin is Mary Garrett Professor of Anthropology at The Johns Hopkins University and has taught at Yale University and at the University of California, Irvine. Results of her earlier fieldwork in Taiwan were published in her books, *The Cult of the Dead in a Chinese Village* (Stanford), *Chinese Ritual and Politics* (Cambridge), and *The Anthropology of Taiwanese Society*, edited with Hill Gates (Stanford). Her most recent book, *The Woman in the Body: A Cultural Analysis of Reproduction* (Beacon), is based on new fieldwork in the United States.

Vieda Skultans is lecturer in mental health, Department of Mental Health, University of Bristol. She has done fieldwork in Wales, India, and England. She is the author of *Intimacy and Ritual: A Study of Spiritualism, Mediums and Groups; Madness and Morals: Ideas of Insanity in the 19th Century;* and, most recently, *English Madness: Ideas on Insanity, 1580–1890* (all Routledge & Kegan Paul). Her current research concerns include women's religious groups in India and England, and ethnicity, incarceration, and mental health care in England.

Index

Aborigines, Australian: intercourse avoided among, 238; late menstruation cured among, 236; male power among, 232, 247–253; menstrual seclusion among, 241; menstrual synchrony among, 232–237, 244–247, 249–250; menstrual taboos among, 246, 247; menstruation among, 45, 118; red symbolism among, 236, 240, 241; rock engravings of, 236, 251; and snake symbolism, 232, 233, 235, 237–238, 239–241, 242–244; wet/dry symbolism among, 237–238, 240, 242, 245, 246–247

Abraham, story of, 91

Ahern, Emily Martin, 35. *See also* Martin, Emily

Alawa Aborigines (of Arnhem Land, Australia), 237

Amenorrhea: as abnormal vs. normal condition, 44–45; Beng remedy for, 71; in nonindustrial societies, 225–226; as punishment for violating taboos, 32–33

Anderson, Peter, 44

Androcentrism, of ethnographic explanations, 5, 9, 30–31, 33, 49, 193, 201–202

Anger, during PMS, 173–180

Aranda (of Australia), 236

Ardener, Edwin, 193

Aristotle, 38, 259 n. 9

Asante (of Ghana), 37

Augé, Marc, 49

Azande (of the Sudan), 38, 259 n. 8

Bacdayan, Albert, 9

Balzer, Marjorie Mandelstam, 29

Barbot, Jean, 223, 226

Barrenness, Beng remedies for, 70

Barrett, Samuel Alfred, 13

Basketmaking, menstrual taboos affecting, 13

Bathing, during menstruation, 64, 143–144, 190, 191, 193, 194–195, 196, 224

Battered women, and PMS, 174

Baule (of Ivory Coast), 262 n. 10, 277–278 n. 10

Bean, Lowell, 187, 188

Bears, influence of menstrual odor on, 22

Becker, Ernest, 156

Bell, Diane, 45

Beng (of Ivory Coast): bathing required among, 64; described, 55–57; food taboos among, 57, 59, 63–72, 73; intercourse taboos among, 58–59, 62–64; menarche among, 56–57, 60; menstrual blood as life force among, 58, 64–67, 73; menstrual blood positively used among, 35; menstrual intercourse among, 58–59; menstrual taboos among, 57–58, 59, 67–68, 168; polluting substances among, 58, 59–60, 61–64; punishments for violations of taboos among, 60–64; rape among, 63–64; religions among, 56; rules vs. taboos among, 24

Berndt, Catherine H., 235, 248, 249

Berndt, Ronald M., 235, 238, 242, 248, 249

Bettelheim, Bruno, 17

Biological determinism, 5

Birth control, in Portugal, 133. *See also* Condoms; Contraceptive pills

Blackburn, Thomas, 187, 188

Blacker, C., 253

Designer:	U.C. Press Staff
Compositor:	Janet Sheila Brown
Text:	10/12 Palatino
Display:	Palatino
Printer:	Maple-Vail Book Mfg. Group
Binder:	Maple-Vail Book Mfg. Group